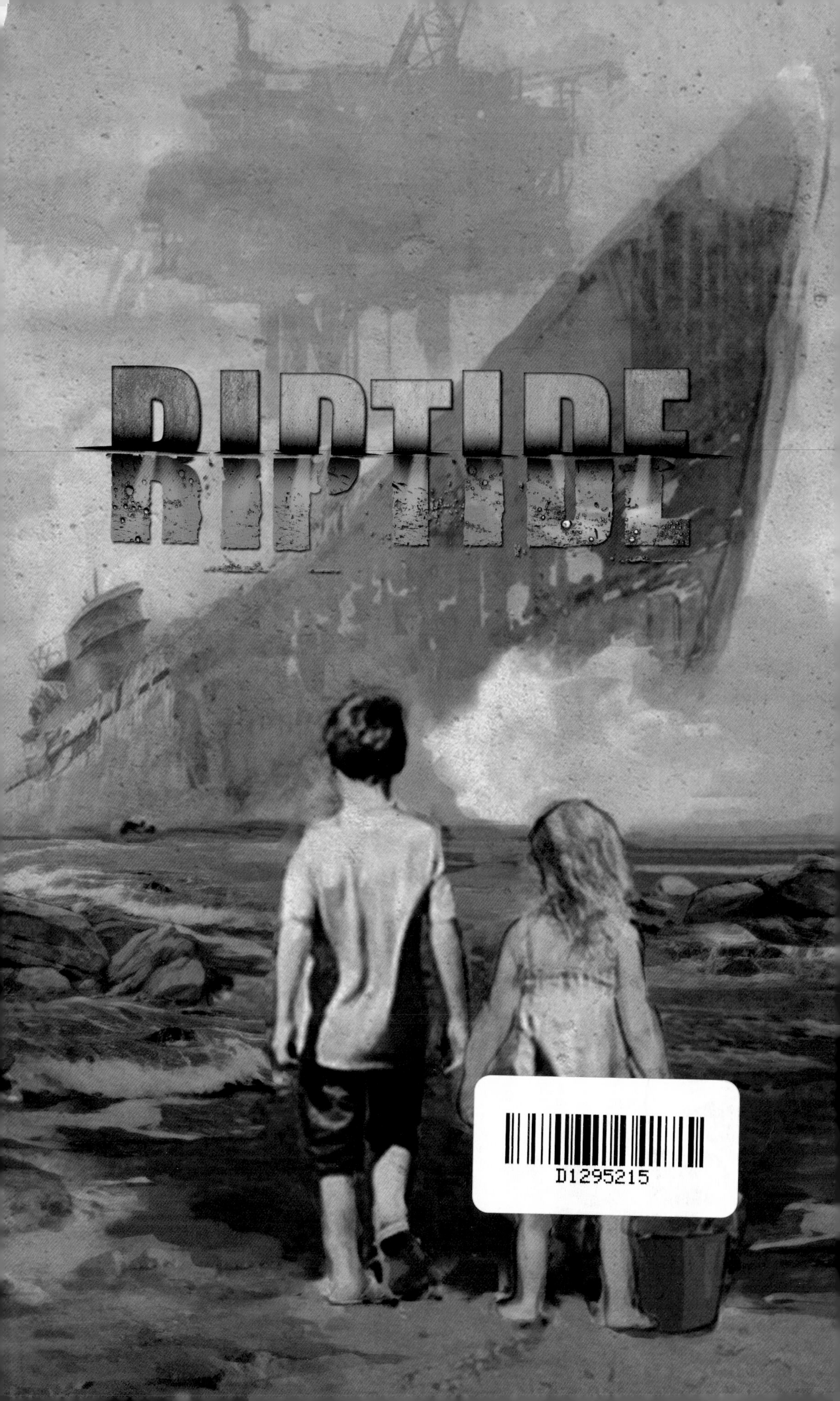
RIPTIDE

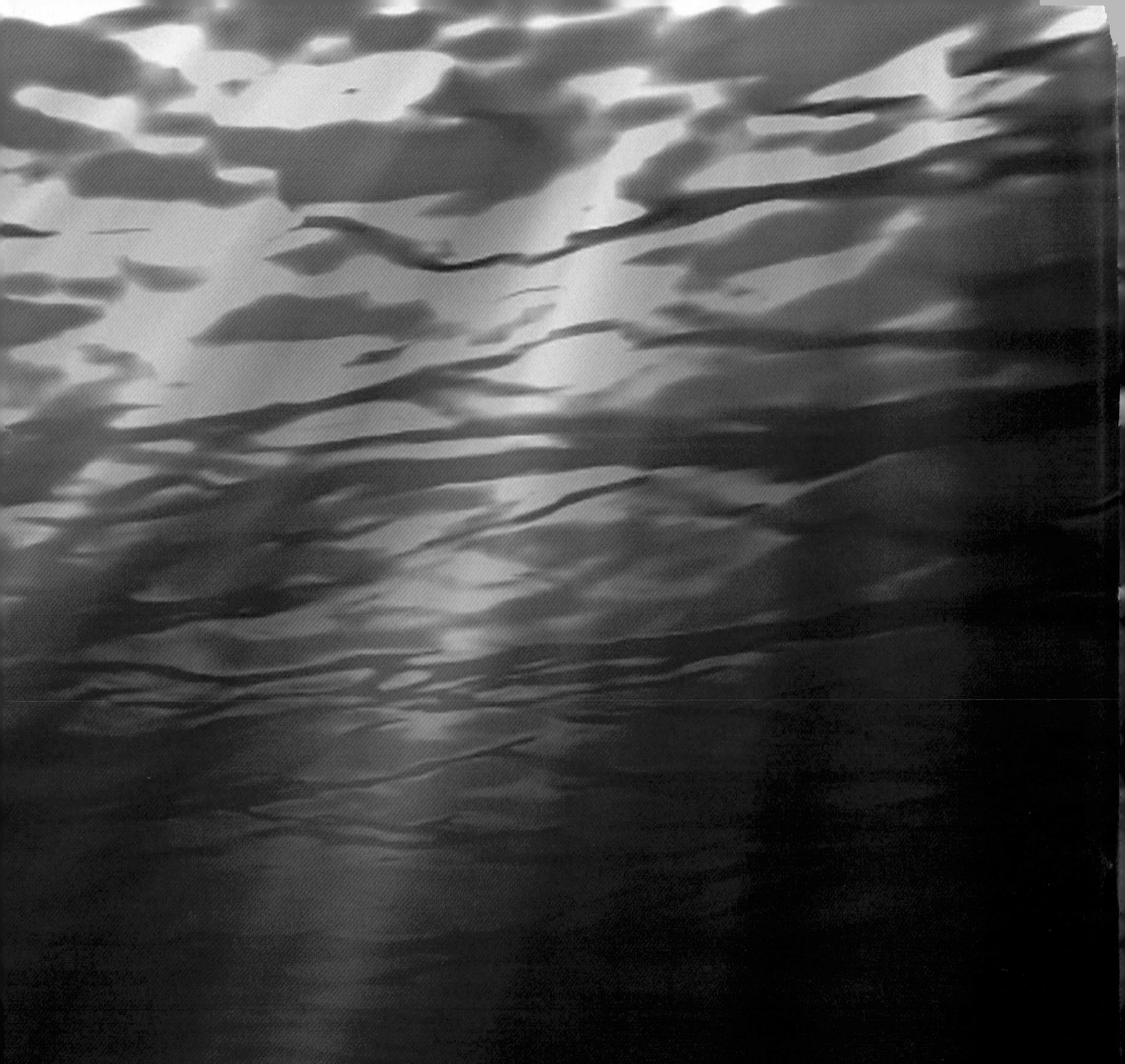

publishers
PAUL ENS, JOSHUA STARNES and SCOTT CHITWOOD

RIPTIDE

This volume collects RIPTIDE #1 through #4 of the comic-book series originally printed by Red 5 Comics.

Published by
RED 5 COMICS
27103 Kelsey Woods Court, Cypress, Texas 77433

www.red5comics.com

To find a comics shop in your area, call the Comic Shop Locator Service toll-free at 1-888-266-4226

RIPTIDE

SCRIPT
SCOTT CHITWOOD

ART
DANNY LUCKERT

COLORS
RONDA PATTISON

LETTERS
TROY PETERI

COVER ART
PAUL ALLEN BALLARD

WWW.RED5COMICS.COM

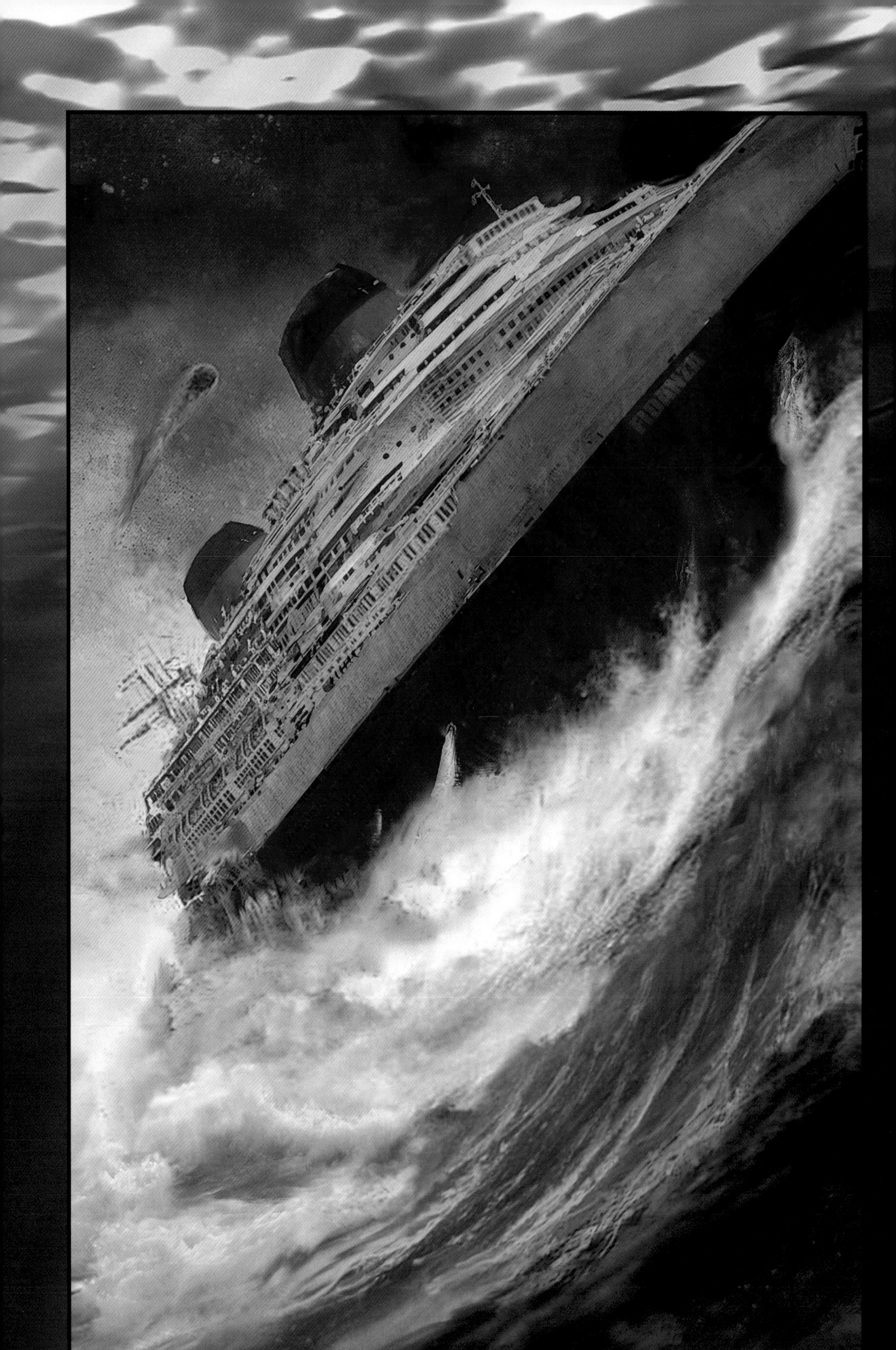

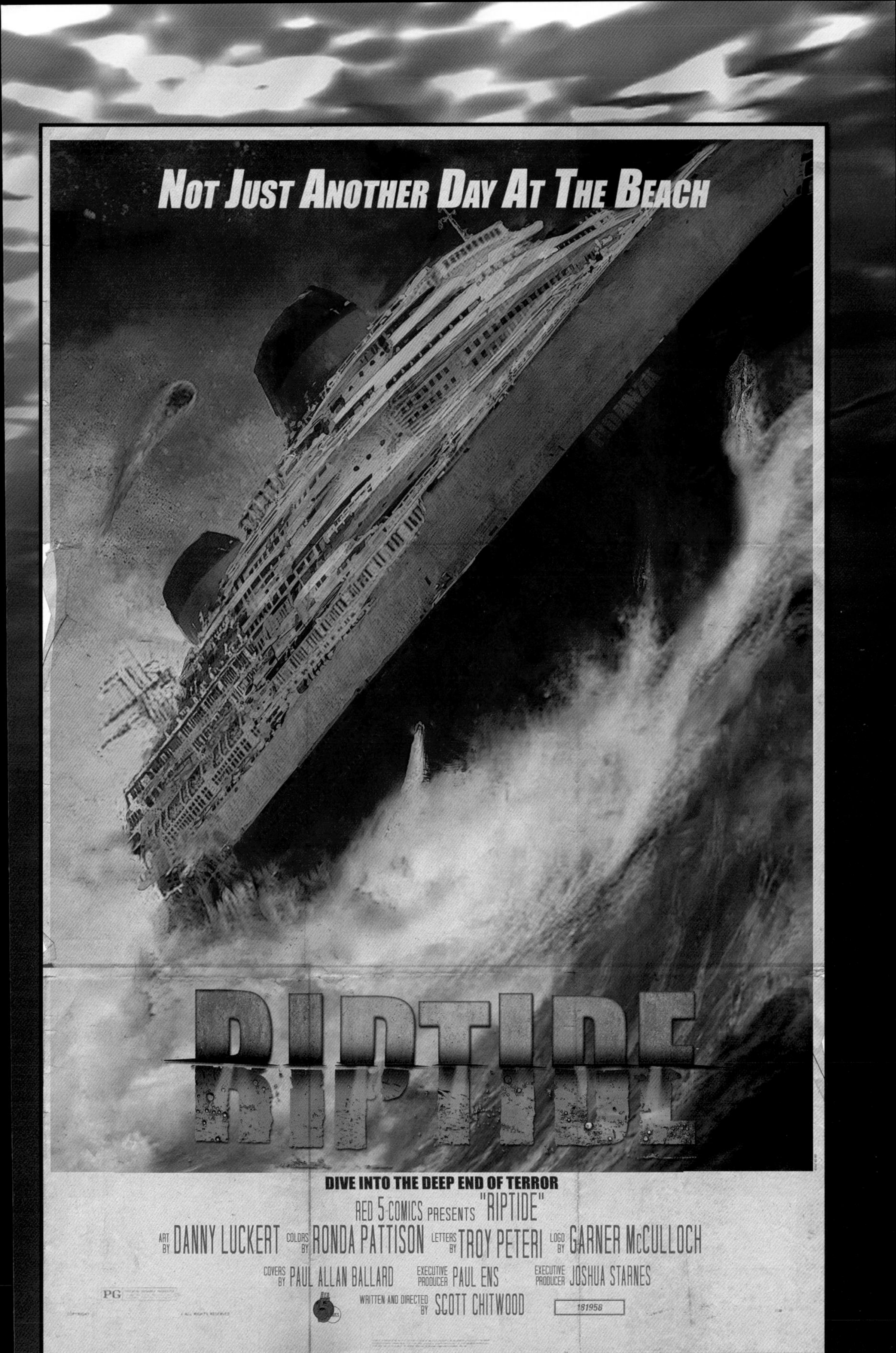
NOT JUST ANOTHER DAY AT THE BEACH
RIPTIDE
DIVE INTO THE DEEP END OF TERROR
RED 5 COMICS PRESENTS "RIPTIDE"
ART BY DANNY LUCKERT
COLORS BY RONDA PATTISON
LETTERS BY TROY PETERI
LOGO BY GARNER McCULLOCH
COVERS BY PAUL ALLAN BALLARD
EXECUTIVE PRODUCER PAUL ENS
EXECUTIVE PRODUCER JOSHUA STARNES
PG
WRITTEN AND DIRECTED BY SCOTT CHITWOOD
181958

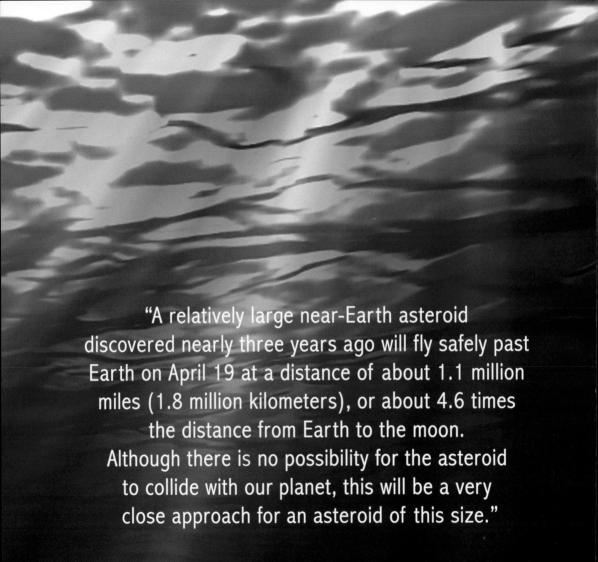

"A relatively large near-Earth asteroid
discovered nearly three years ago will fly safely past
Earth on April 19 at a distance of about 1.1 million
miles (1.8 million kilometers), or about 4.6 times
the distance from Earth to the moon.
Although there is no possibility for the asteroid
to collide with our planet, this will be a very
close approach for an asteroid of this size."

"At this time very little else is known about the object's
physical properties, even though its trajectory is well known."

NASA.Gov, April 16, 2017

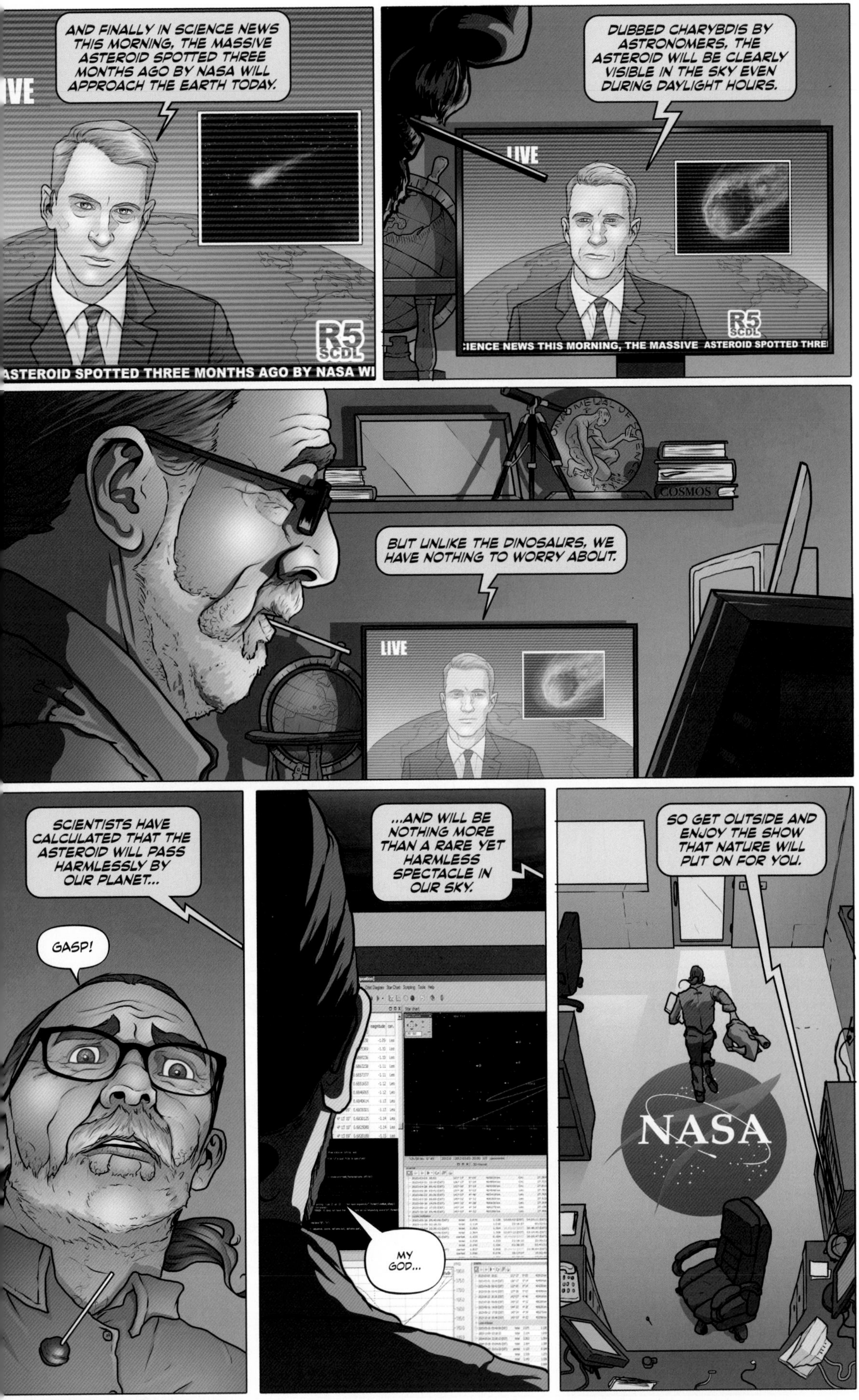
AND FINALLY IN SCIENCE NEWS THIS MORNING, THE MASSIVE ASTEROID SPOTTED THREE MONTHS AGO BY NASA WILL APPROACH THE EARTH TODAY.
IVE
R5 SCDL
ASTEROID SPOTTED THREE MONTHS AGO BY NASA WI
DUBBED CHARYBDIS BY ASTRONOMERS, THE ASTEROID WILL BE CLEARLY VISIBLE IN THE SKY EVEN DURING DAYLIGHT HOURS.
LIVE
R5 SCDL
CIENCE NEWS THIS MORNING, THE MASSIVE ASTEROID SPOTTED THRE
COSMOS
BUT UNLIKE THE DINOSAURS, WE HAVE NOTHING TO WORRY ABOUT.
LIVE
SCIENTISTS HAVE CALCULATED THAT THE ASTEROID WILL PASS HARMLESSLY BY OUR PLANET...
GASP!
...AND WILL BE NOTHING MORE THAN A RARE YET HARMLESS SPECTACLE IN OUR SKY.
MY GOD...
SO GET OUTSIDE AND ENJOY THE SHOW THAT NATURE WILL PUT ON FOR YOU.
NASA

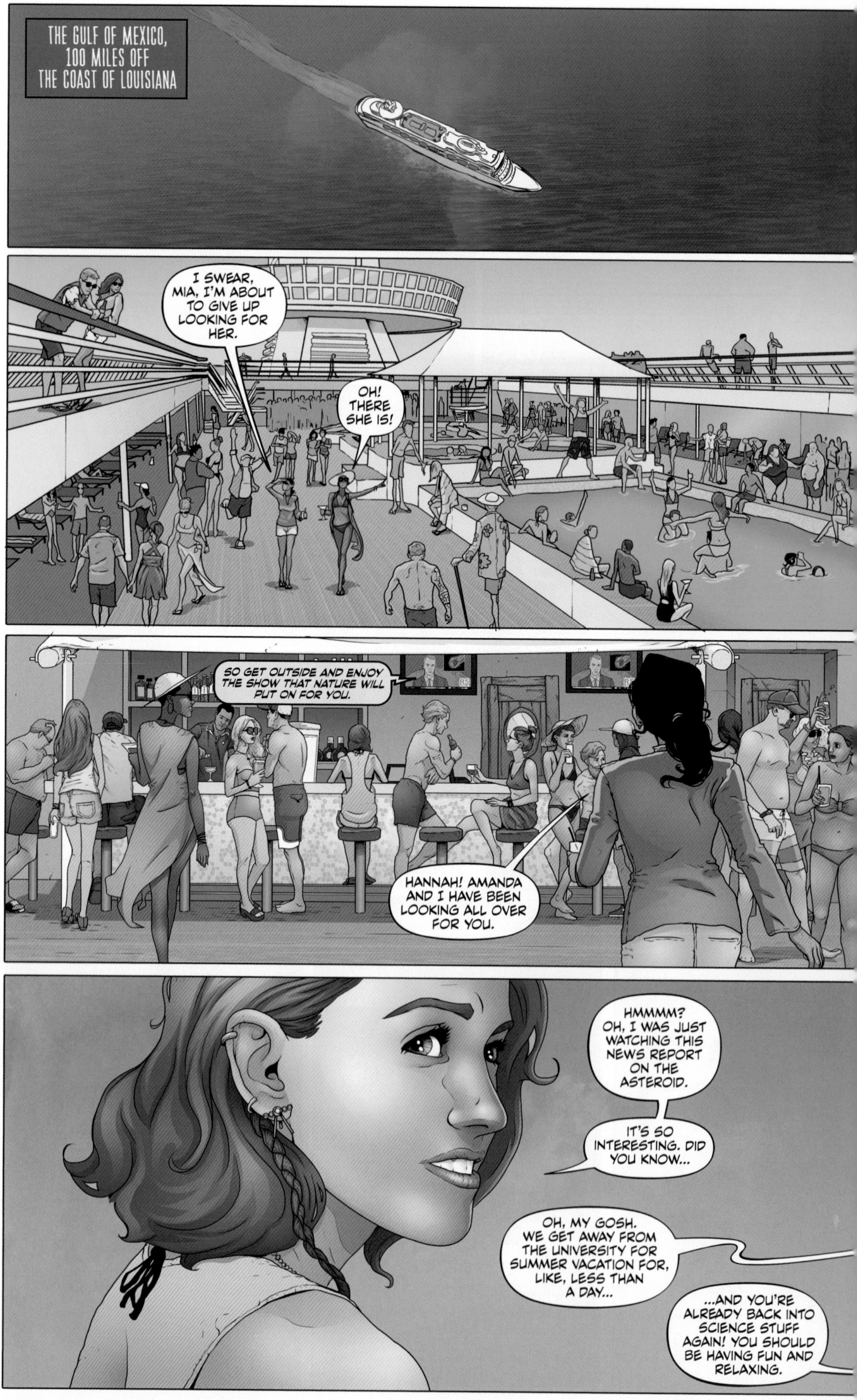
THE GULF OF MEXICO, 100 MILES OFF THE COAST OF LOUISIANA
I SWEAR, MIA, I'M ABOUT TO GIVE UP LOOKING FOR HER.
OH! THERE SHE IS!
SO GET OUTSIDE AND ENJOY THE SHOW THAT NATURE WILL PUT ON FOR YOU.
HANNAH! AMANDA AND I HAVE BEEN LOOKING ALL OVER FOR YOU.
HMMMM? OH, I WAS JUST WATCHING THIS NEWS REPORT ON THE ASTEROID.
IT'S SO INTERESTING. DID YOU KNOW...
OH, MY GOSH. WE GET AWAY FROM THE UNIVERSITY FOR SUMMER VACATION FOR, LIKE, LESS THAN A DAY...
...AND YOU'RE ALREADY BACK INTO SCIENCE STUFF AGAIN! YOU SHOULD BE HAVING FUN AND RELAXING.

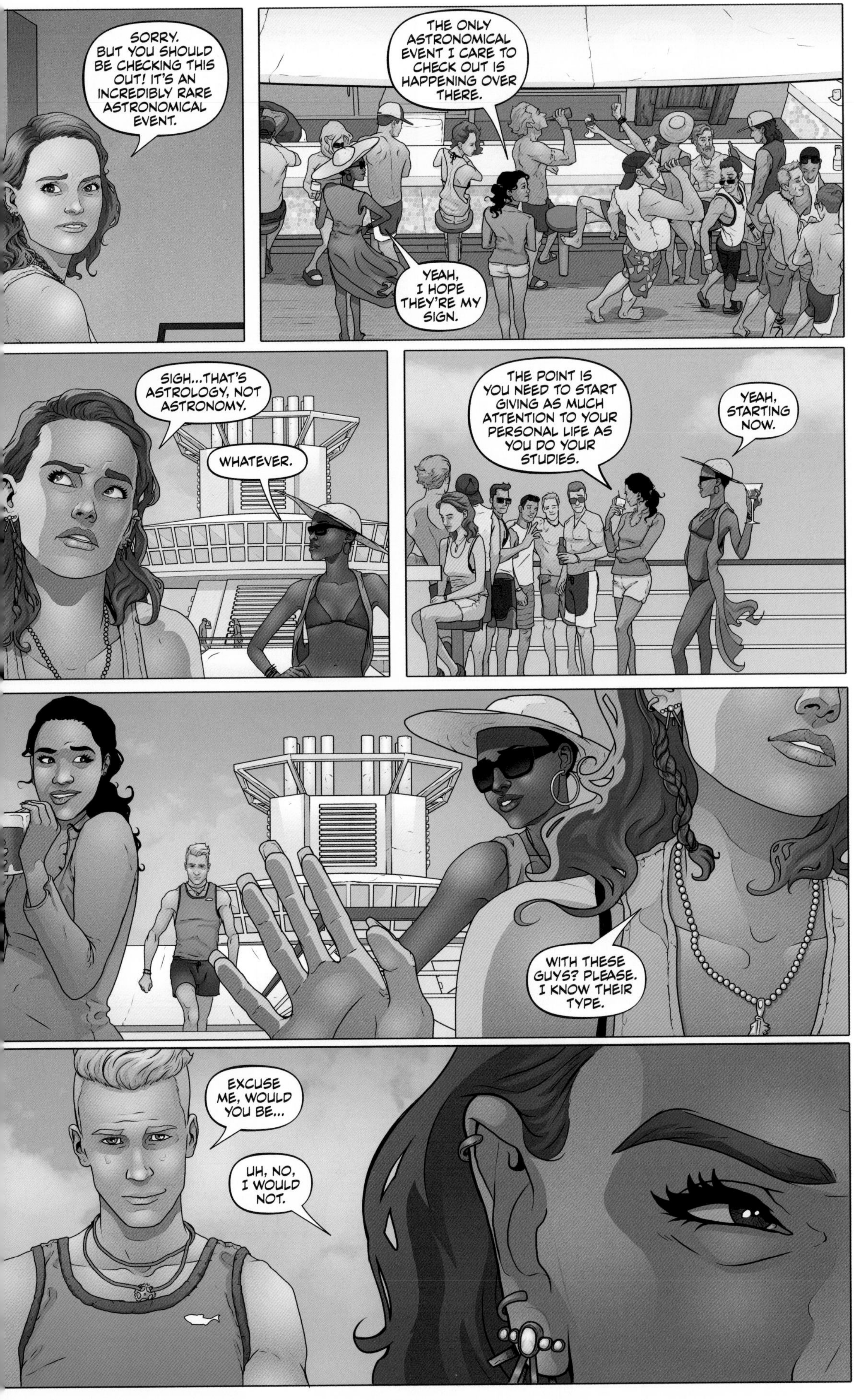
SORRY. BUT YOU SHOULD BE CHECKING THIS OUT! IT'S AN INCREDIBLY RARE ASTRONOMICAL EVENT.
THE ONLY ASTRONOMICAL EVENT I CARE TO CHECK OUT IS HAPPENING OVER THERE.
YEAH, I HOPE THEY'RE MY SIGN.
SIGH...THAT'S ASTROLOGY, NOT ASTRONOMY.
WHATEVER.
THE POINT IS YOU NEED TO START GIVING AS MUCH ATTENTION TO YOUR PERSONAL LIFE AS YOU DO YOUR STUDIES.
YEAH, STARTING NOW.
WITH THESE GUYS? PLEASE. I KNOW THEIR TYPE.
EXCUSE ME, WOULD YOU BE...
UH, NO, I WOULD NOT.

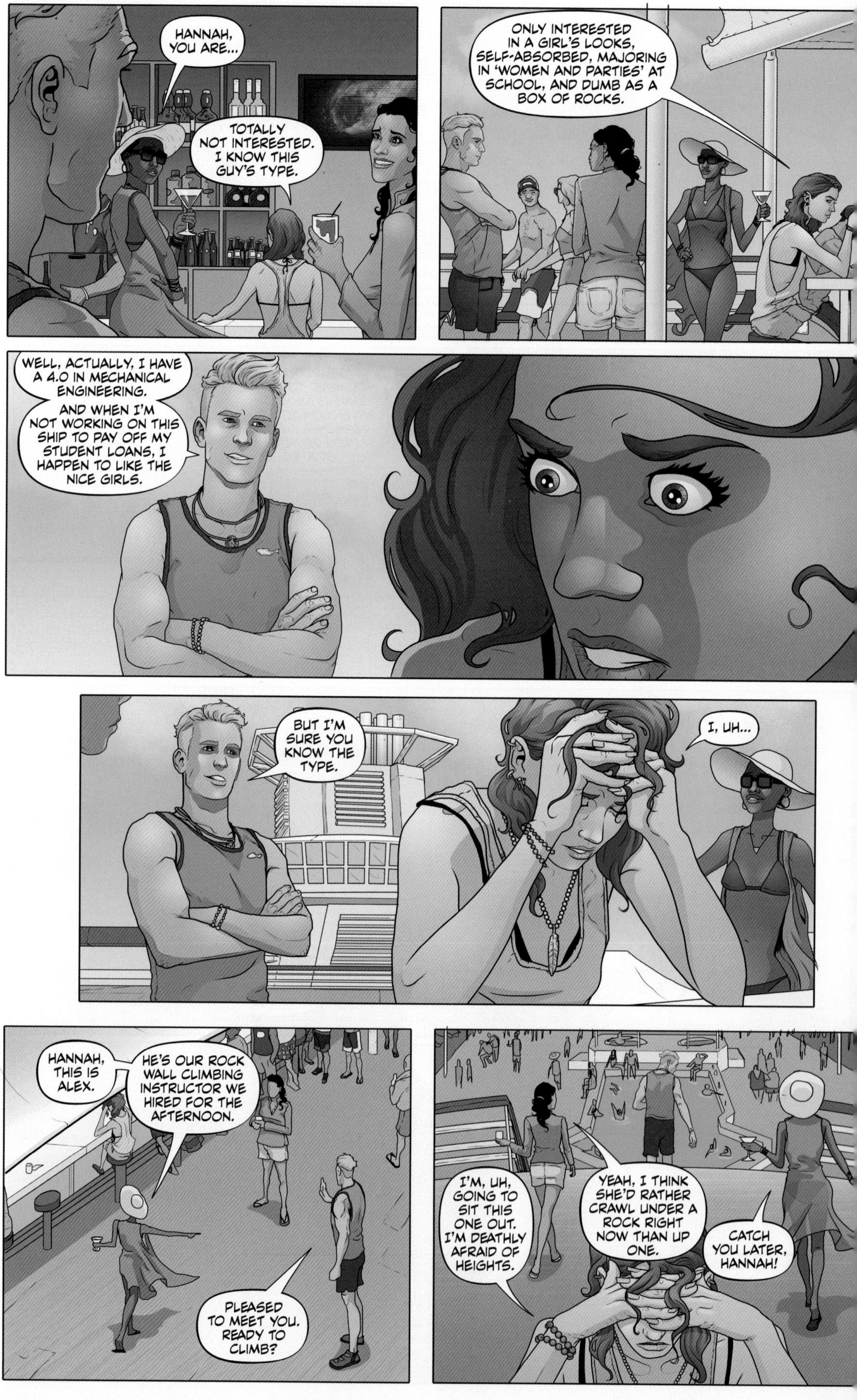
HANNAH, YOU ARE...
TOTALLY NOT INTERESTED. I KNOW THIS GUY'S TYPE.
ONLY INTERESTED IN A GIRL'S LOOKS, SELF-ABSORBED, MAJORING IN 'WOMEN AND PARTIES' AT SCHOOL, AND DUMB AS A BOX OF ROCKS.
WELL, ACTUALLY, I HAVE A 4.0 IN MECHANICAL ENGINEERING.
AND WHEN I'M NOT WORKING ON THIS SHIP TO PAY OFF MY STUDENT LOANS, I HAPPEN TO LIKE THE NICE GIRLS.
BUT I'M SURE YOU KNOW THE TYPE.
I, UH...
HANNAH, THIS IS ALEX.
HE'S OUR ROCK WALL CLIMBING INSTRUCTOR WE HIRED FOR THE AFTERNOON.
PLEASED TO MEET YOU. READY TO CLIMB?
I'M, UH, GOING TO SIT THIS ONE OUT. I'M DEATHLY AFRAID OF HEIGHTS.
YEAH, I THINK SHE'D RATHER CRAWL UNDER A ROCK RIGHT NOW THAN UP ONE.
CATCH YOU LATER, HANNAH!

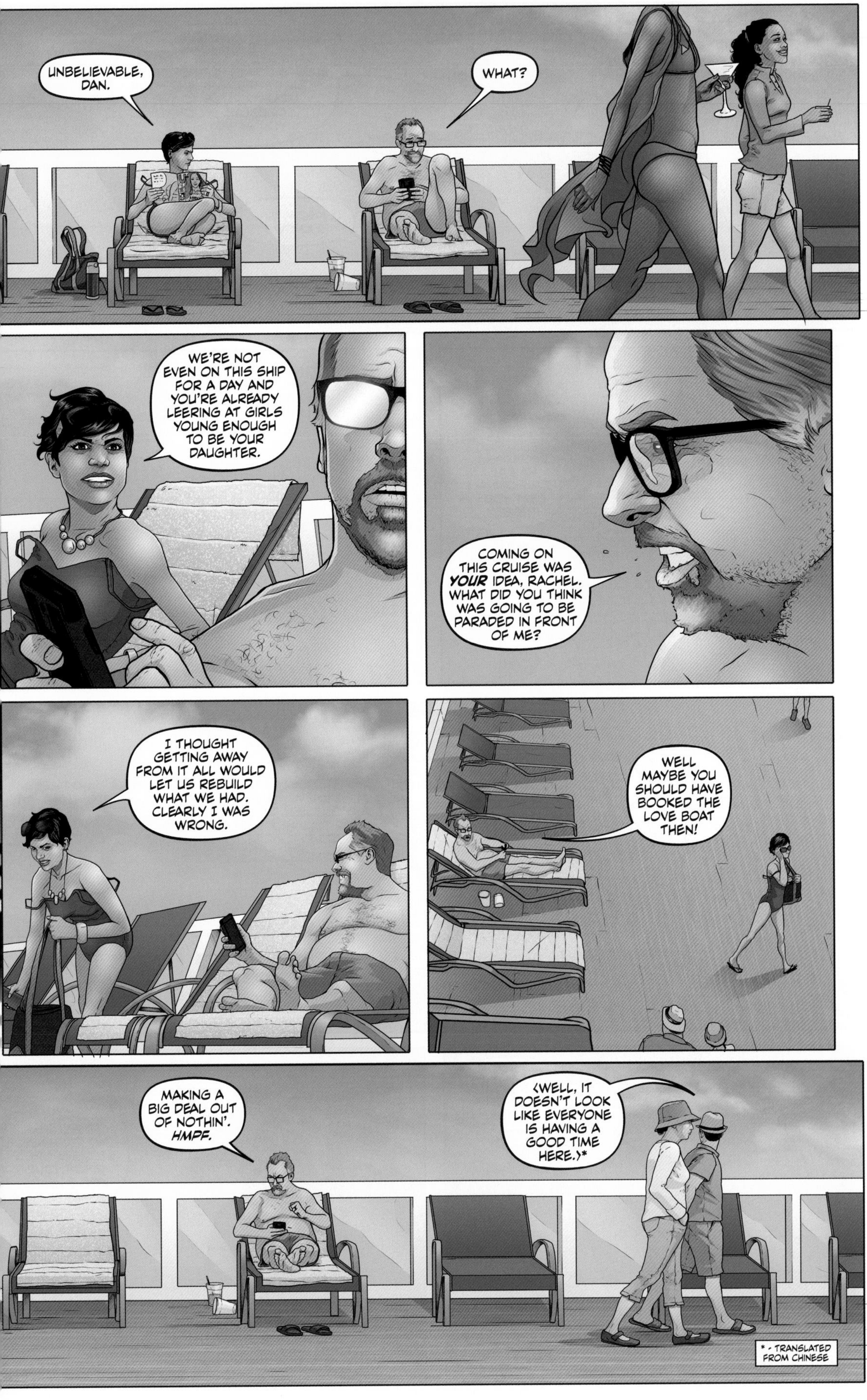
UNBELIEVABLE, DAN.
WHAT?
WE'RE NOT EVEN ON THIS SHIP FOR A DAY AND YOU'RE ALREADY LEERING AT GIRLS YOUNG ENOUGH TO BE YOUR DAUGHTER.
COMING ON THIS CRUISE WAS ***YOUR*** IDEA, RACHEL. WHAT DID YOU THINK WAS GOING TO BE PARADED IN FRONT OF ME?
I THOUGHT GETTING AWAY FROM IT ALL WOULD LET US REBUILD WHAT WE HAD. CLEARLY I WAS WRONG.
WELL MAYBE YOU SHOULD HAVE BOOKED THE LOVE BOAT THEN!
MAKING A BIG DEAL OUT OF NOTHIN'. *HMPF.*
<WELL, IT DOESN'T LOOK LIKE EVERYONE IS HAVING A GOOD TIME HERE.>*
* - TRANSLATED FROM CHINESE

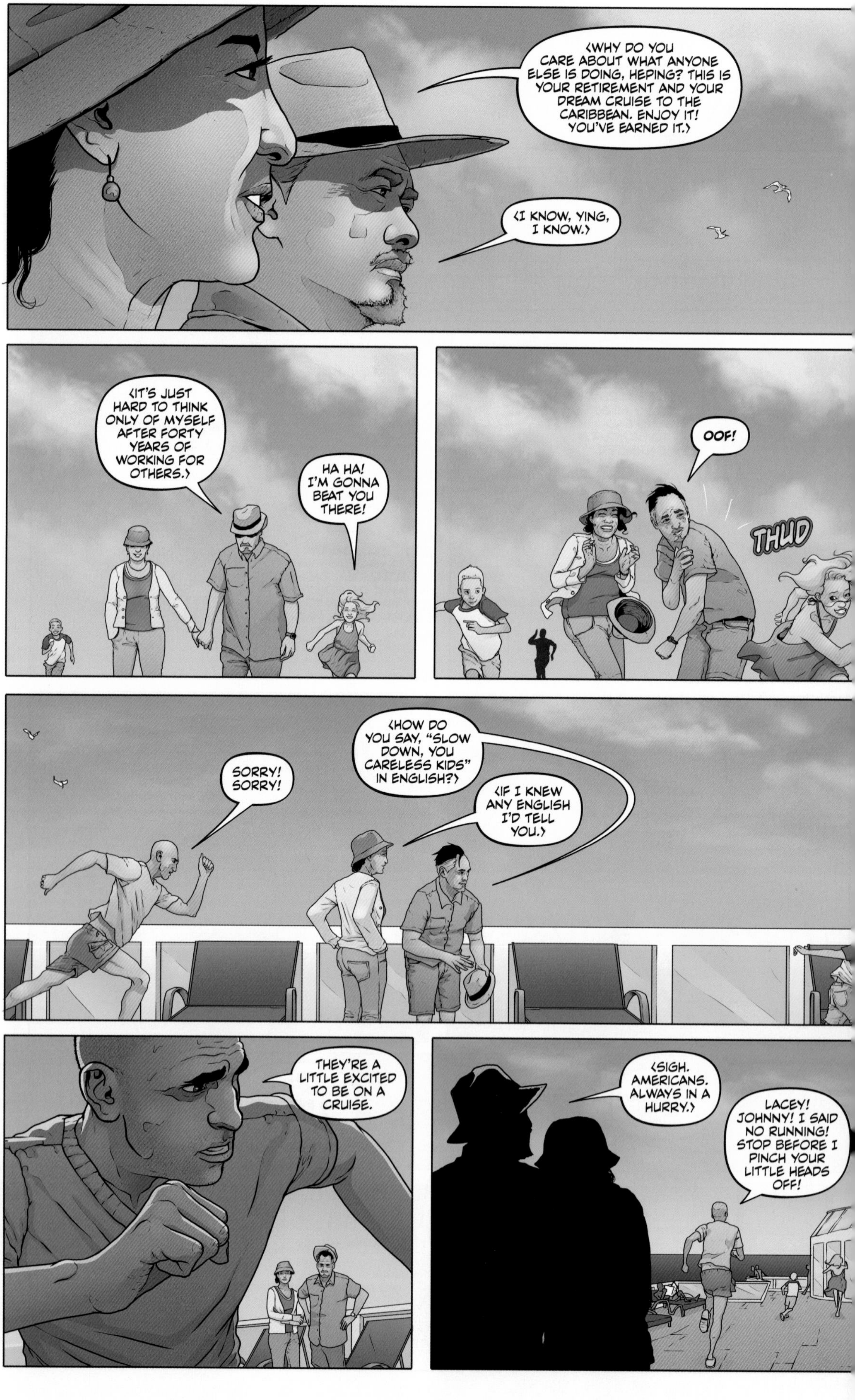

<WHY DO YOU CARE ABOUT WHAT ANYONE ELSE IS DOING, HEPING? THIS IS YOUR RETIREMENT AND YOUR DREAM CRUISE TO THE CARIBBEAN. ENJOY IT! YOU'VE EARNED IT.>
<I KNOW, YING, I KNOW.>
<IT'S JUST HARD TO THINK ONLY OF MYSELF AFTER FORTY YEARS OF WORKING FOR OTHERS.>
HA HA! I'M GONNA BEAT YOU THERE!
OOF!
THUD
SORRY! SORRY!
<HOW DO YOU SAY, "SLOW DOWN, YOU CARELESS KIDS" IN ENGLISH?>
<IF I KNEW ANY ENGLISH I'D TELL YOU.>
THEY'RE A LITTLE EXCITED TO BE ON A CRUISE.
<SIGH. AMERICANS. ALWAYS IN A HURRY.>
LACEY! JOHNNY! I SAID NO RUNNING! STOP BEFORE I PINCH YOUR LITTLE HEADS OFF!

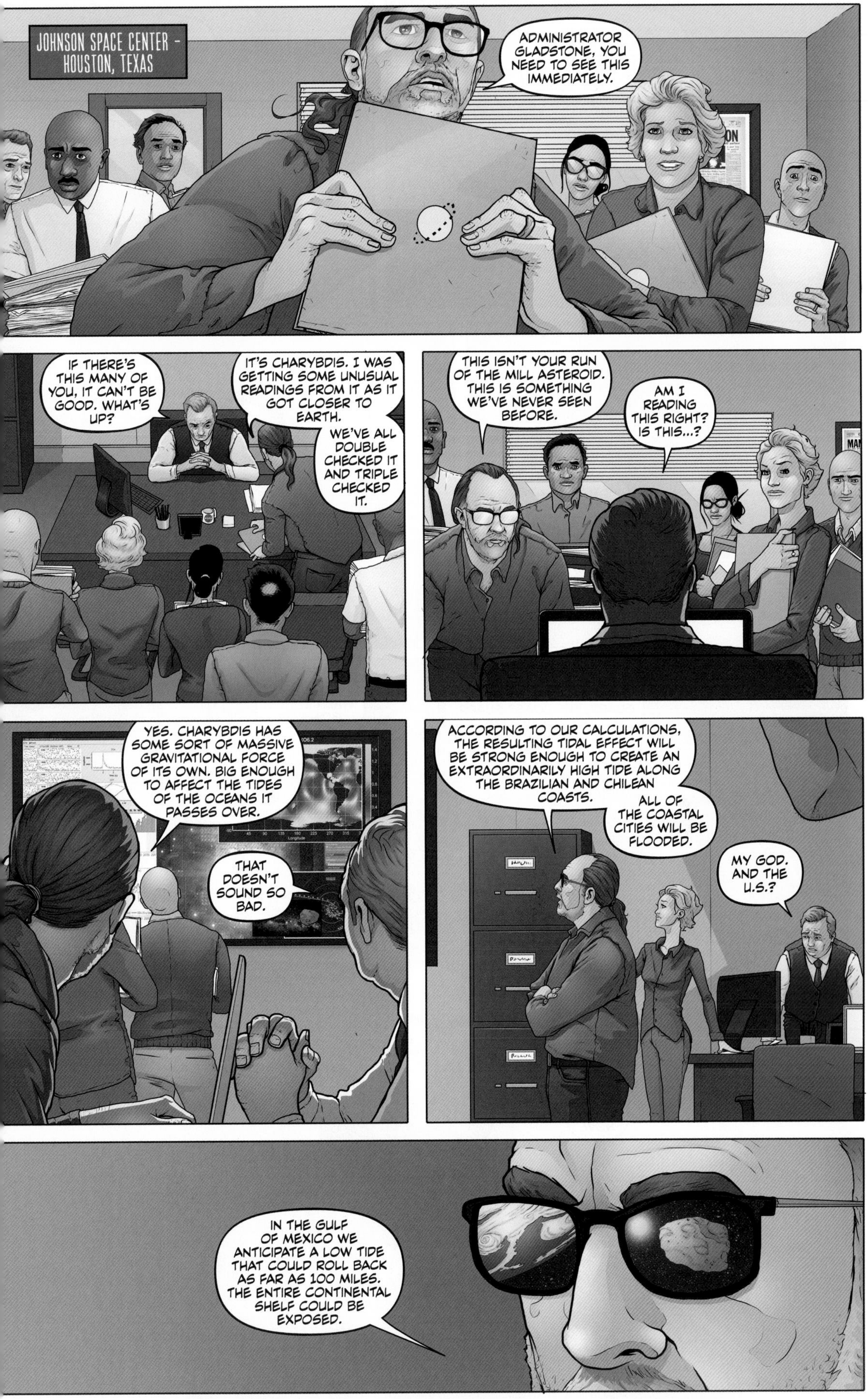
JOHNSON SPACE CENTER - HOUSTON, TEXAS
ADMINISTRATOR GLADSTONE, YOU NEED TO SEE THIS IMMEDIATELY.
IF THERE'S THIS MANY OF YOU, IT CAN'T BE GOOD. WHAT'S UP?
IT'S CHARYBDIS. I WAS GETTING SOME UNUSUAL READINGS FROM IT AS IT GOT CLOSER TO EARTH.
WE'VE ALL DOUBLE CHECKED IT AND TRIPLE CHECKED IT.
THIS ISN'T YOUR RUN OF THE MILL ASTEROID. THIS IS SOMETHING WE'VE NEVER SEEN BEFORE.
AM I READING THIS RIGHT? IS THIS...?
YES. CHARYBDIS HAS SOME SORT OF MASSIVE GRAVITATIONAL FORCE OF ITS OWN. BIG ENOUGH TO AFFECT THE TIDES OF THE OCEANS IT PASSES OVER.
THAT DOESN'T SOUND SO BAD.
ACCORDING TO OUR CALCULATIONS, THE RESULTING TIDAL EFFECT WILL BE STRONG ENOUGH TO CREATE AN EXTRAORDINARILY HIGH TIDE ALONG THE BRAZILIAN AND CHILEAN COASTS.
ALL OF THE COASTAL CITIES WILL BE FLOODED.
MY GOD. AND THE U.S.?
IN THE GULF OF MEXICO WE ANTICIPATE A LOW TIDE THAT COULD ROLL BACK AS FAR AS 100 MILES. THE ENTIRE CONTINENTAL SHELF COULD BE EXPOSED.

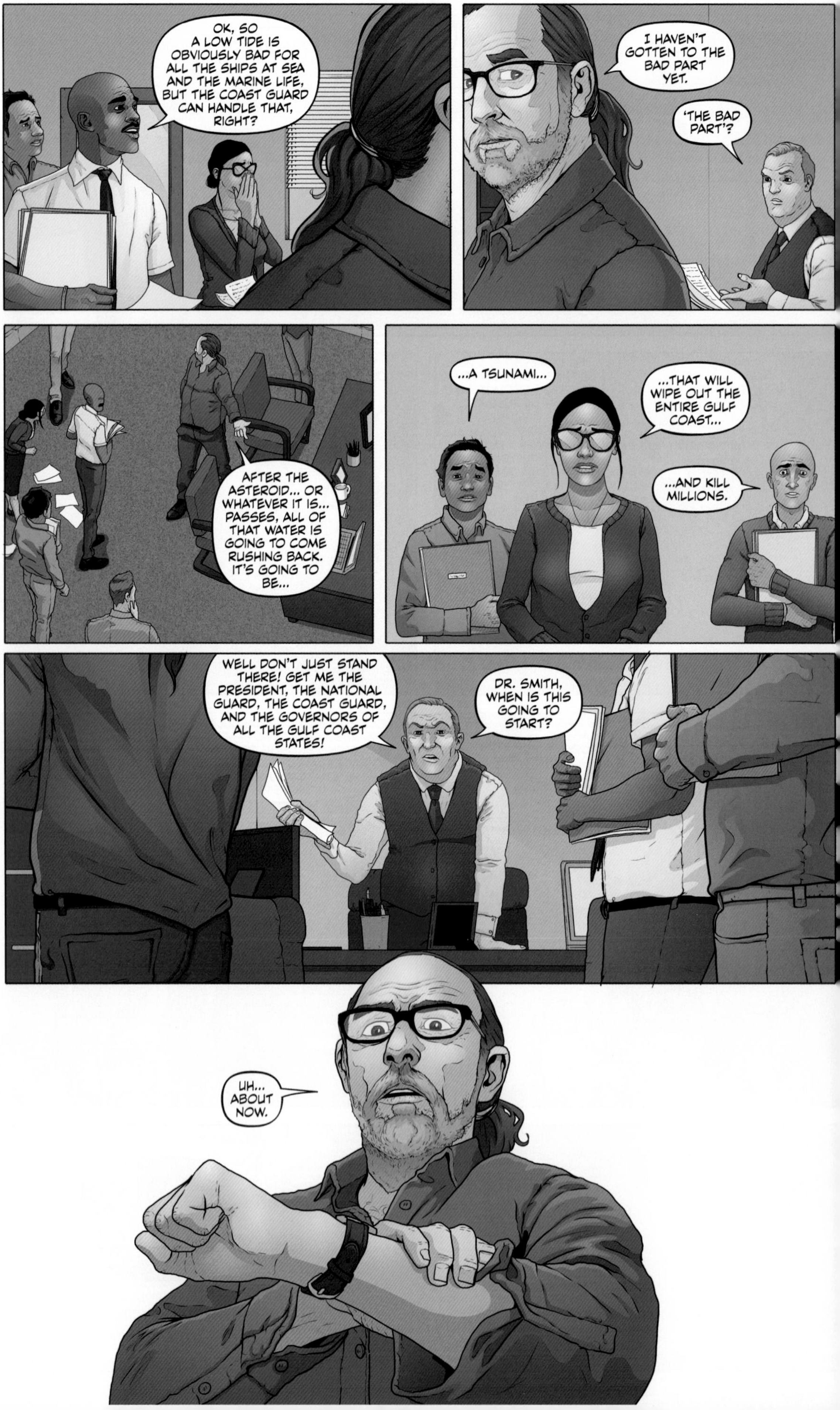
OK, SO A LOW TIDE IS OBVIOUSLY BAD FOR ALL THE SHIPS AT SEA AND THE MARINE LIFE, BUT THE COAST GUARD CAN HANDLE THAT, RIGHT?
I HAVEN'T GOTTEN TO THE BAD PART YET.
'THE BAD PART'?
AFTER THE ASTEROID... OR WHATEVER IT IS... PASSES, ALL OF THAT WATER IS GOING TO COME RUSHING BACK. IT'S GOING TO BE...
...A TSUNAMI...
...THAT WILL WIPE OUT THE ENTIRE GULF COAST...
...AND KILL MILLIONS.
WELL DON'T JUST STAND THERE! GET ME THE PRESIDENT, THE NATIONAL GUARD, THE COAST GUARD, AND THE GOVERNORS OF ALL THE GULF COAST STATES!
DR. SMITH, WHEN IS THIS GOING TO START?
UH... ABOUT NOW.

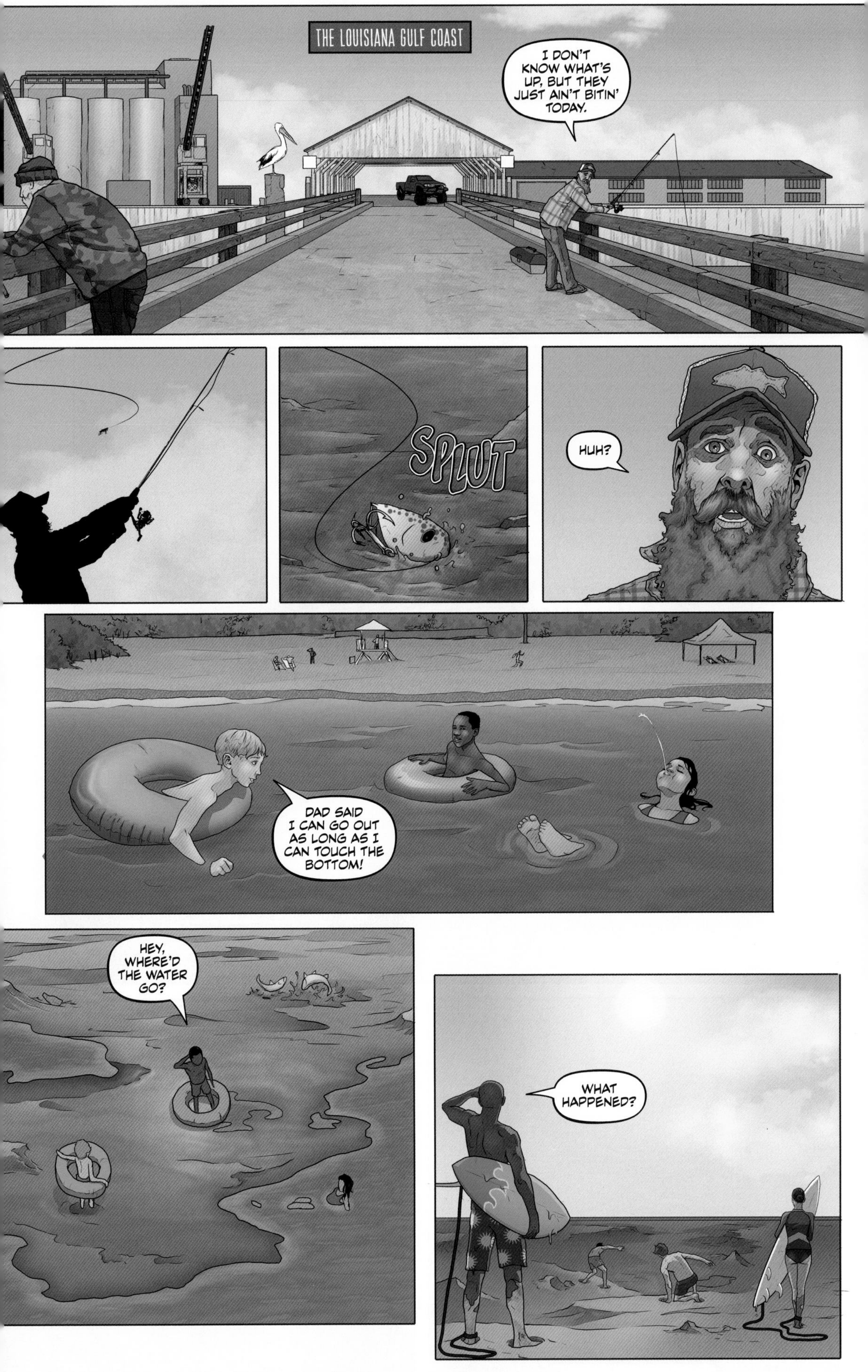
THE LOUISIANA GULF COAST
I DON'T KNOW WHAT'S UP, BUT THEY JUST AIN'T BITIN' TODAY.
SPLUT
HUH?
DAD SAID I CAN GO OUT AS LONG AS I CAN TOUCH THE BOTTOM!
HEY, WHERE'D THE WATER GO?
WHAT HAPPENED?

VRMMMMMMM

HEY, YOU FEEL THAT CURRENT?

AAAAHHH!

THUD

PETE! BRING IT AROUND BEFORE WE...

VRMMMMMMM

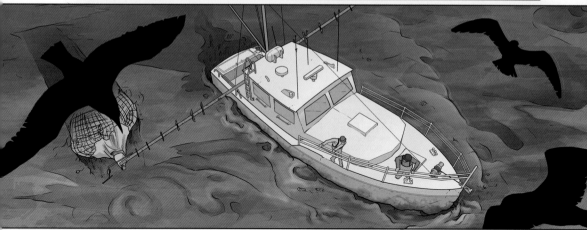

CAW! CAW! CAW!

THE TIDE JUST ROLLED OUT!

AIN'T SEEN NOTHIN' LIKE DAT BEFORE.

BWAAAAAMM

SHE'S HEADED RIGHT FOR US!

SOUND THE COLLISION ALARM!

KA-THOOM

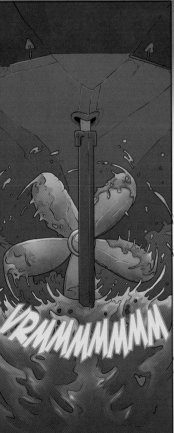

VRMMMMMMM

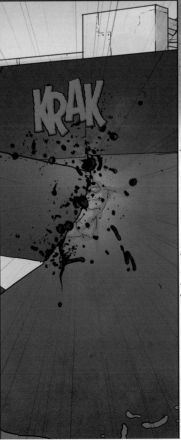

KRAK

WE HAVE A HULL BREACH!

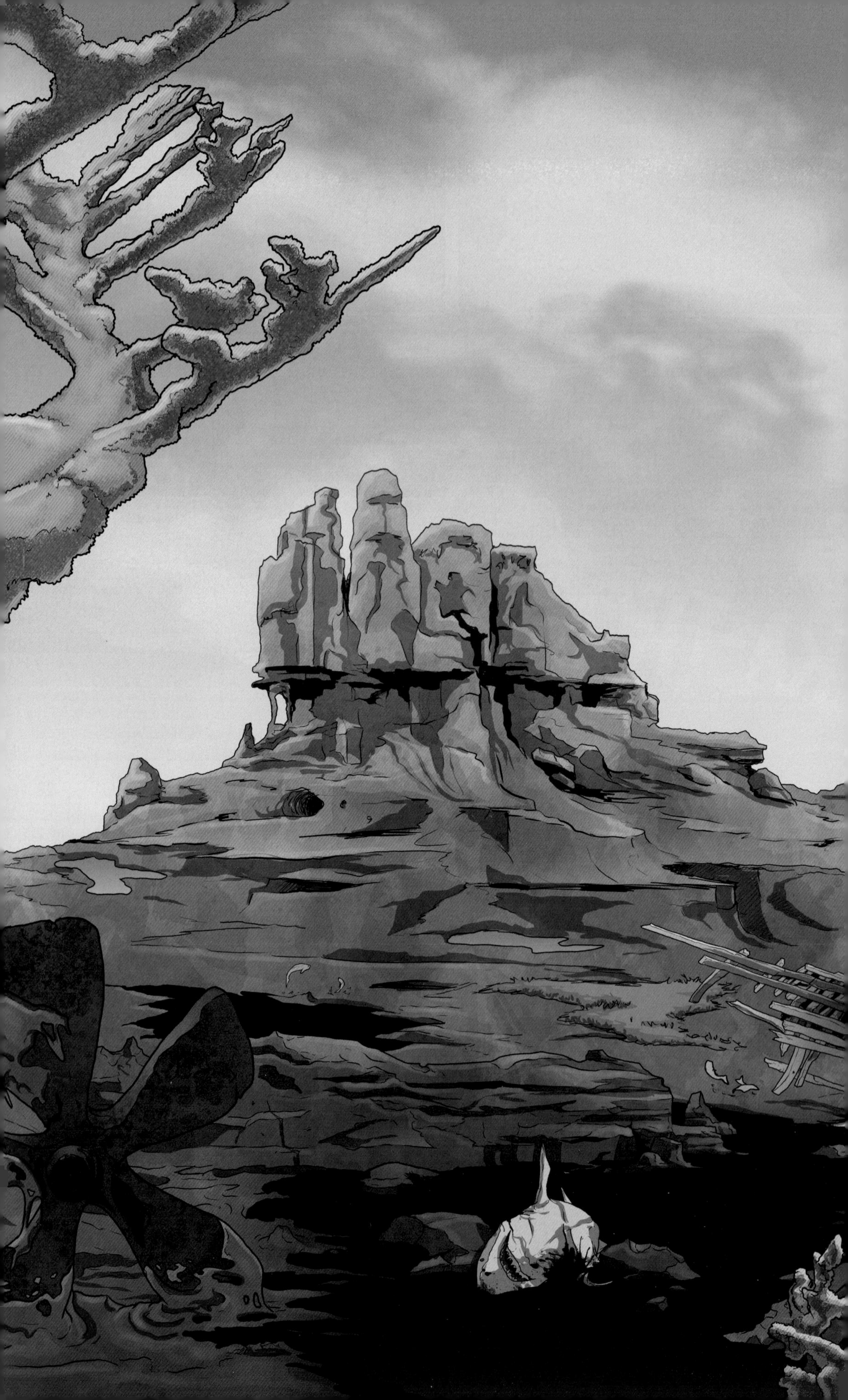

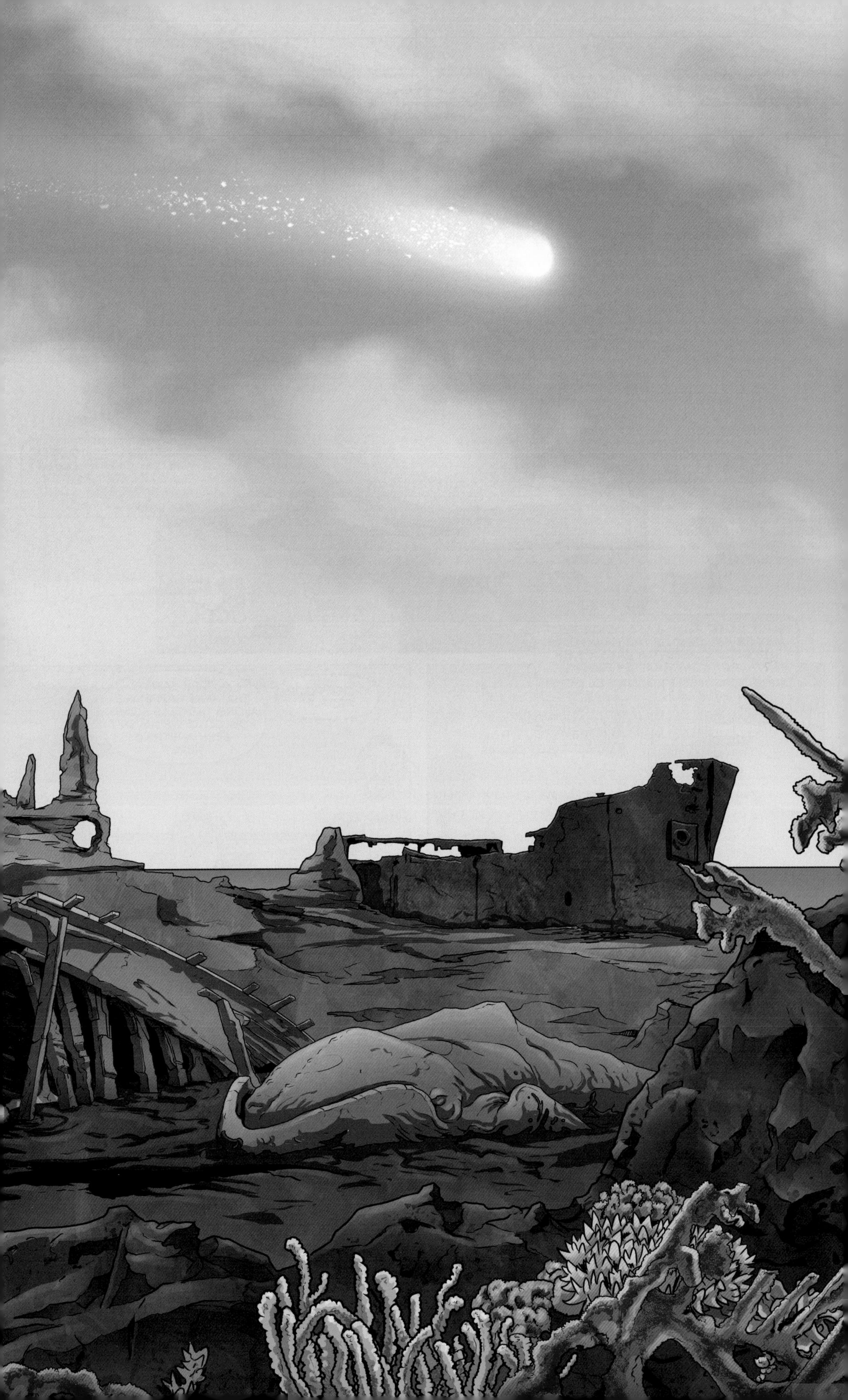

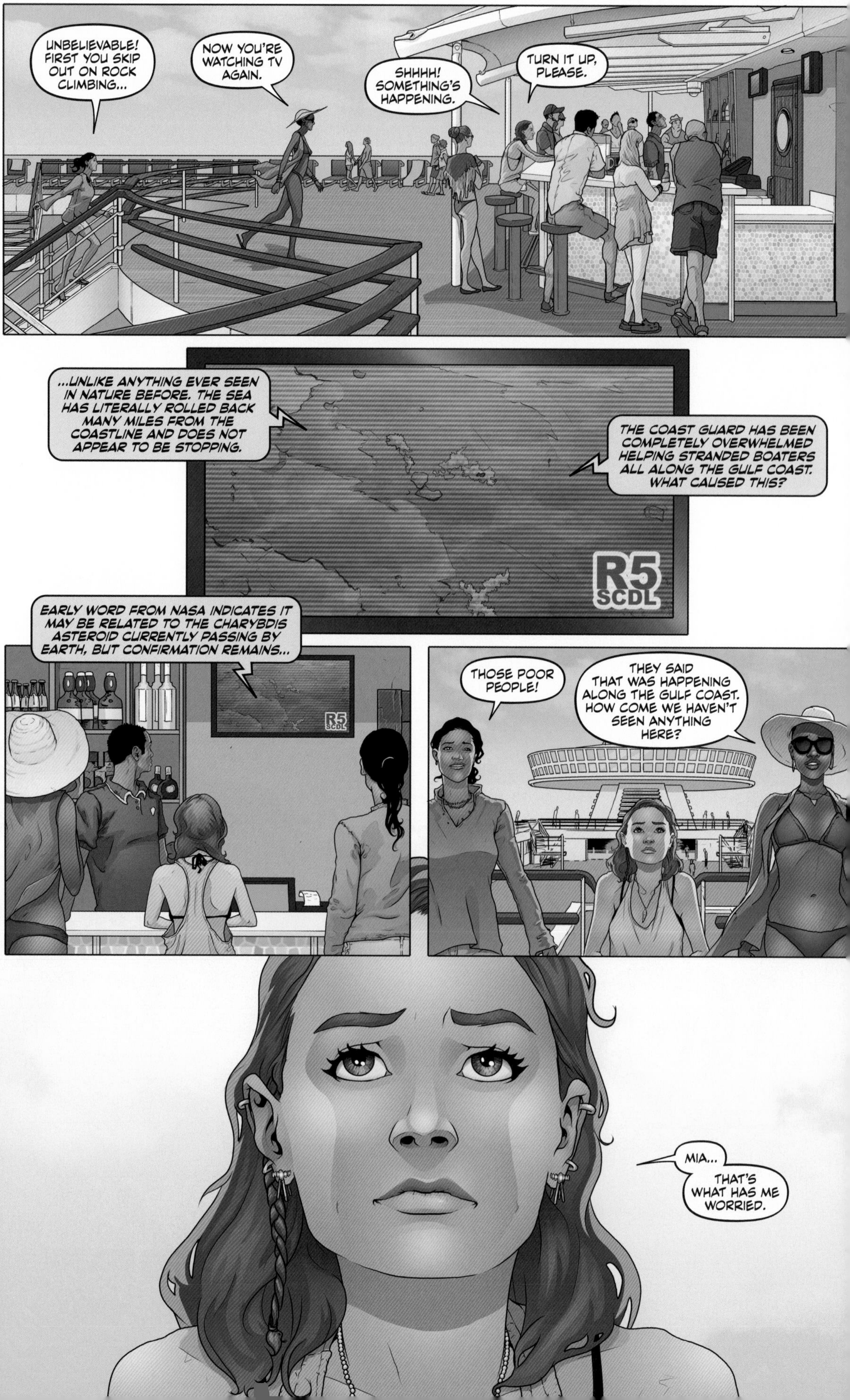
UNBELIEVABLE! FIRST YOU SKIP OUT ON ROCK CLIMBING...
NOW YOU'RE WATCHING TV AGAIN.
SHHHH! SOMETHING'S HAPPENING.
TURN IT UP, PLEASE.
...UNLIKE ANYTHING EVER SEEN IN NATURE BEFORE. THE SEA HAS LITERALLY ROLLED BACK MANY MILES FROM THE COASTLINE AND DOES NOT APPEAR TO BE STOPPING.
THE COAST GUARD HAS BEEN COMPLETELY OVERWHELMED HELPING STRANDED BOATERS ALL ALONG THE GULF COAST. WHAT CAUSED THIS?
R5 SCDL
EARLY WORD FROM NASA INDICATES IT MAY BE RELATED TO THE CHARYBDIS ASTEROID CURRENTLY PASSING BY EARTH, BUT CONFIRMATION REMAINS...
R5 SCDL
THOSE POOR PEOPLE!
THEY SAID THAT WAS HAPPENING ALONG THE GULF COAST. HOW COME WE HAVEN'T SEEN ANYTHING HERE?
MIA... THAT'S WHAT HAS ME WORRIED.

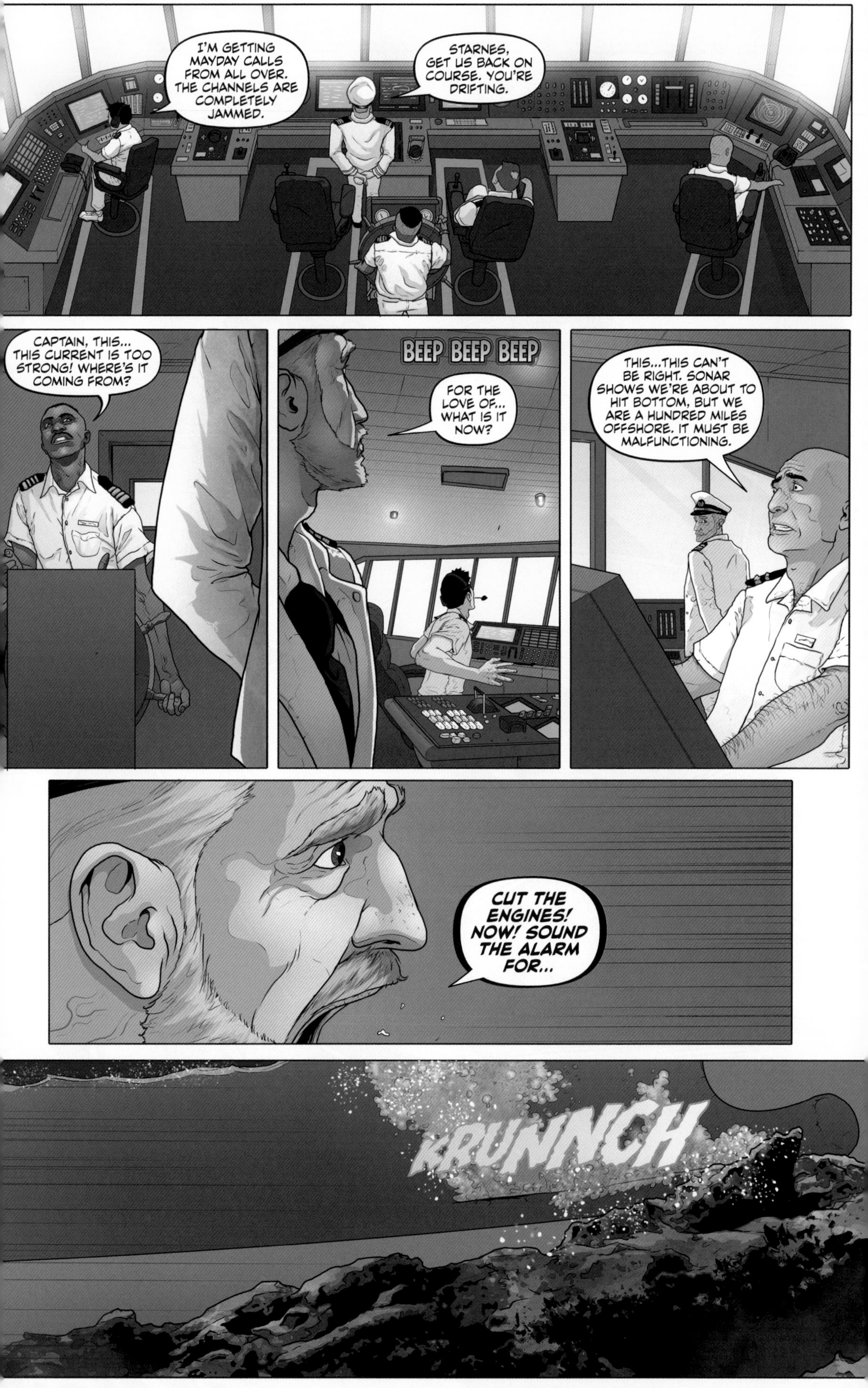
I'M GETTING MAYDAY CALLS FROM ALL OVER. THE CHANNELS ARE COMPLETELY JAMMED.
STARNES, GET US BACK ON COURSE. YOU'RE DRIFTING.
CAPTAIN, THIS... THIS CURRENT IS TOO STRONG! WHERE'S IT COMING FROM?
BEEP BEEP BEEP
FOR THE LOVE OF... WHAT IS IT NOW?
THIS...THIS CAN'T BE RIGHT. SONAR SHOWS WE'RE ABOUT TO HIT BOTTOM, BUT WE ARE A HUNDRED MILES OFFSHORE. IT MUST BE MALFUNCTIONING.
CUT THE ENGINES! NOW! SOUND THE ALARM FOR...
KRUNNCH

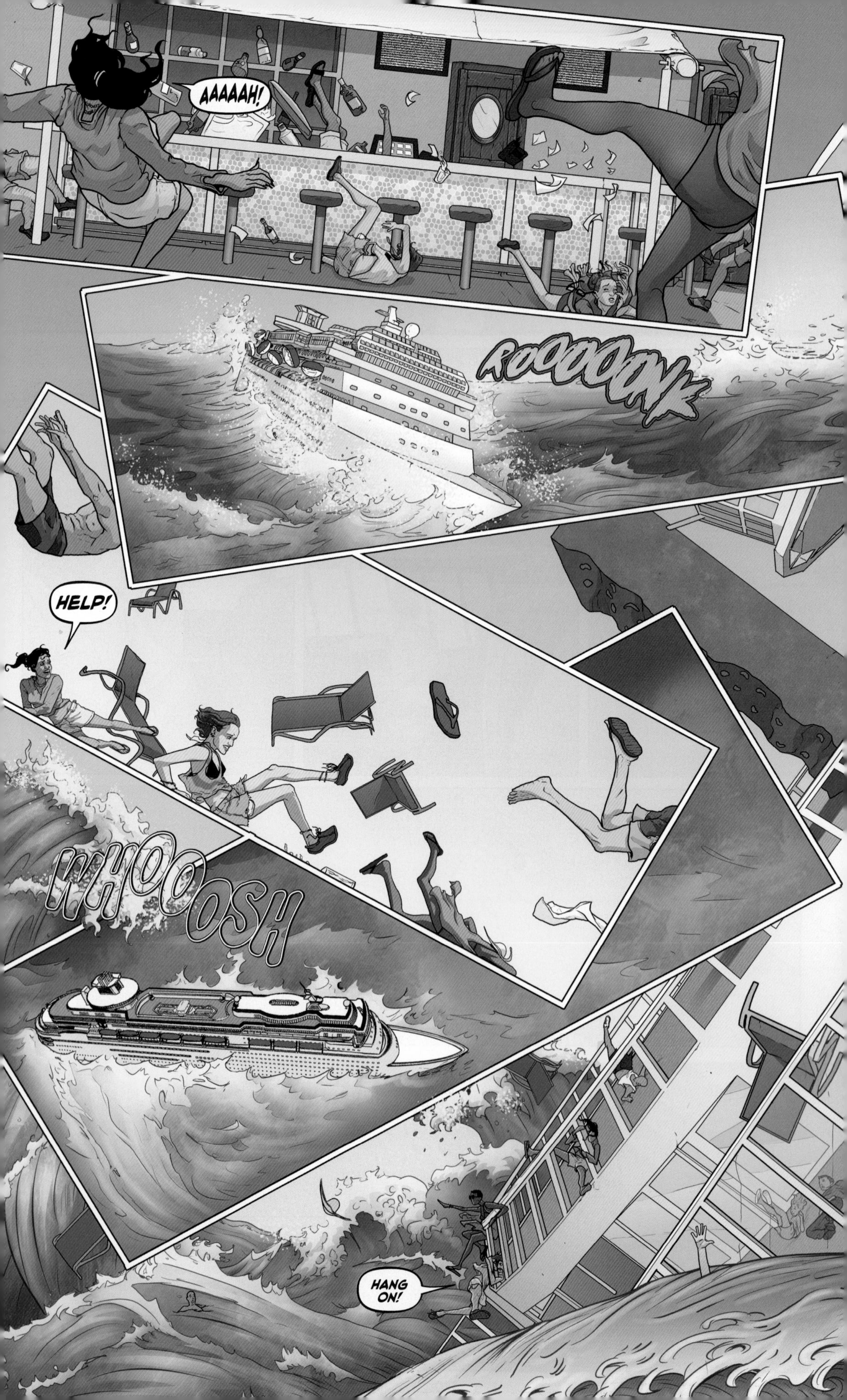
AAAAAH!
ROOOOONK
HELP!
WHOOOSH
HANG ON!

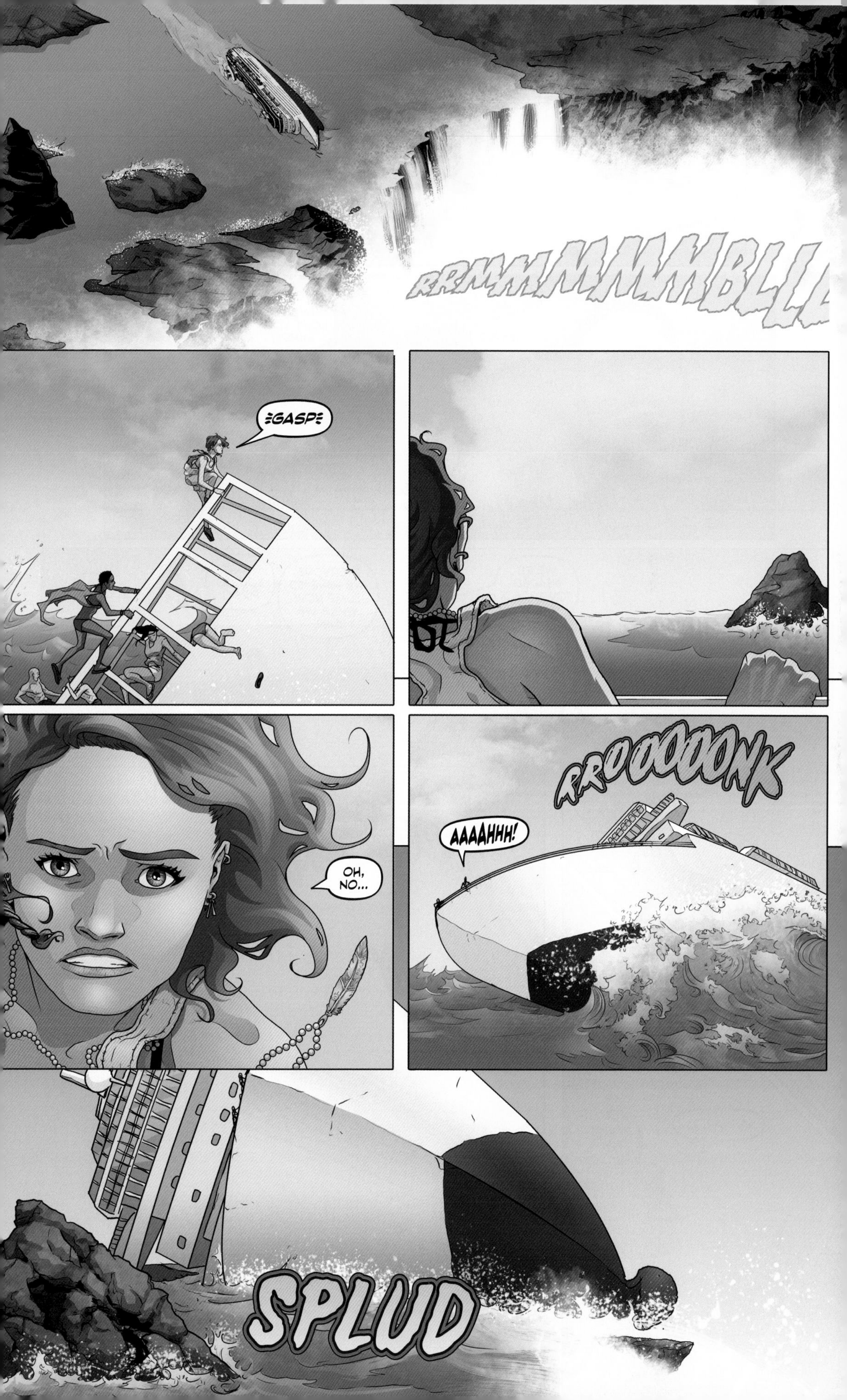
RRMMMMMMMBLLL
GASP
OH, NO...
RROOOOONK
AAAAHHH!
SPLUD

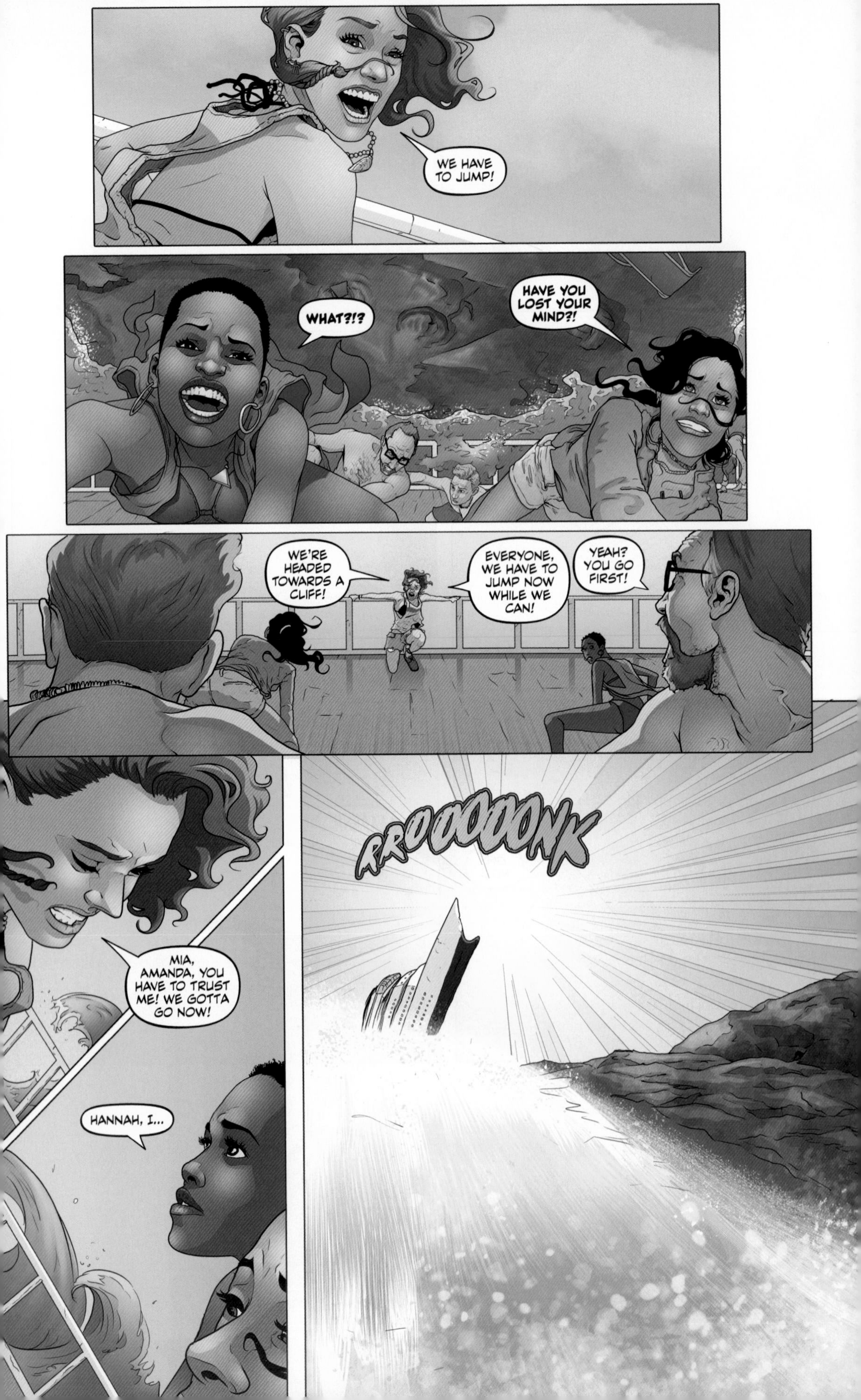
WE HAVE TO JUMP!
WHAT?!?
HAVE YOU LOST YOUR MIND?!
WE'RE HEADED TOWARDS A CLIFF!
EVERYONE, WE HAVE TO JUMP NOW WHILE WE CAN!
YEAH? YOU GO FIRST!
MIA, AMANDA, YOU HAVE TO TRUST ME! WE GOTTA GO NOW!
HANNAH, I...
RROOOOOONK

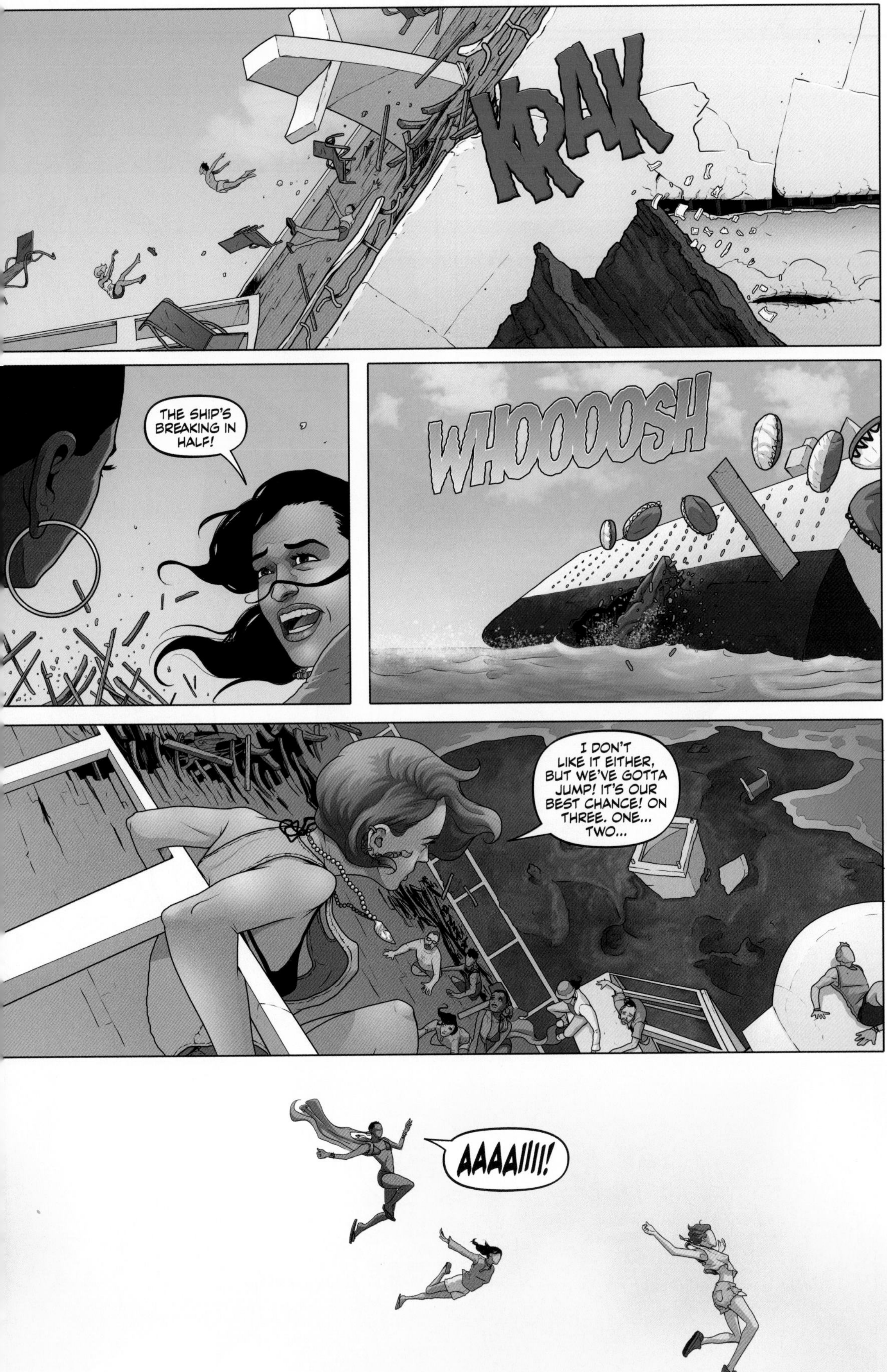
KRAK
THE SHIP'S BREAKING IN HALF!
WHOOOOSH
I DON'T LIKE IT EITHER, BUT WE'VE GOTTA JUMP! IT'S OUR BEST CHANCE! ON THREE. ONE... TWO...
AAAAIIII!

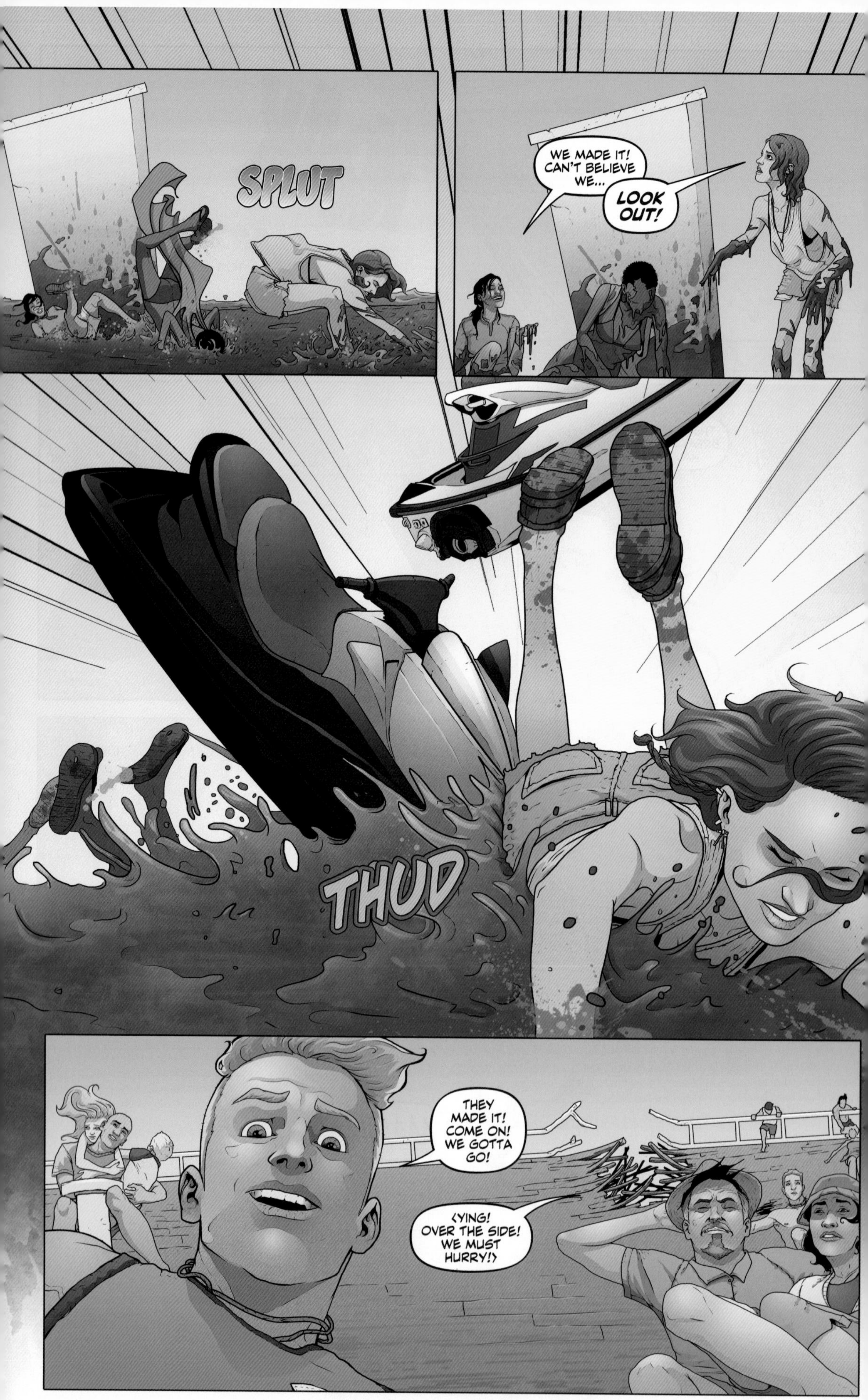
SPLUT
WE MADE IT! CAN'T BELIEVE WE...
LOOK OUT!
THUD
THEY MADE IT! COME ON! WE GOTTA GO!
‹YING! OVER THE SIDE! WE MUST HURRY!›

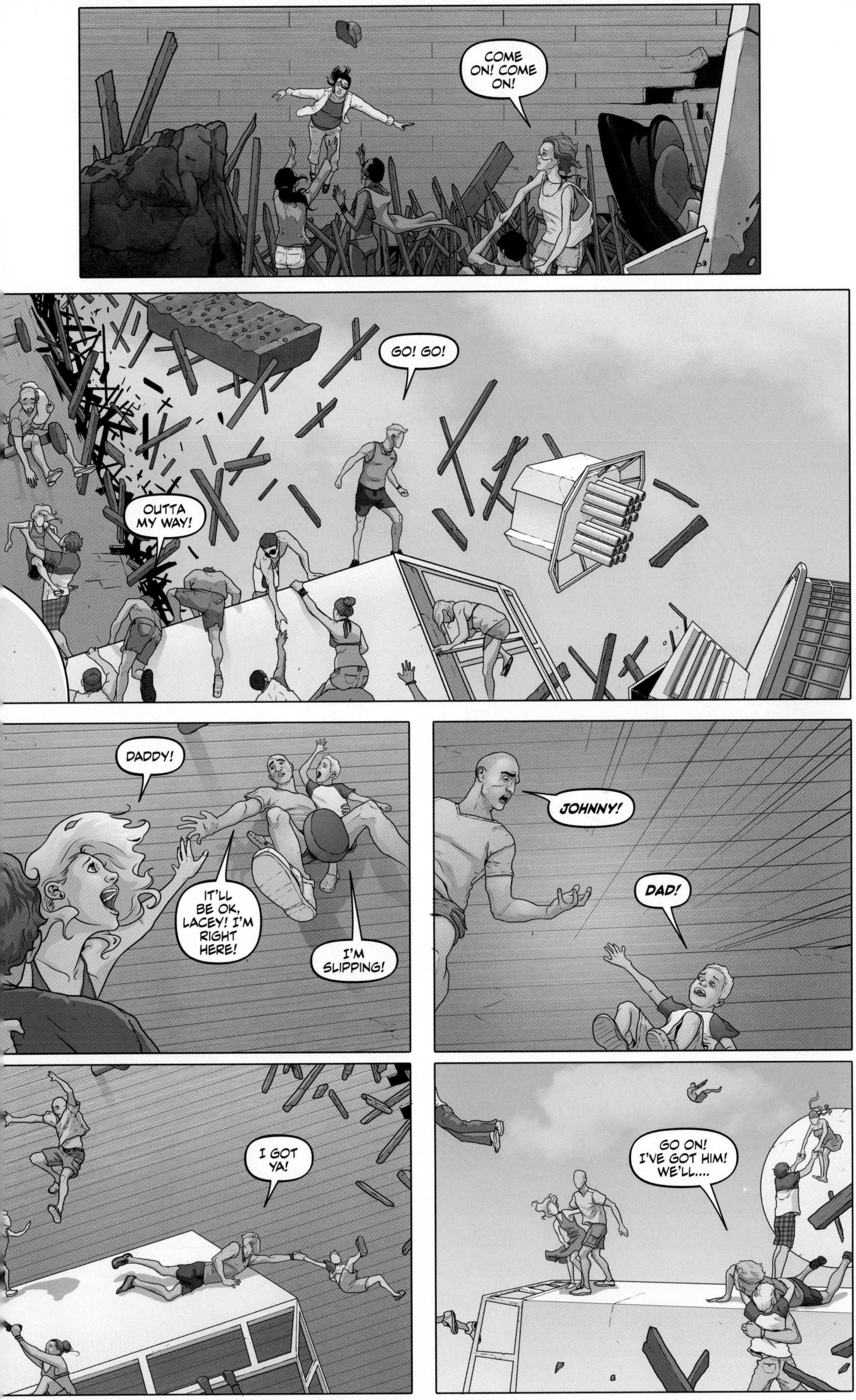
COME ON! COME ON!
GO! GO!
OUTTA MY WAY!
DADDY!
IT'LL BE OK, LACEY! I'M RIGHT HERE!
I'M SLIPPING!
JOHNNY!
DAD!
I GOT YA!
GO ON! I'VE GOT HIM! WE'LL....

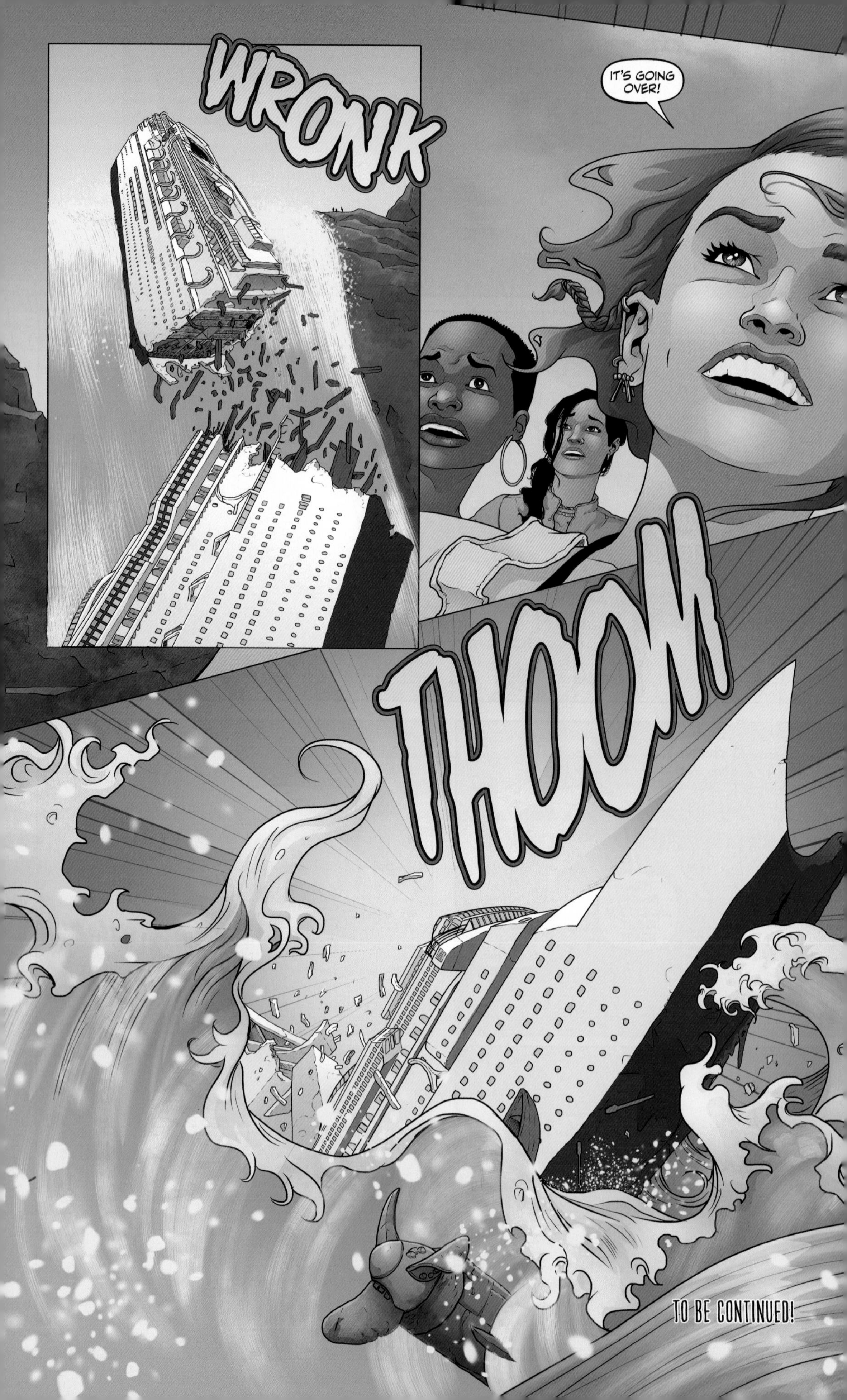
WRONK
IT'S GOING OVER!
THOOM
TO BE CONTINUED!

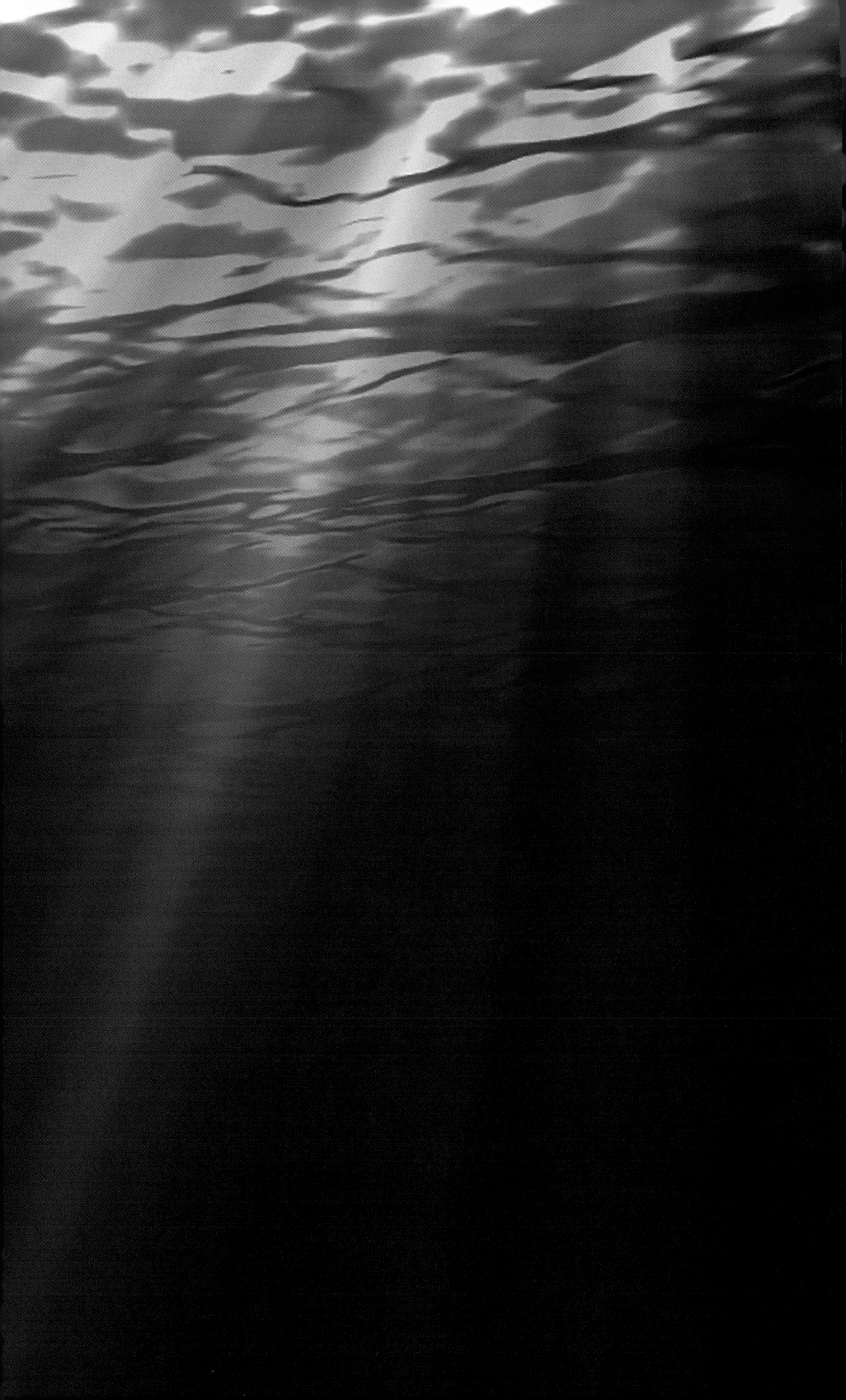

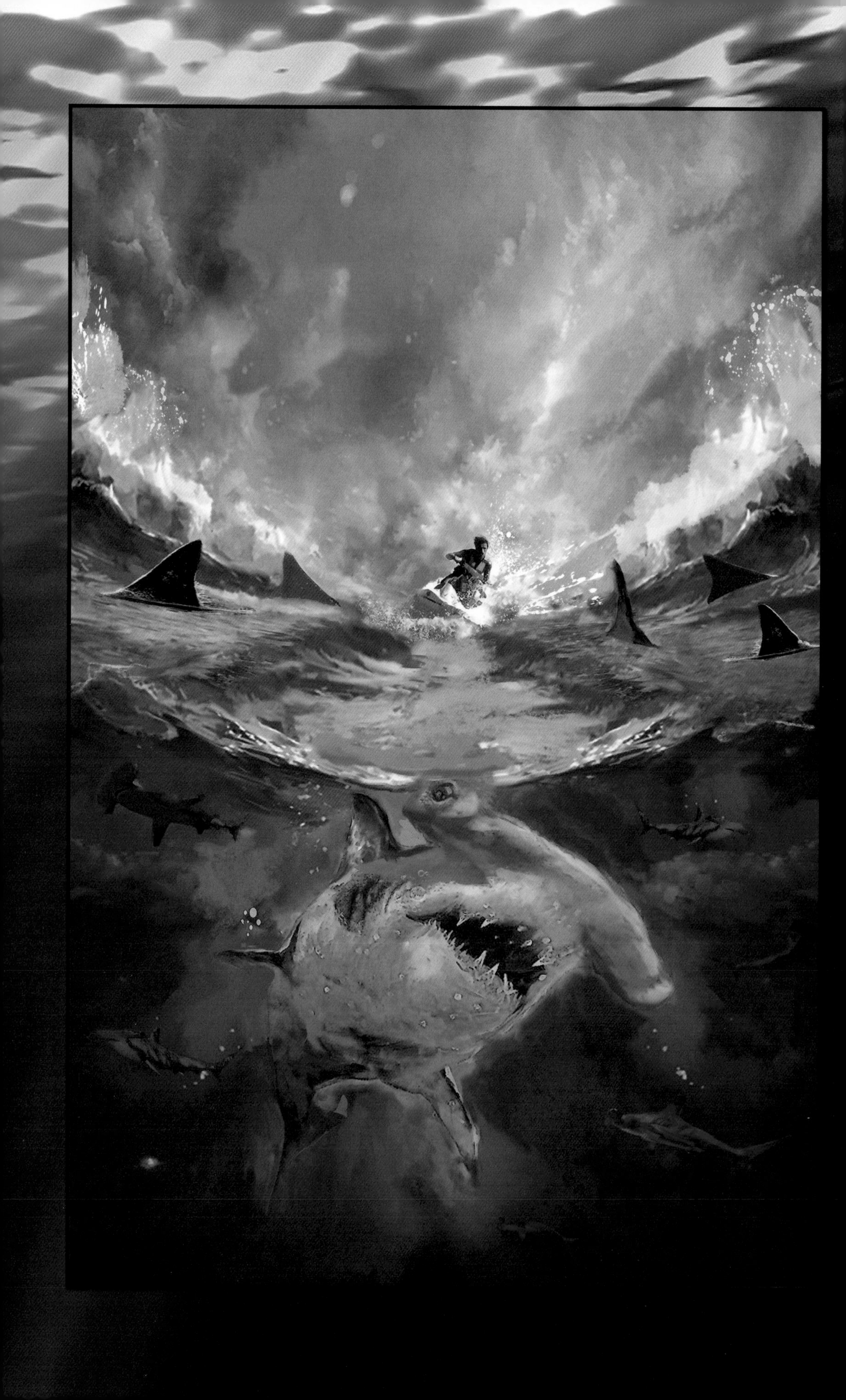

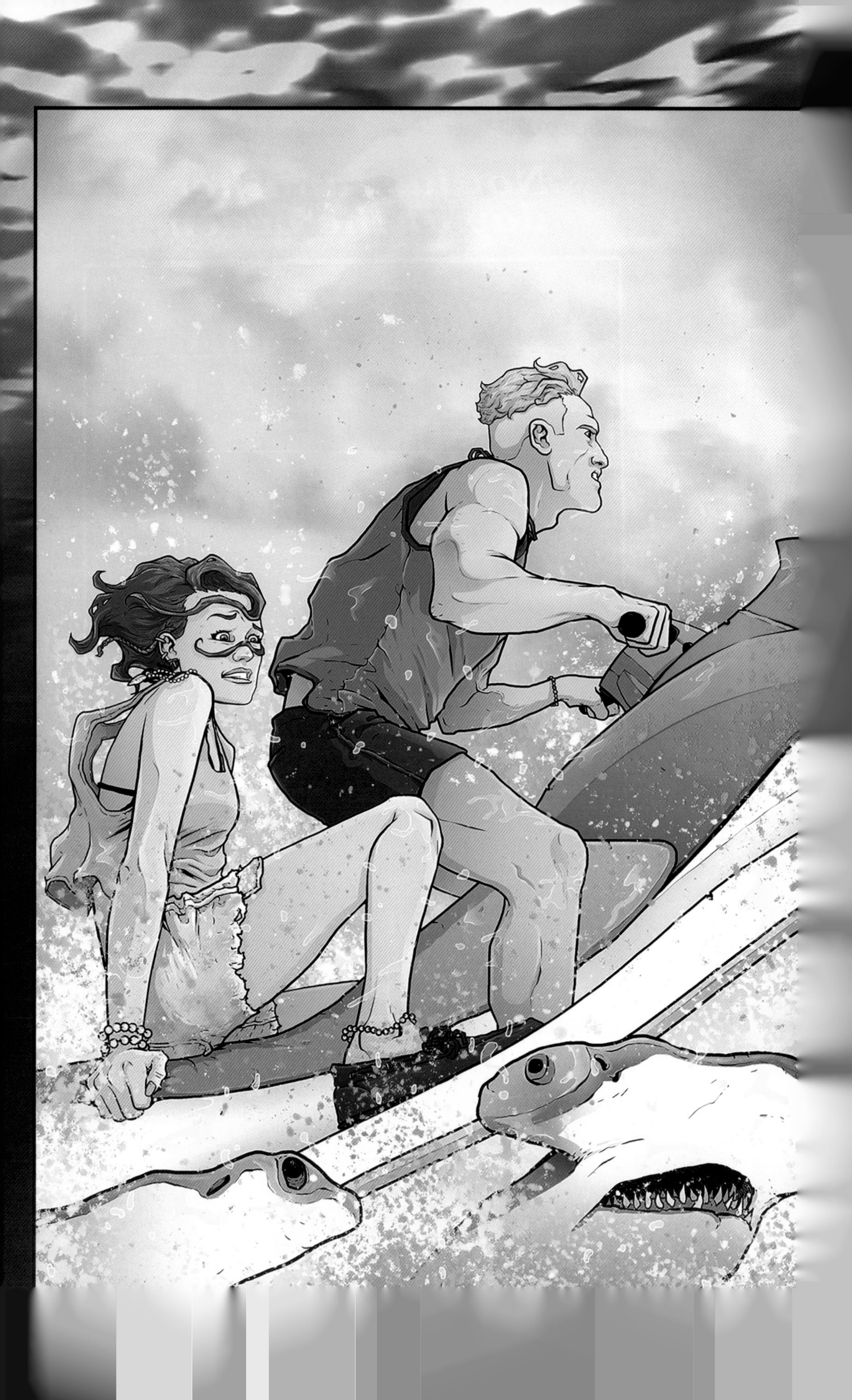

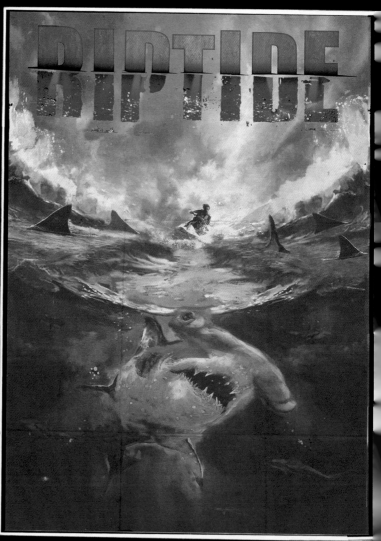

Not just another
day at the beach.

CHITWOOD RIPTIDE **LUCKERT**

ART BY DANNY LUCKERT COLORS BY RONDA PATTISON LETTERS BY TROY PETERI LOGO BY GARNER McCULLOCH

COVERS BY PAUL ALLAN BALLARD EXECUTIVE PRODUCER PAUL ENS EXECUTIVE PRODUCER JOSHUA STARNES

WRITTEN AND DIRECTED BY SCOTT CHITWOOD

PG PARENTAL GUIDANCE SUGGESTED
SOME MATERIAL MAY NOT BE SUITABLE FOR CHILDREN

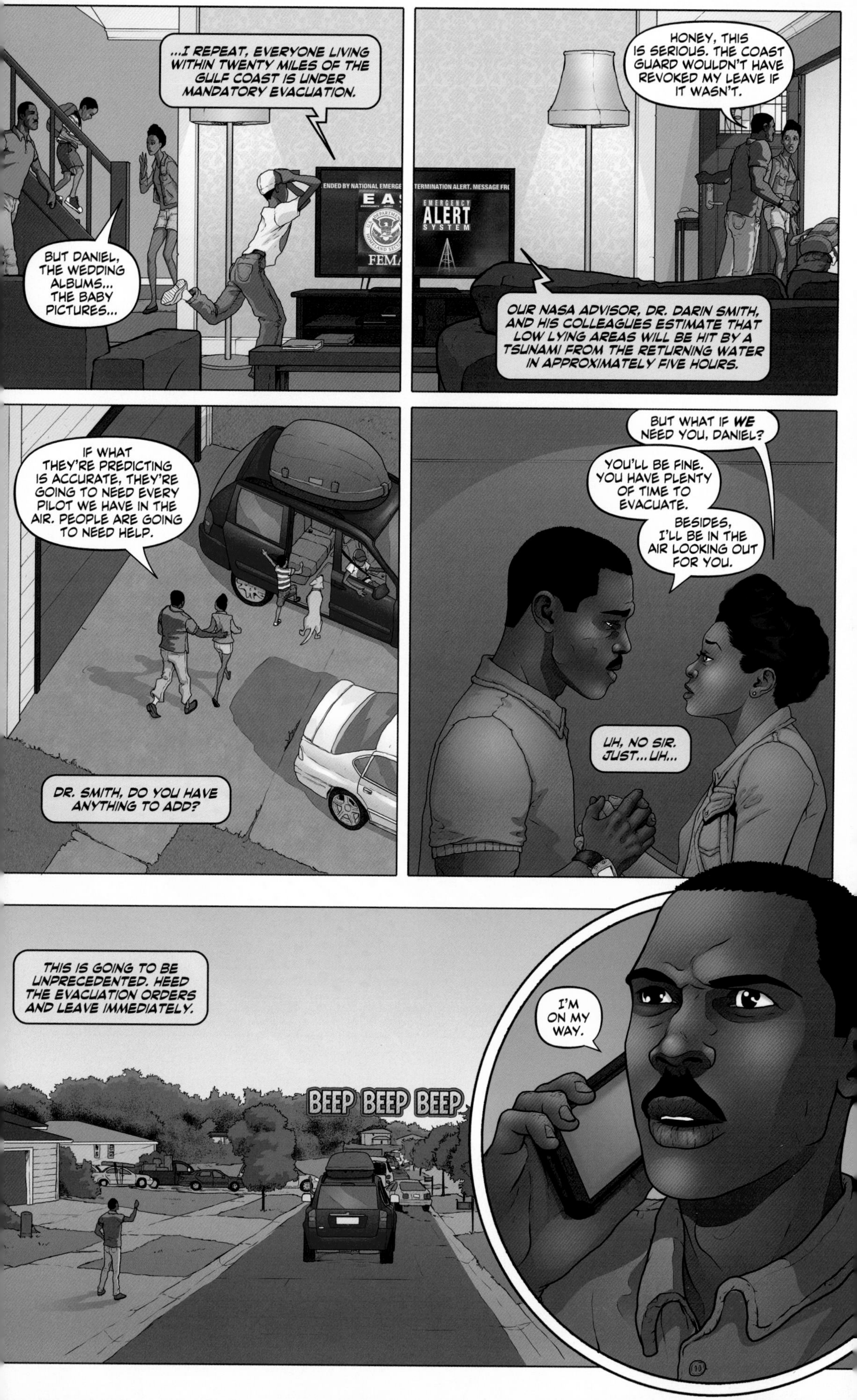
...I REPEAT, EVERYONE LIVING WITHIN TWENTY MILES OF THE GULF COAST IS UNDER MANDATORY EVACUATION.
BUT DANIEL, THE WEDDING ALBUMS... THE BABY PICTURES...
ENDED BY NATIONAL EMERGE TERMINATION ALERT. MESSAGE FR
EAS
FEMA
EMERGENCY ALERT SYSTEM
HONEY, THIS IS SERIOUS. THE COAST GUARD WOULDN'T HAVE REVOKED MY LEAVE IF IT WASN'T.
OUR NASA ADVISOR, DR. DARIN SMITH, AND HIS COLLEAGUES ESTIMATE THAT LOW LYING AREAS WILL BE HIT BY A TSUNAMI FROM THE RETURNING WATER IN APPROXIMATELY FIVE HOURS.
IF WHAT THEY'RE PREDICTING IS ACCURATE, THEY'RE GOING TO NEED EVERY PILOT WE HAVE IN THE AIR. PEOPLE ARE GOING TO NEED HELP.
DR. SMITH, DO YOU HAVE ANYTHING TO ADD?
BUT WHAT IF WE NEED YOU, DANIEL?
YOU'LL BE FINE. YOU HAVE PLENTY OF TIME TO EVACUATE.
BESIDES, I'LL BE IN THE AIR LOOKING OUT FOR YOU.
UH, NO SIR. JUST...UH...
THIS IS GOING TO BE UNPRECEDENTED. HEED THE EVACUATION ORDERS AND LEAVE IMMEDIATELY.
BEEP BEEP BEEP
I'M ON MY WAY.

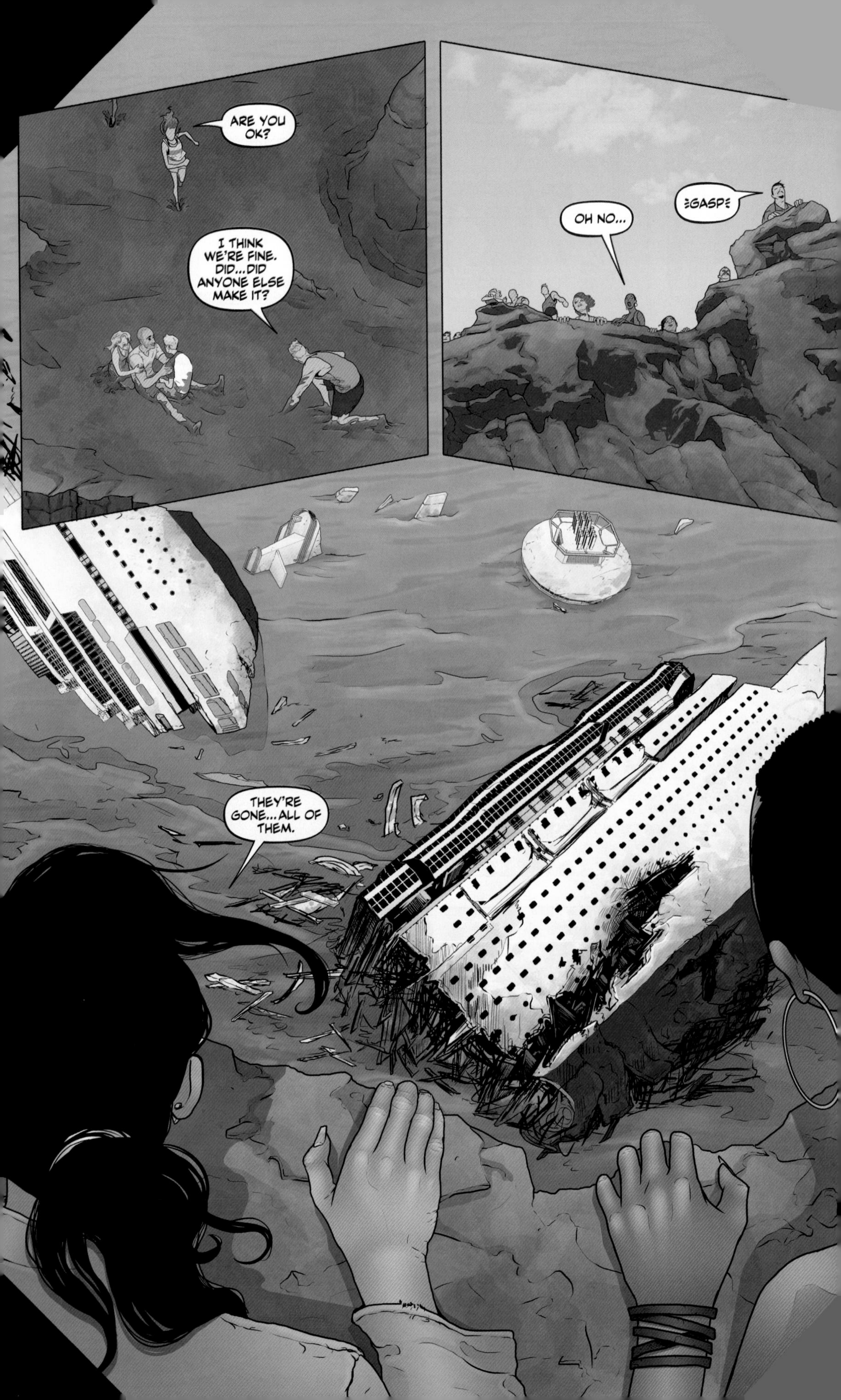
ARE YOU OK?
I THINK WE'RE FINE. DID...DID ANYONE ELSE MAKE IT?
≡GASP≡
OH NO...
THEY'RE GONE...ALL OF THEM.

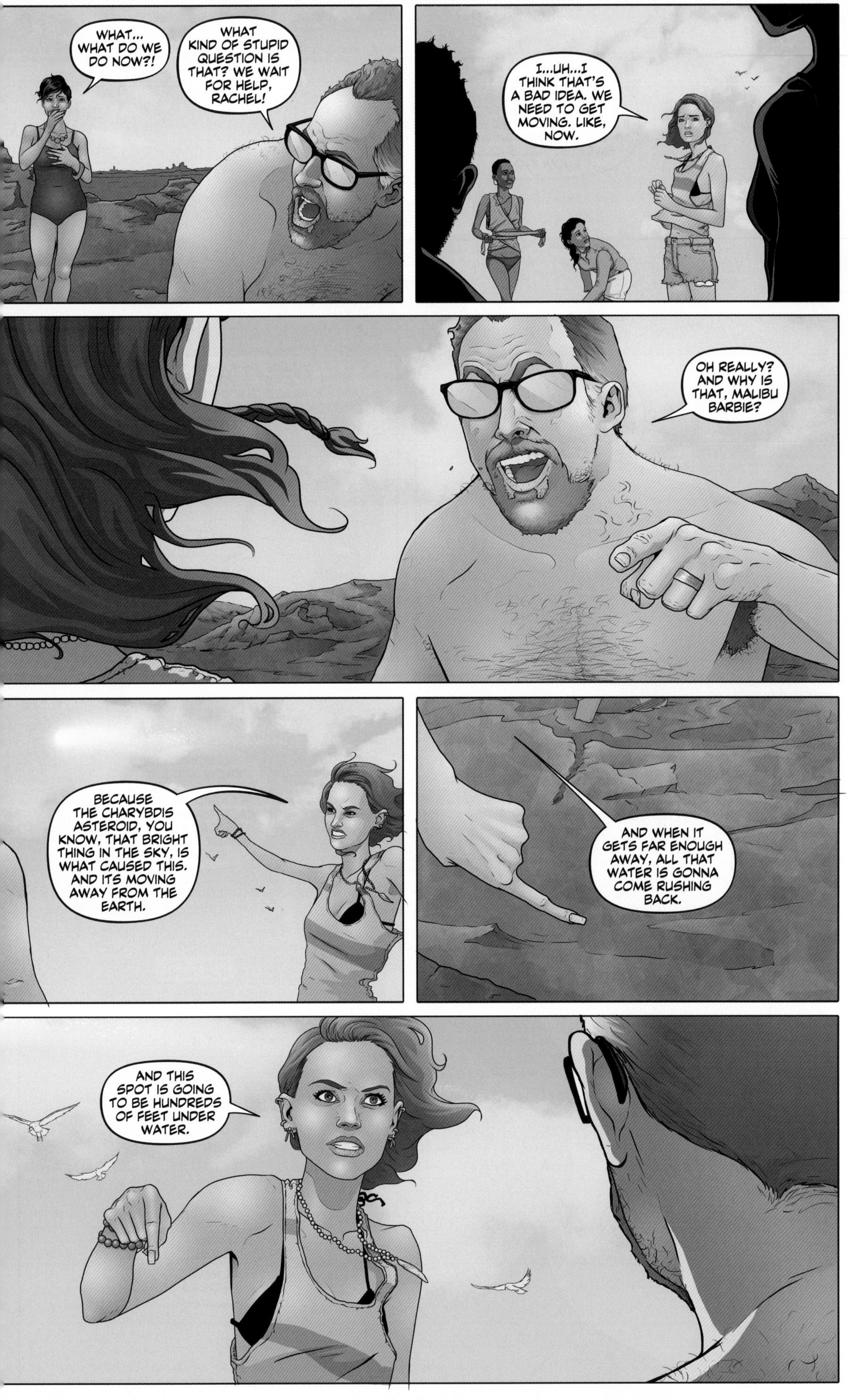
WHAT... WHAT DO WE DO NOW?!
WHAT KIND OF STUPID QUESTION IS THAT? WE WAIT FOR HELP, RACHEL!
I...UH...I THINK THAT'S A BAD IDEA. WE NEED TO GET MOVING. LIKE, NOW.
OH REALLY? AND WHY IS THAT, MALIBU BARBIE?
BECAUSE THE CHARYBDIS ASTEROID, YOU KNOW, THAT BRIGHT THING IN THE SKY, IS WHAT CAUSED THIS. AND ITS MOVING AWAY FROM THE EARTH.
AND WHEN IT GETS FAR ENOUGH AWAY, ALL THAT WATER IS GONNA COME RUSHING BACK.
AND THIS SPOT IS GOING TO BE HUNDREDS OF FEET UNDER WATER.

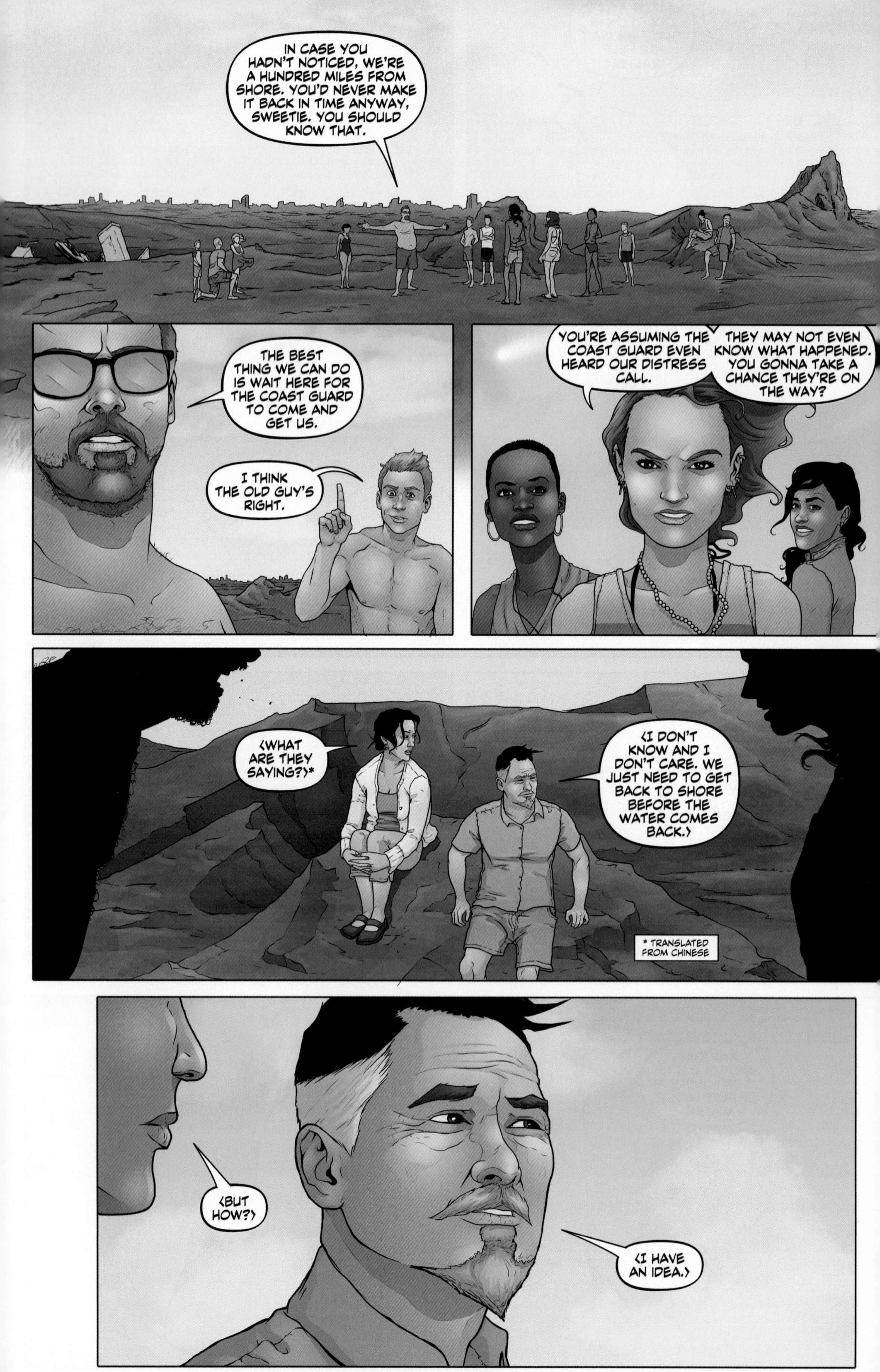
IN CASE YOU HADN'T NOTICED, WE'RE A HUNDRED MILES FROM SHORE. YOU'D NEVER MAKE IT BACK IN TIME ANYWAY, SWEETIE. YOU SHOULD KNOW THAT.
THE BEST THING WE CAN DO IS WAIT HERE FOR THE COAST GUARD TO COME AND GET US.
I THINK THE OLD GUY'S RIGHT.
YOU'RE ASSUMING THE COAST GUARD EVEN HEARD OUR DISTRESS CALL.
THEY MAY NOT EVEN KNOW WHAT HAPPENED. YOU GONNA TAKE A CHANCE THEY'RE ON THE WAY?
‹WHAT ARE THEY SAYING?›*
‹I DON'T KNOW AND I DON'T CARE. WE JUST NEED TO GET BACK TO SHORE BEFORE THE WATER COMES BACK.›
* TRANSLATED FROM CHINESE
‹BUT HOW?›
‹I HAVE AN IDEA.›

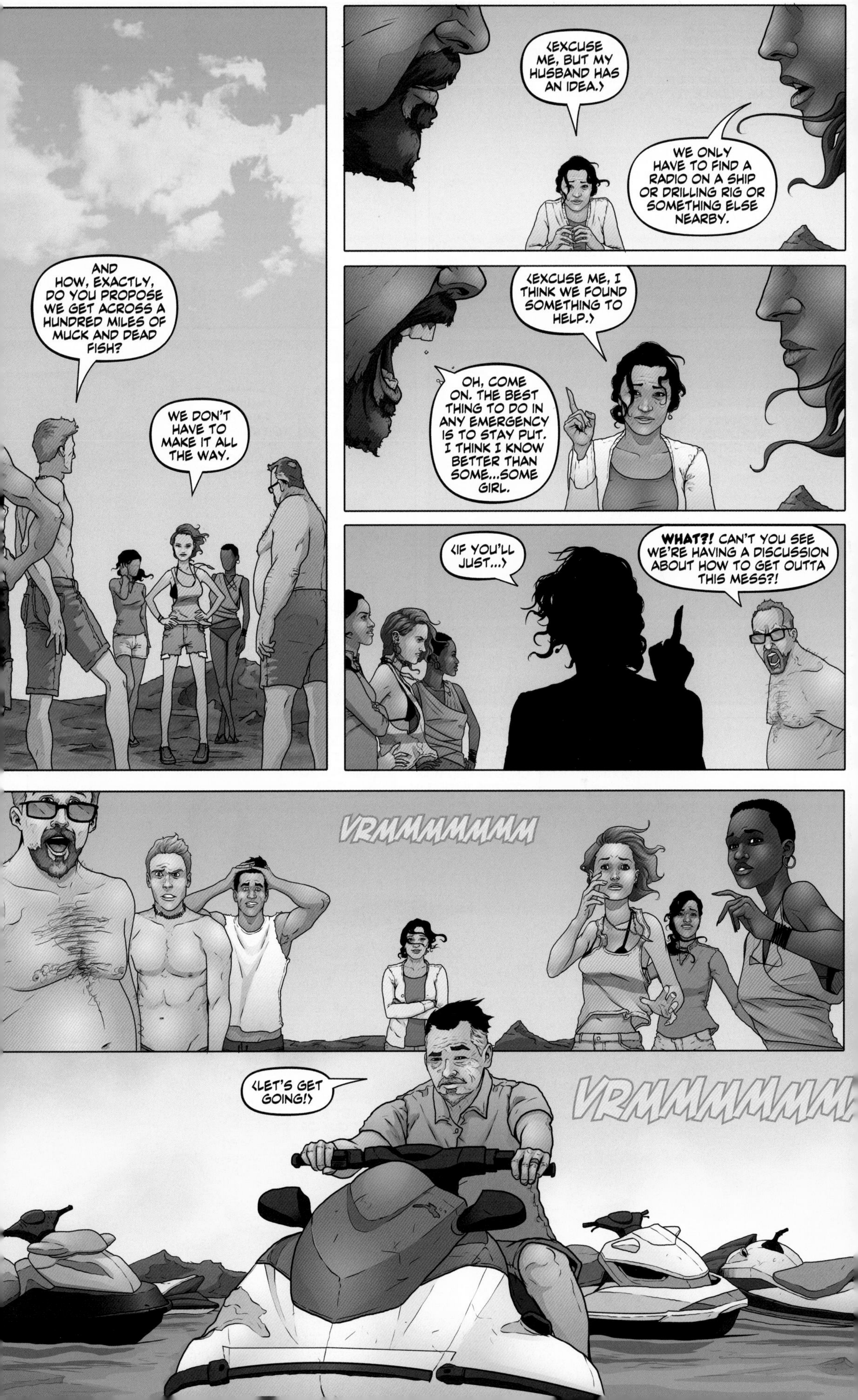
AND HOW, EXACTLY, DO YOU PROPOSE WE GET ACROSS A HUNDRED MILES OF MUCK AND DEAD FISH?
WE DON'T HAVE TO MAKE IT ALL THE WAY.
<EXCUSE ME, BUT MY HUSBAND HAS AN IDEA.>
WE ONLY HAVE TO FIND A RADIO ON A SHIP OR DRILLING RIG OR SOMETHING ELSE NEARBY.
<EXCUSE ME, I THINK WE FOUND SOMETHING TO HELP.>
OH, COME ON. THE BEST THING TO DO IN ANY EMERGENCY IS TO STAY PUT. I THINK I KNOW BETTER THAN SOME...SOME GIRL.
<IF YOU'LL JUST...>
WHAT?! CAN'T YOU SEE WE'RE HAVING A DISCUSSION ABOUT HOW TO GET OUTTA THIS MESS?!
VRMMMMMMM
<LET'S GET GOING!>
VRMMMMMMM

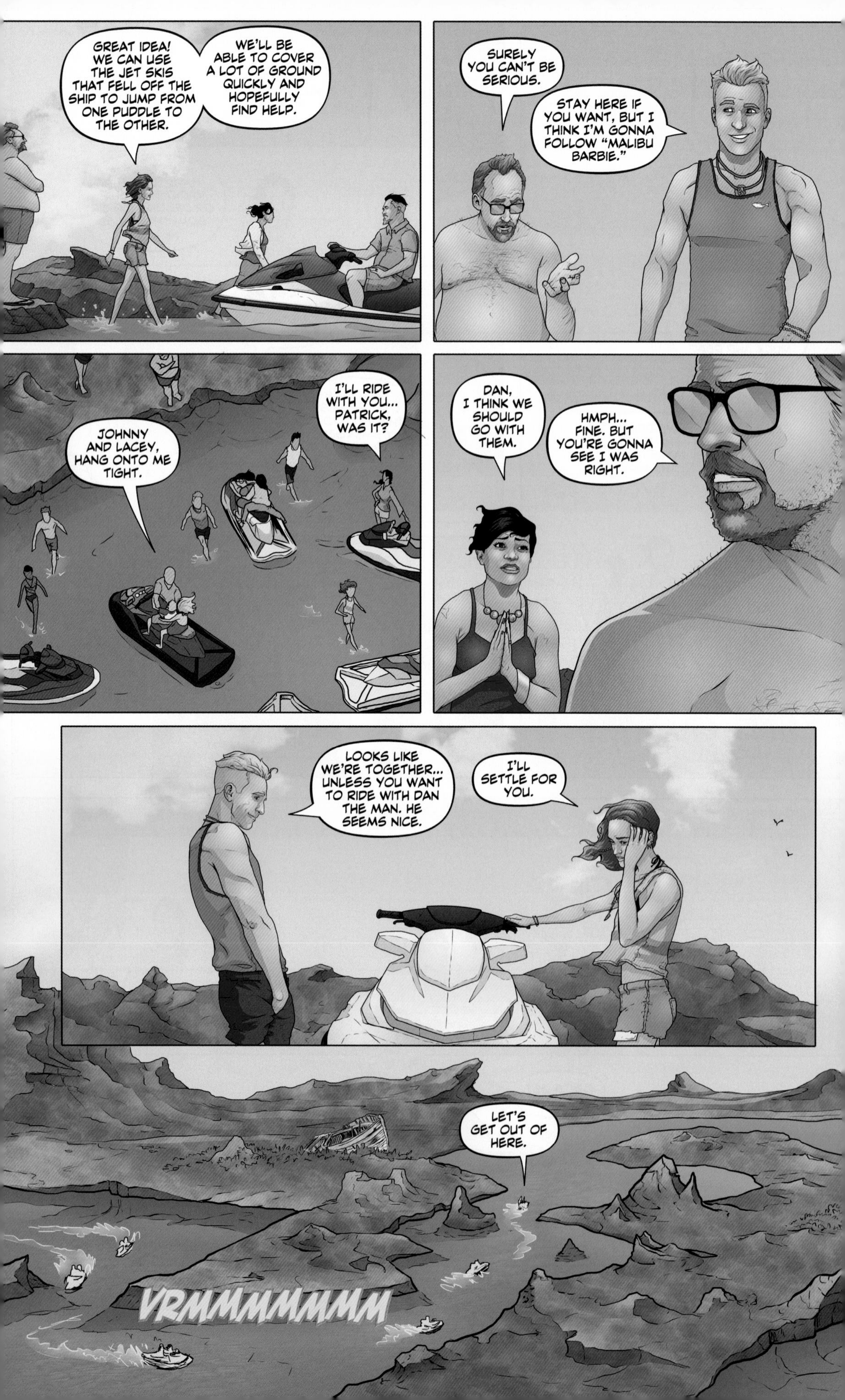
GREAT IDEA! WE CAN USE THE JET SKIS THAT FELL OFF THE SHIP TO JUMP FROM ONE PUDDLE TO THE OTHER.
WE'LL BE ABLE TO COVER A LOT OF GROUND QUICKLY AND HOPEFULLY FIND HELP.
SURELY YOU CAN'T BE SERIOUS.
STAY HERE IF YOU WANT, BUT I THINK I'M GONNA FOLLOW "MALIBU BARBIE."
JOHNNY AND LACEY, HANG ONTO ME TIGHT.
I'LL RIDE WITH YOU... PATRICK, WAS IT?
DAN, I THINK WE SHOULD GO WITH THEM.
HMPH... FINE. BUT YOU'RE GONNA SEE I WAS RIGHT.
LOOKS LIKE WE'RE TOGETHER... UNLESS YOU WANT TO RIDE WITH DAN THE MAN. HE SEEMS NICE.
I'LL SETTLE FOR YOU.
LET'S GET OUT OF HERE.
VRMMMMMMMM

U.S. COAST GUARD - LOUISIANA

...MISSISSIPPI RIVER IS RAPIDS NOW....

...GUESS YOU CAN WALK TO CUBA...

...CARACAS AND CARTAGENA ARE COMPLETELY UNDERWATER...

...PANAMA'S GONE. THE PACIFIC AND CARIBBEAN ARE CONNECTED NOW...

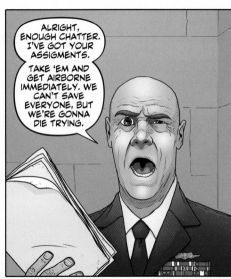

ALRIGHT, ENOUGH CHATTER. I'VE GOT YOUR ASSIGMENTS.

TAKE 'EM AND GET AIRBORNE IMMEDIATELY. WE CAN'T SAVE EVERYONE, BUT WE'RE GONNA DIE TRYING.

COME ON! COME ON! WE'VE GOT PLACES TO GO, PEOPLE TO RESCUE!

I'M COMIN'!

MAN, LOOK AT ALL THAT TRAFFIC! HOW ARE THEY GOING TO...

STAY FOCUSED, DAVID. KEEP AN EYE OUT FOR THAT DISABLED TRAWLER WE'RE LOOKIN' FOR.

INCREDIBLE. THE SEA ROLLED BACK, BUT THE MISSISSIPPI RIVER KEEPS DUMPING WATER ONTO THE DRY SEABED. YOU READY?

YOU KNOW ME, MAN. "SEMPER PARATUS!"

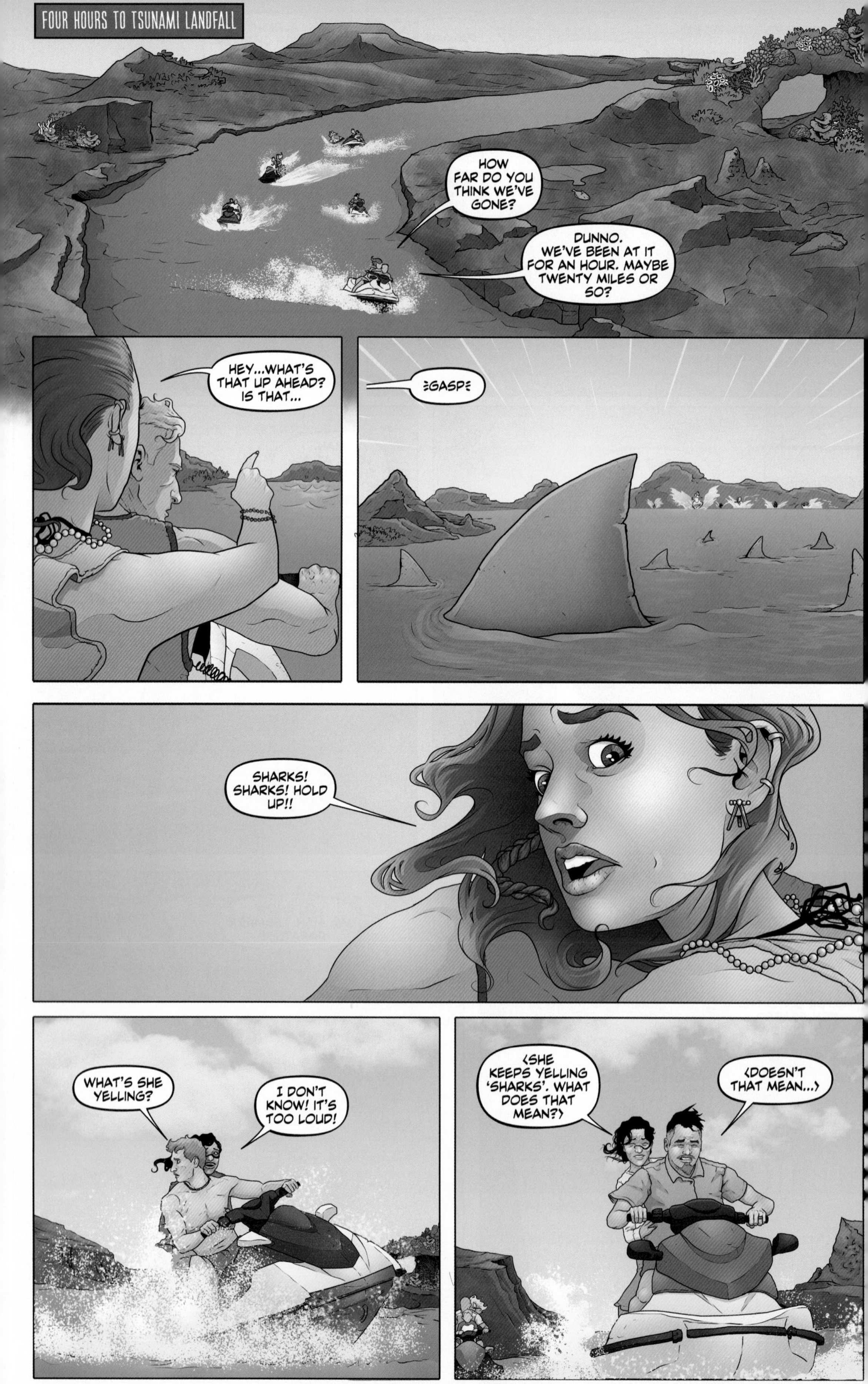
FOUR HOURS TO TSUNAMI LANDFALL
HOW FAR DO YOU THINK WE'VE GONE?
DUNNO. WE'VE BEEN AT IT FOR AN HOUR. MAYBE TWENTY MILES OR SO?
HEY...WHAT'S THAT UP AHEAD? IS THAT...
GASP
SHARKS! SHARKS! HOLD UP!!
WHAT'S SHE YELLING?
I DON'T KNOW! IT'S TOO LOUD!
‹SHE KEEPS YELLING 'SHARKS'. WHAT DOES THAT MEAN?›
‹DOESN'T THAT MEAN...›

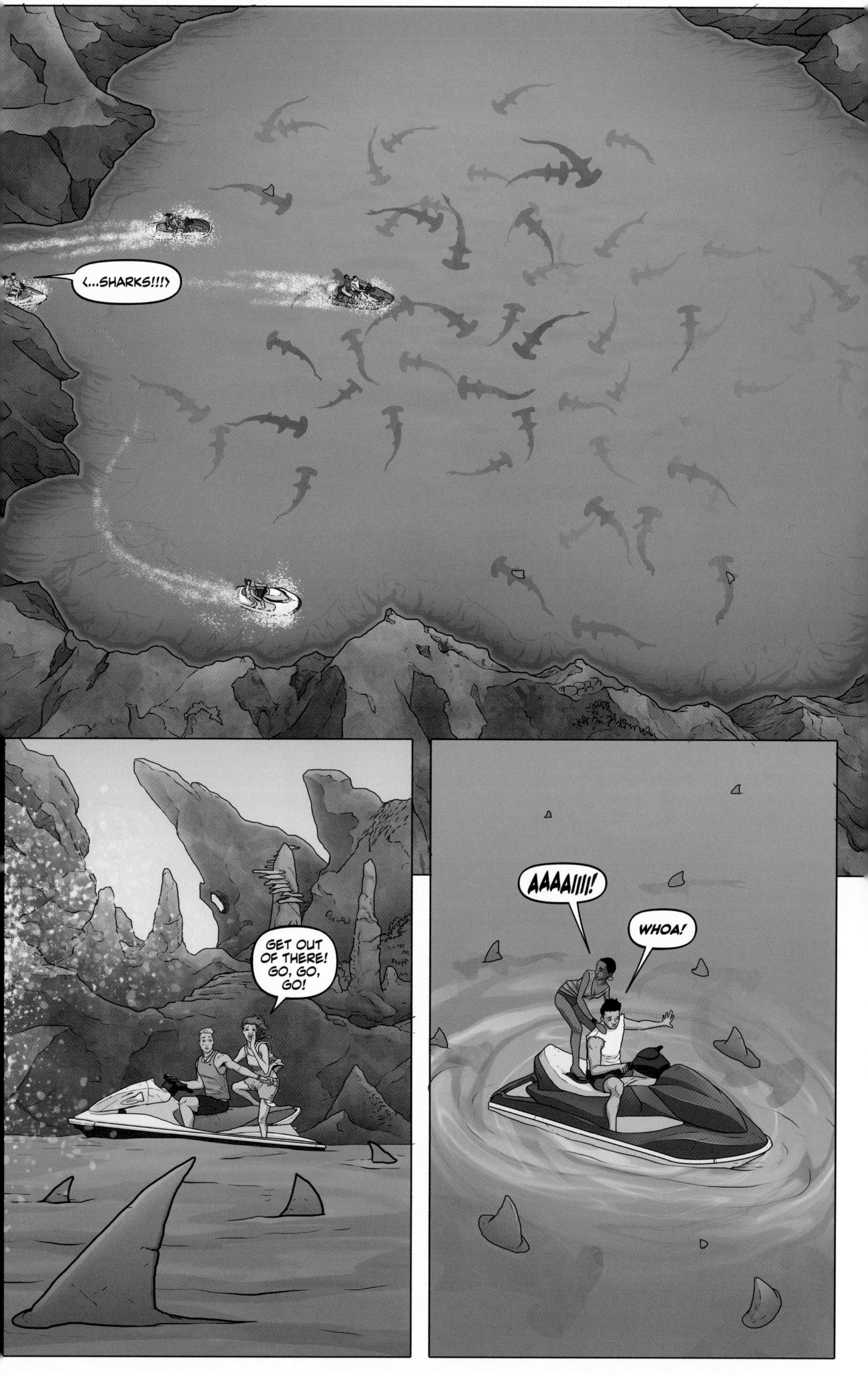

‹...SHARKS!!!›
GET OUT OF THERE! GO, GO, GO!
AAAAIIII!
WHOA!

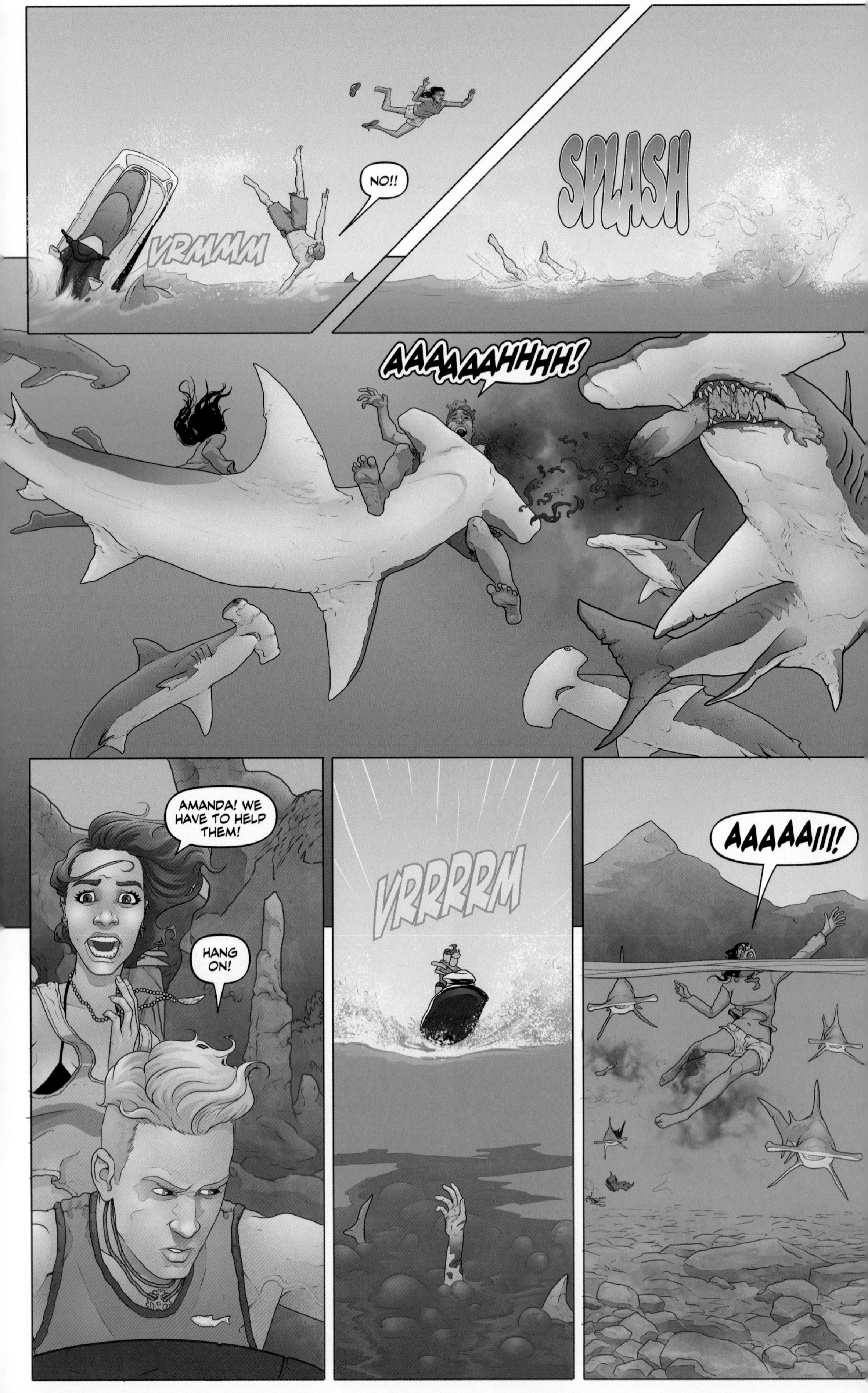
NO!!
VRMMM
SPLASH
AAAAAAHHHH!
AMANDA! WE HAVE TO HELP THEM!
HANG ON!
VRRRRM
AAAAAIII!

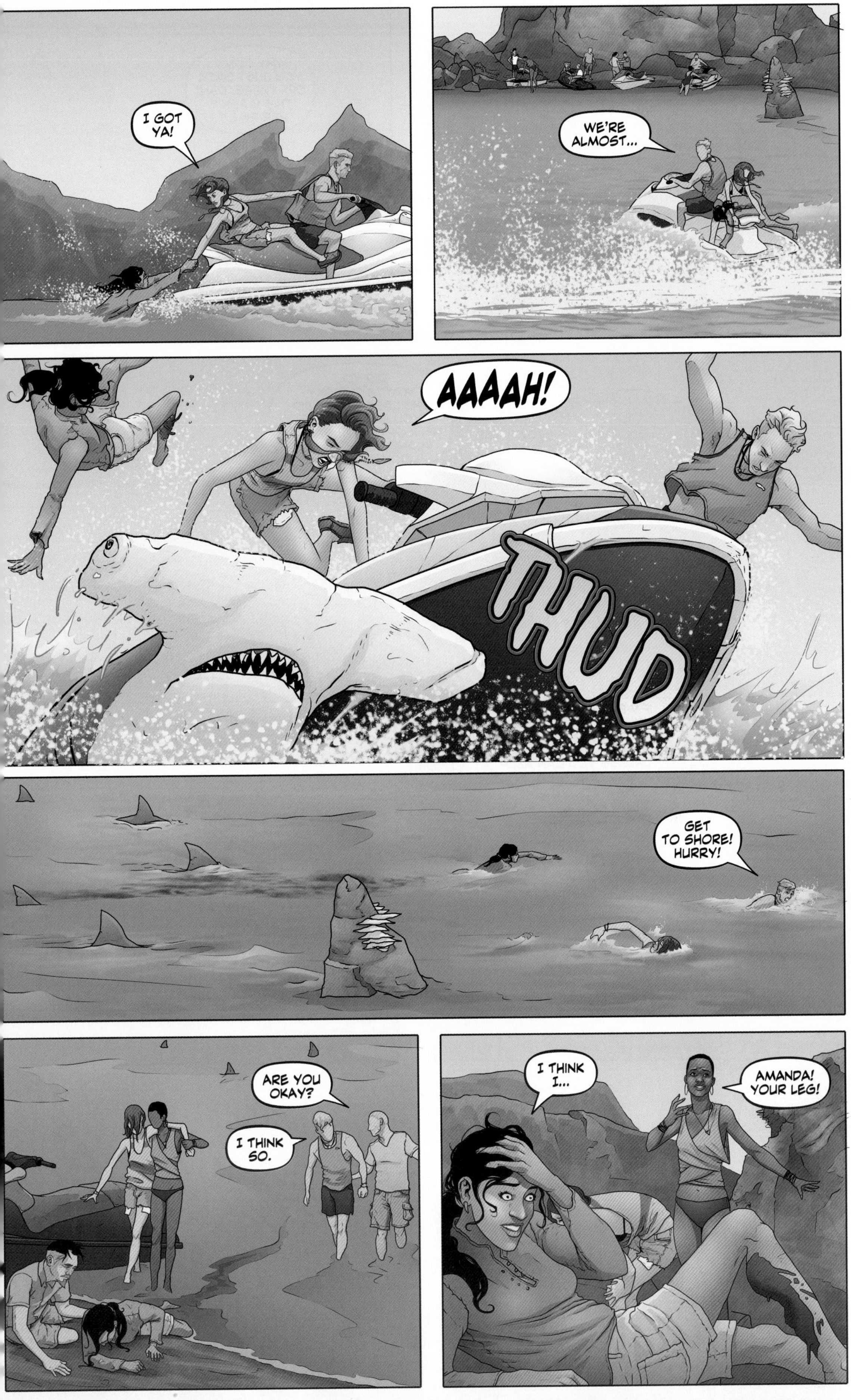
I GOT YA!
WE'RE ALMOST...
AAAAH!
THUD
GET TO SHORE! HURRY!
ARE YOU OKAY?
I THINK SO.
I THINK I...
AMANDA! YOUR LEG!

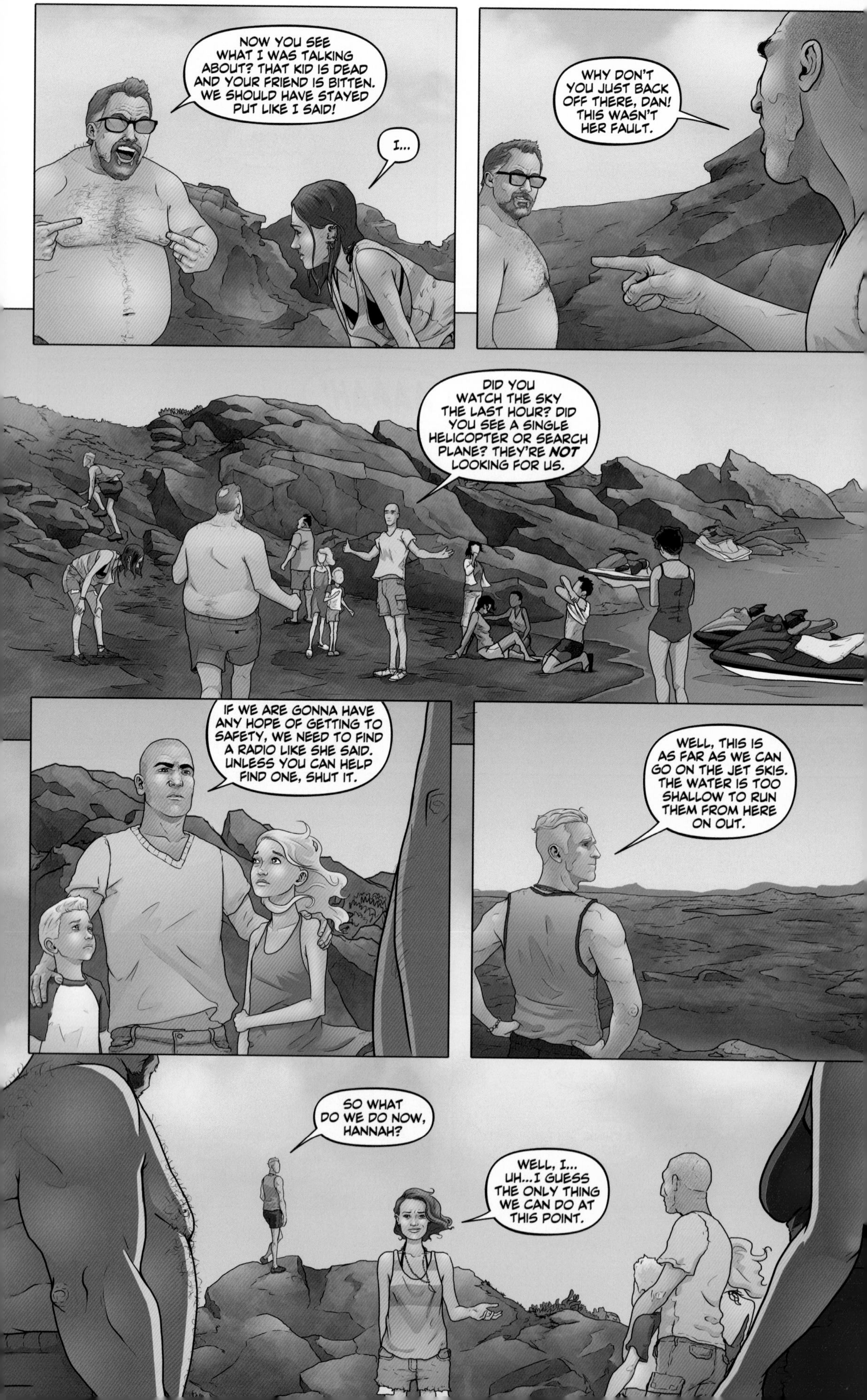
NOW YOU SEE WHAT I WAS TALKING ABOUT? THAT KID IS DEAD AND YOUR FRIEND IS BITTEN. WE SHOULD HAVE STAYED PUT LIKE I SAID!
I...
WHY DON'T YOU JUST BACK OFF THERE, DAN! THIS WASN'T HER FAULT.
DID YOU WATCH THE SKY THE LAST HOUR? DID YOU SEE A SINGLE HELICOPTER OR SEARCH PLANE? THEY'RE ***NOT*** LOOKING FOR US.
IF WE ARE GONNA HAVE ANY HOPE OF GETTING TO SAFETY, WE NEED TO FIND A RADIO LIKE SHE SAID. UNLESS YOU CAN HELP FIND ONE, SHUT IT.
WELL, THIS IS AS FAR AS WE CAN GO ON THE JET SKIS. THE WATER IS TOO SHALLOW TO RUN THEM FROM HERE ON OUT.
SO WHAT DO WE DO NOW, HANNAH?
WELL, I... UH...I GUESS THE ONLY THING WE CAN DO AT THIS POINT.

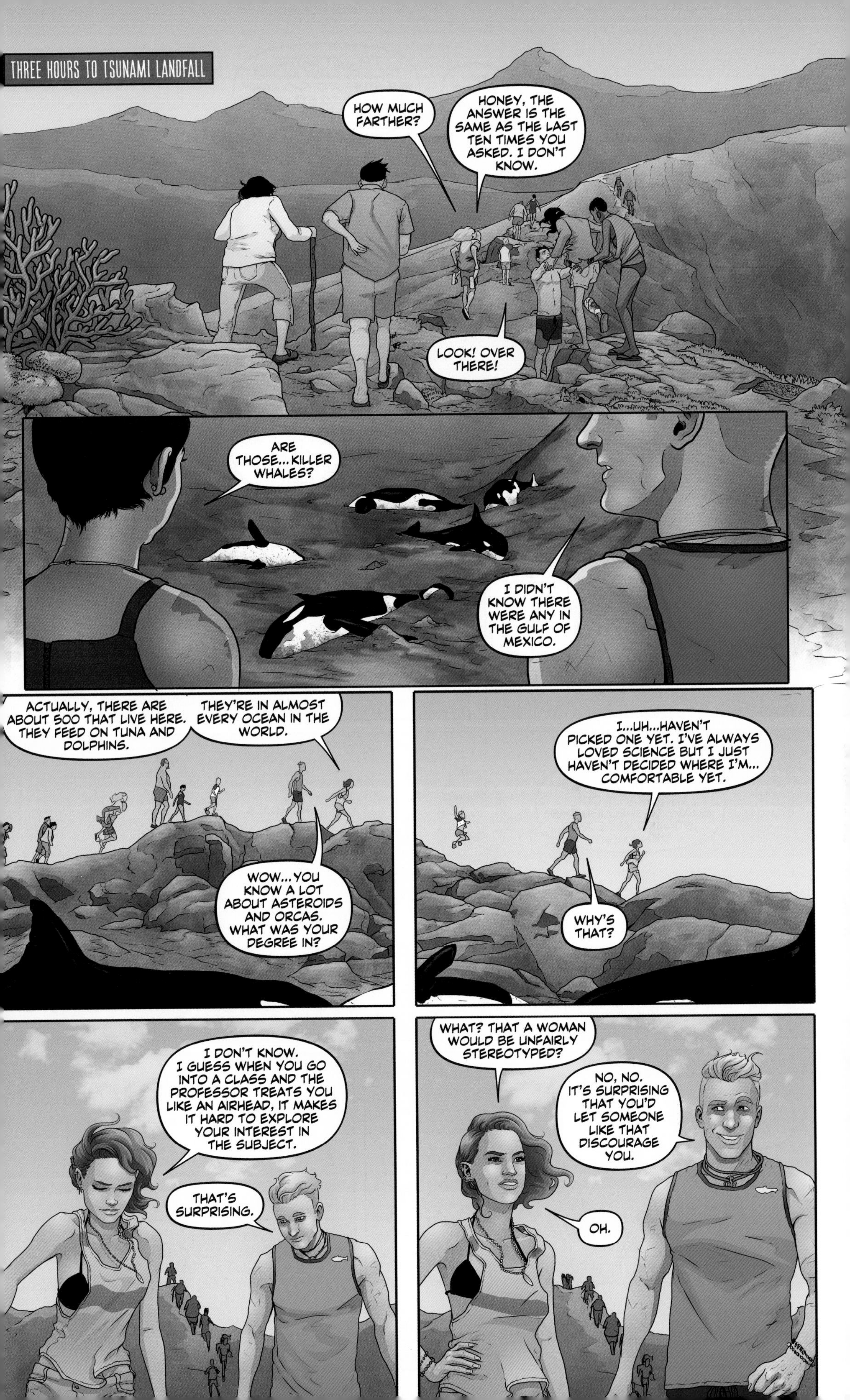
THREE HOURS TO TSUNAMI LANDFALL
HOW MUCH FARTHER?
HONEY, THE ANSWER IS THE SAME AS THE LAST TEN TIMES YOU ASKED. I DON'T KNOW.
LOOK! OVER THERE!
ARE THOSE... KILLER WHALES?
I DIDN'T KNOW THERE WERE ANY IN THE GULF OF MEXICO.
ACTUALLY, THERE ARE ABOUT 500 THAT LIVE HERE. THEY FEED ON TUNA AND DOLPHINS.
THEY'RE IN ALMOST EVERY OCEAN IN THE WORLD.
WOW... YOU KNOW A LOT ABOUT ASTEROIDS AND ORCAS. WHAT WAS YOUR DEGREE IN?
I...UH...HAVEN'T PICKED ONE YET. I'VE ALWAYS LOVED SCIENCE BUT I JUST HAVEN'T DECIDED WHERE I'M... COMFORTABLE YET.
WHY'S THAT?
I DON'T KNOW. I GUESS WHEN YOU GO INTO A CLASS AND THE PROFESSOR TREATS YOU LIKE AN AIRHEAD, IT MAKES IT HARD TO EXPLORE YOUR INTEREST IN THE SUBJECT.
THAT'S SURPRISING.
WHAT? THAT A WOMAN WOULD BE UNFAIRLY STEREOTYPED?
NO, NO. IT'S SURPRISING THAT YOU'D LET SOMEONE LIKE THAT DISCOURAGE YOU.
OH.

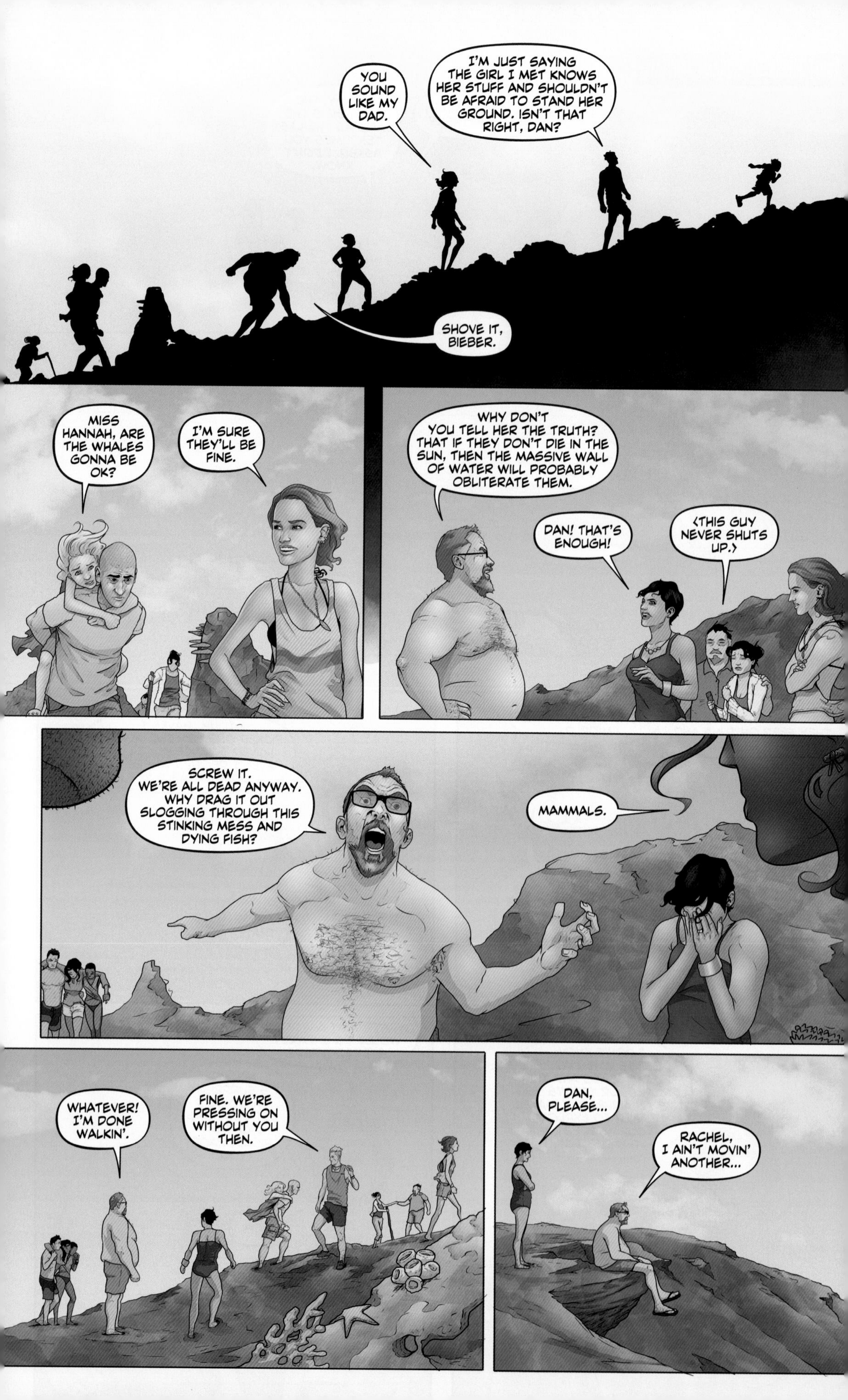
YOU SOUND LIKE MY DAD.
I'M JUST SAYING THE GIRL I MET KNOWS HER STUFF AND SHOULDN'T BE AFRAID TO STAND HER GROUND. ISN'T THAT RIGHT, DAN?
SHOVE IT, BIEBER.
MISS HANNAH, ARE THE WHALES GONNA BE OK?
I'M SURE THEY'LL BE FINE.
WHY DON'T YOU TELL HER THE TRUTH? THAT IF THEY DON'T DIE IN THE SUN, THEN THE MASSIVE WALL OF WATER WILL PROBABLY OBLITERATE THEM.
DAN! THAT'S ENOUGH!
<THIS GUY NEVER SHUTS UP.>
SCREW IT. WE'RE ALL DEAD ANYWAY. WHY DRAG IT OUT SLOGGING THROUGH THIS STINKING MESS AND DYING FISH?
MAMMALS.
WHATEVER! I'M DONE WALKIN'.
FINE. WE'RE PRESSING ON WITHOUT YOU THEN.
DAN, PLEASE...
RACHEL, I AIN'T MOVIN' ANOTHER...

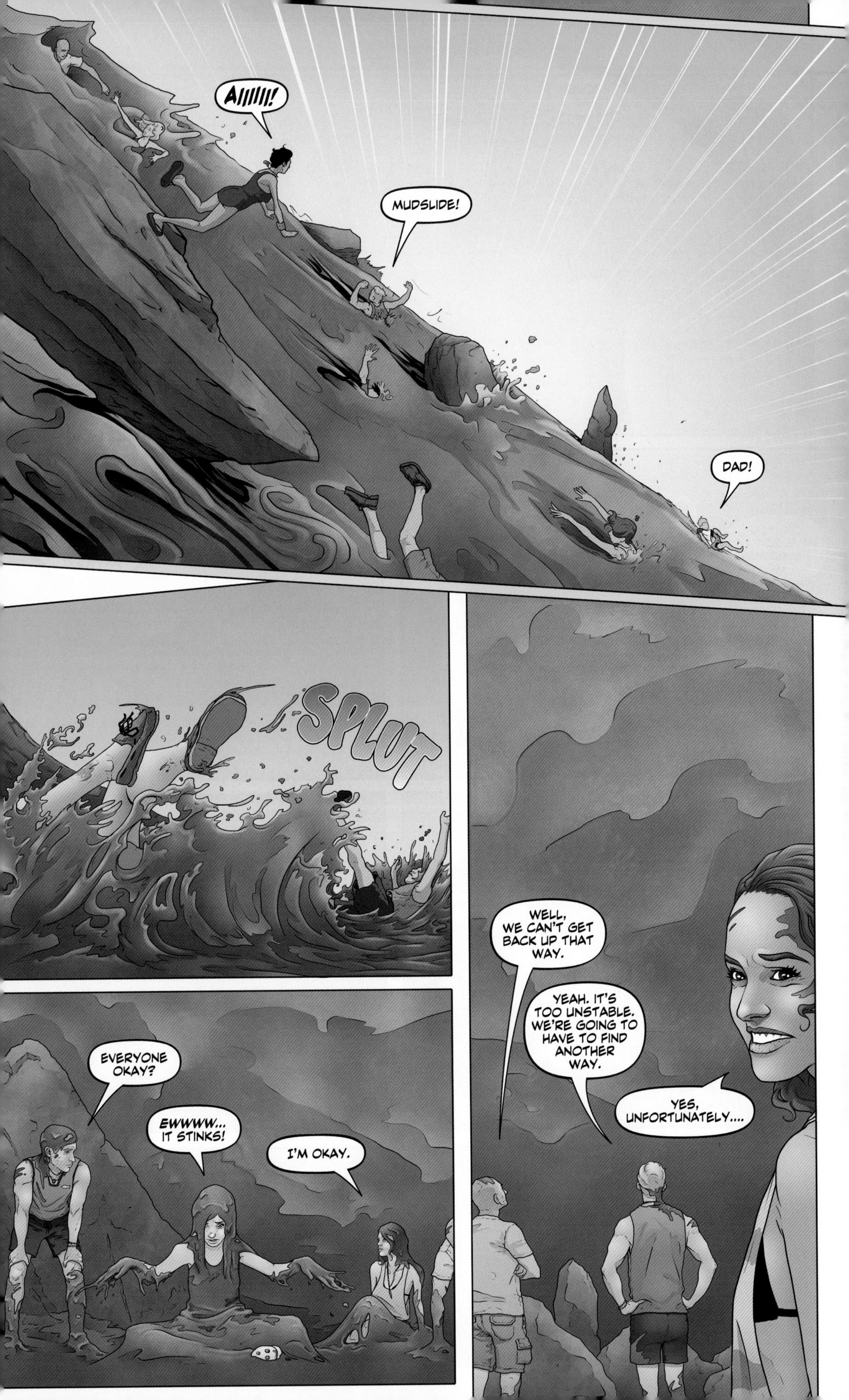
AIIIIII!
MUDSLIDE!
DAD!
SPLUT
EVERYONE OKAY?
EWWWW... IT STINKS!
I'M OKAY.
WELL, WE CAN'T GET BACK UP THAT WAY.
YEAH. IT'S TOO UNSTABLE. WE'RE GOING TO HAVE TO FIND ANOTHER WAY.
YES, UNFORTUNATELY....

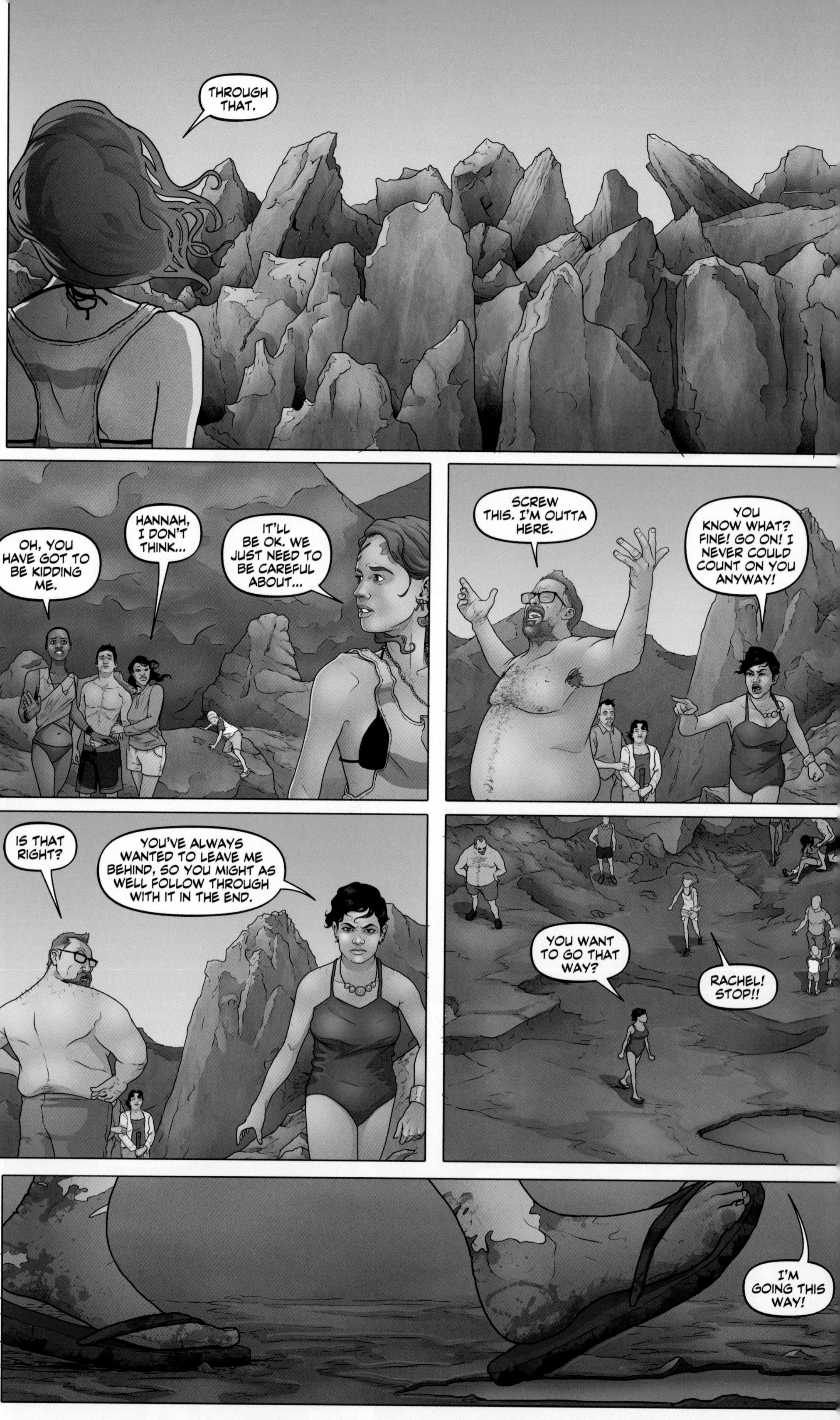
THROUGH THAT.
OH, YOU HAVE GOT TO BE KIDDING ME.
HANNAH, I DON'T THINK...
IT'LL BE OK. WE JUST NEED TO BE CAREFUL ABOUT...
SCREW THIS. I'M OUTTA HERE.
YOU KNOW WHAT? FINE! GO ON! I NEVER COULD COUNT ON YOU ANYWAY!
IS THAT RIGHT?
YOU'VE ALWAYS WANTED TO LEAVE ME BEHIND, SO YOU MIGHT AS WELL FOLLOW THROUGH WITH IT IN THE END.
YOU WANT TO GO THAT WAY?
RACHEL! STOP!!
I'M GOING THIS WAY!

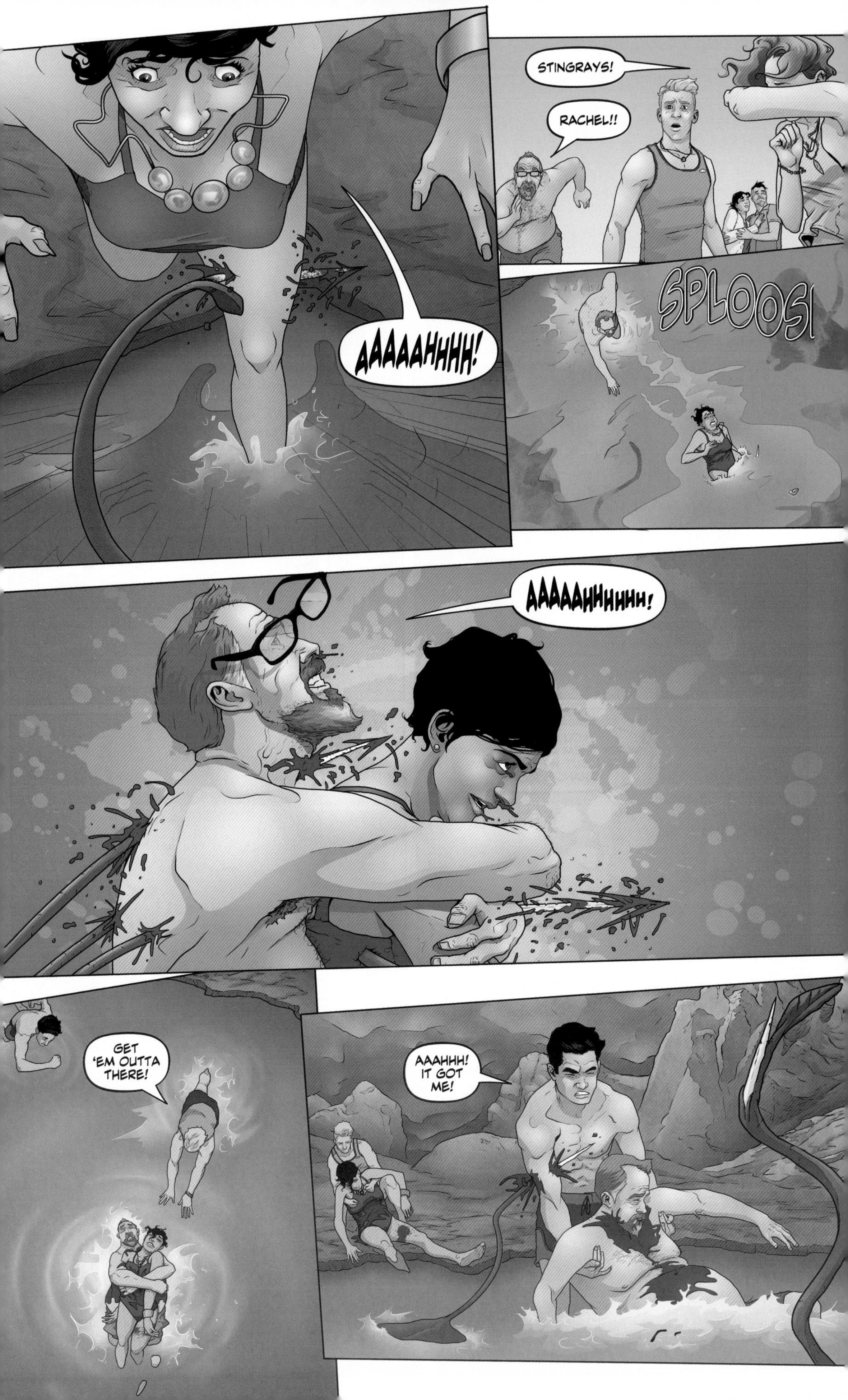
AAAAAHHHH!
STINGRAYS!
RACHEL!!
SPLOOSH
AAAAAHHhhhh!
GET 'EM OUTTA THERE!
AAAHHH! IT GOT ME!

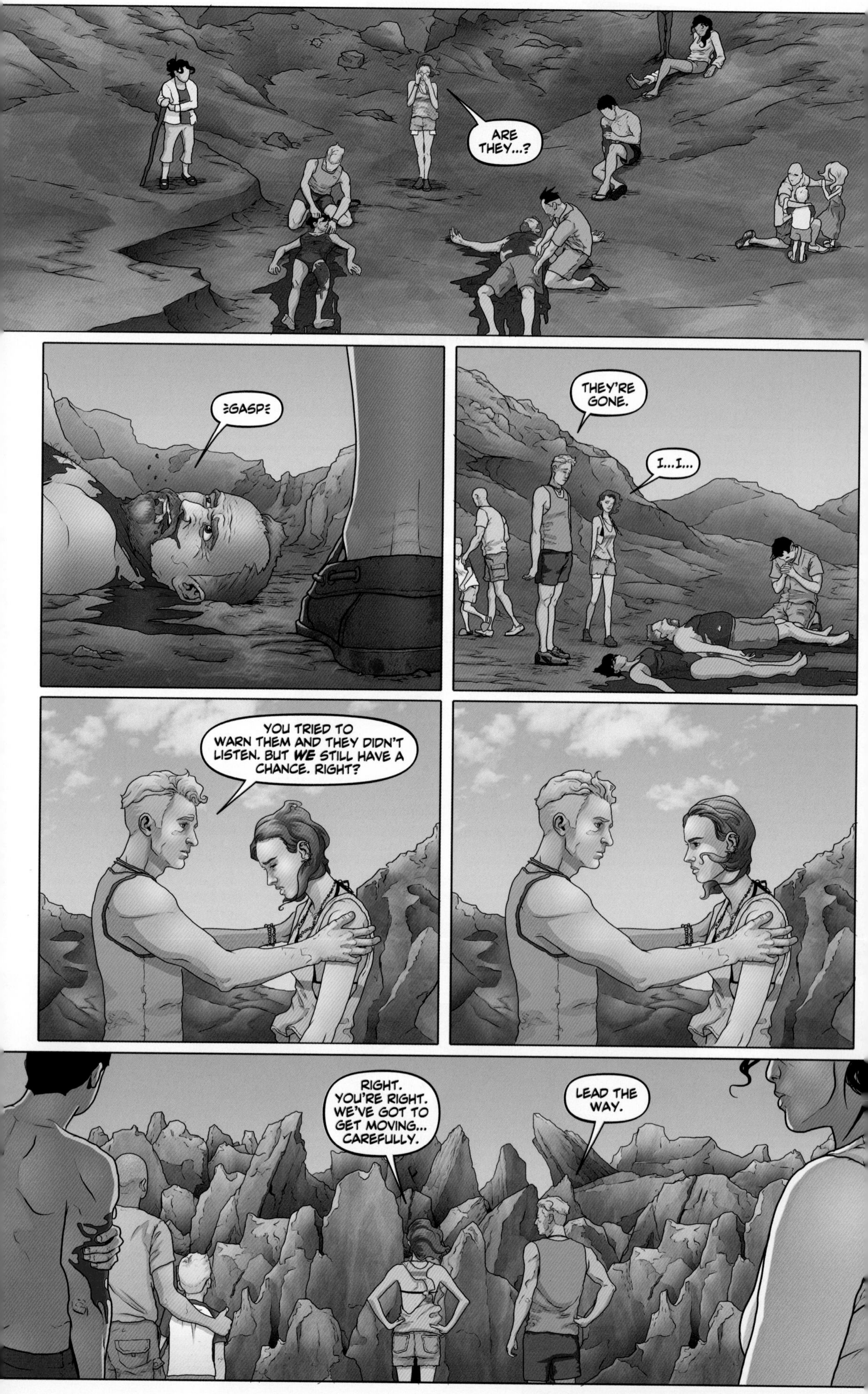
ARE THEY...?
GASP
THEY'RE GONE.
I...I...
YOU TRIED TO WARN THEM AND THEY DIDN'T LISTEN. BUT *WE* STILL HAVE A CHANCE. RIGHT?
RIGHT. YOU'RE RIGHT. WE'VE GOT TO GET MOVING... CAREFULLY.
LEAD THE WAY.

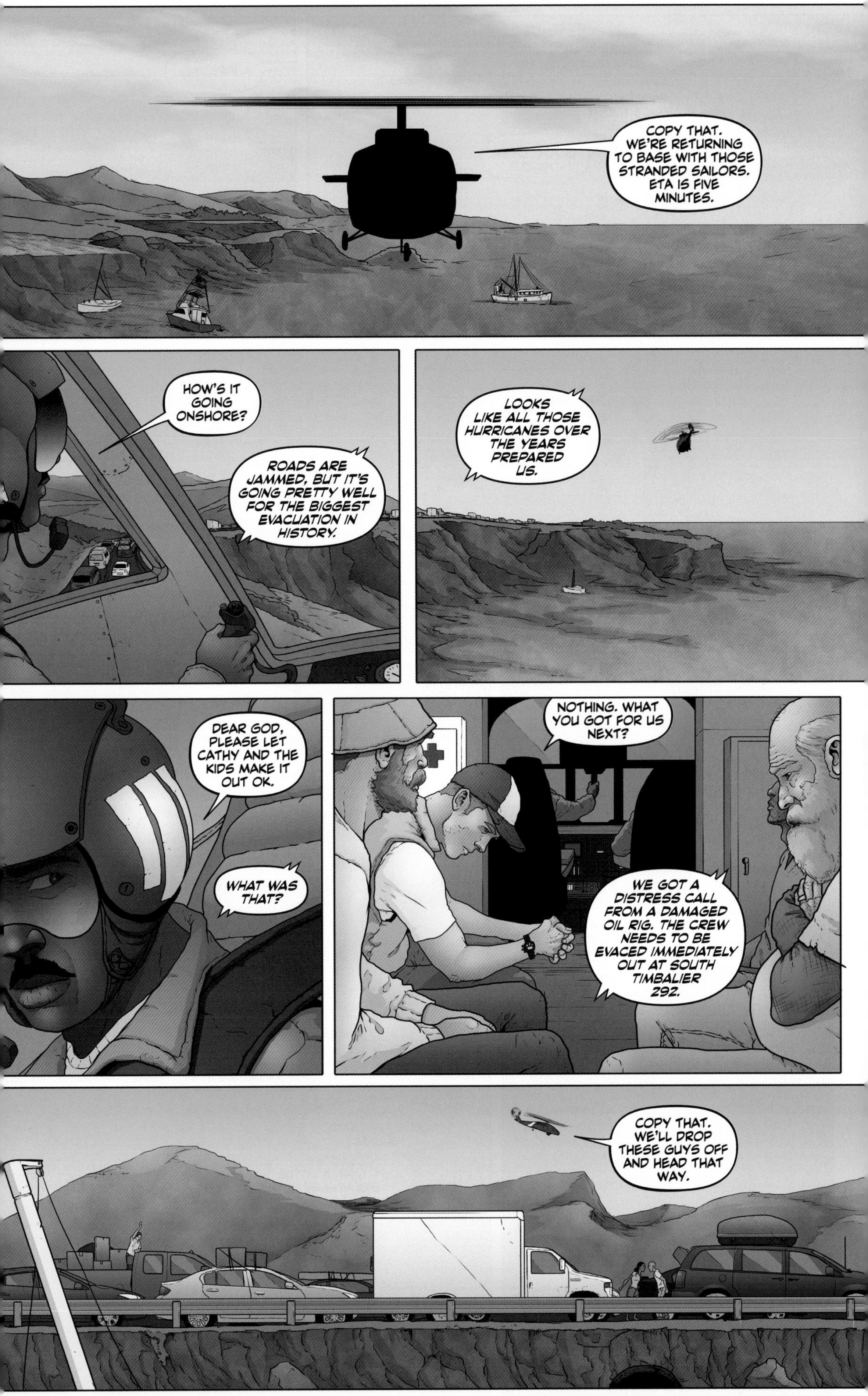
COPY THAT. WE'RE RETURNING TO BASE WITH THOSE STRANDED SAILORS. ETA IS FIVE MINUTES.
HOW'S IT GOING ONSHORE?
ROADS ARE JAMMED, BUT IT'S GOING PRETTY WELL FOR THE BIGGEST EVACUATION IN HISTORY.
LOOKS LIKE ALL THOSE HURRICANES OVER THE YEARS PREPARED US.
DEAR GOD, PLEASE LET CATHY AND THE KIDS MAKE IT OUT OK.
WHAT WAS THAT?
NOTHING. WHAT YOU GOT FOR US NEXT?
WE GOT A DISTRESS CALL FROM A DAMAGED OIL RIG. THE CREW NEEDS TO BE EVACED IMMEDIATELY OUT AT SOUTH TIMBALIER 292.
COPY THAT. WE'LL DROP THESE GUYS OFF AND HEAD THAT WAY.

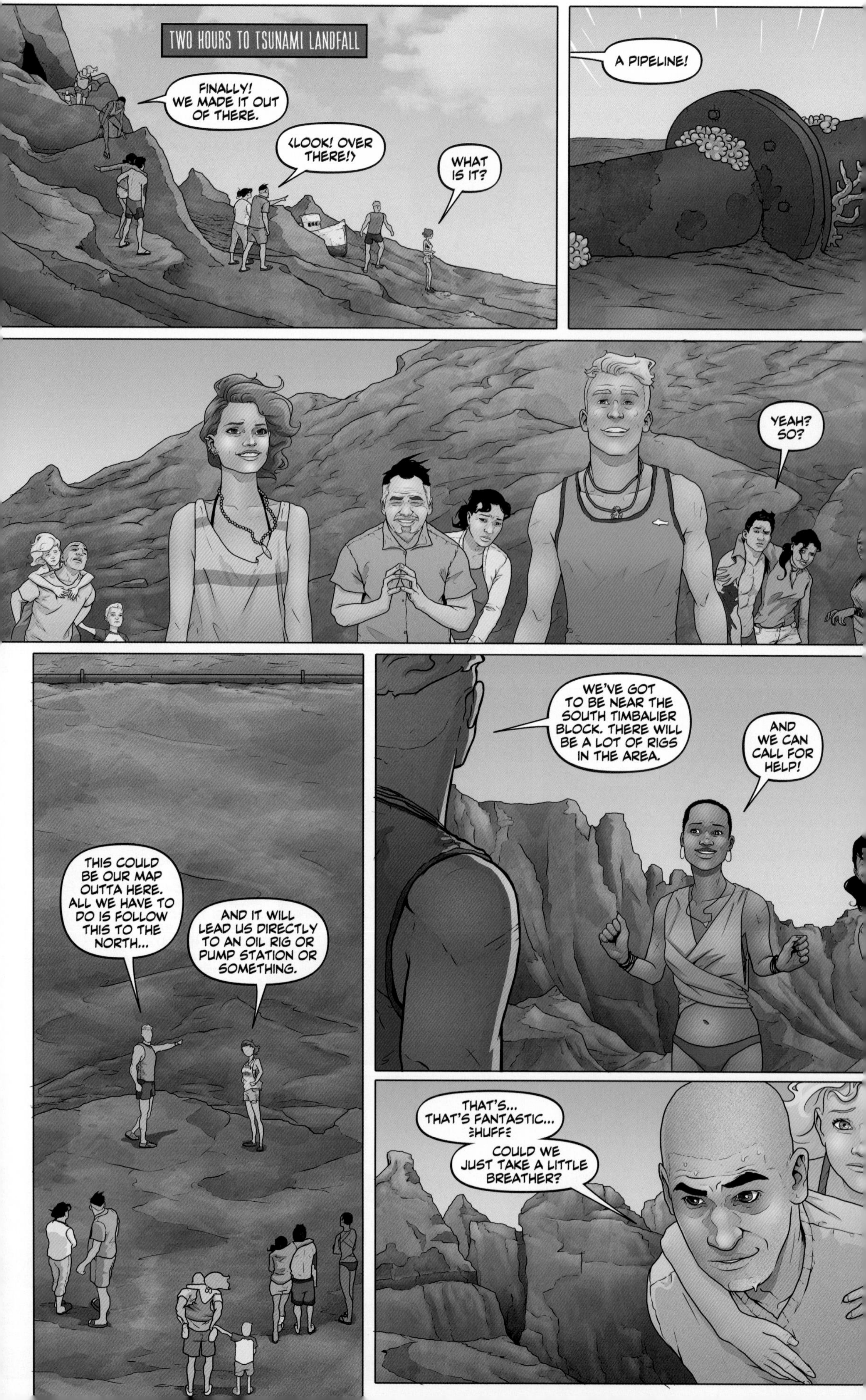
TWO HOURS TO TSUNAMI LANDFALL
FINALLY! WE MADE IT OUT OF THERE.
‹LOOK! OVER THERE!›
WHAT IS IT?
A PIPELINE!
YEAH? SO?
THIS COULD BE OUR MAP OUTTA HERE. ALL WE HAVE TO DO IS FOLLOW THIS TO THE NORTH...
AND IT WILL LEAD US DIRECTLY TO AN OIL RIG OR PUMP STATION OR SOMETHING.
WE'VE GOT TO BE NEAR THE SOUTH TIMBALIER BLOCK. THERE WILL BE A LOT OF RIGS IN THE AREA.
AND WE CAN CALL FOR HELP!
THAT'S... THAT'S FANTASTIC... *HUFF*
COULD WE JUST TAKE A LITTLE BREATHER?

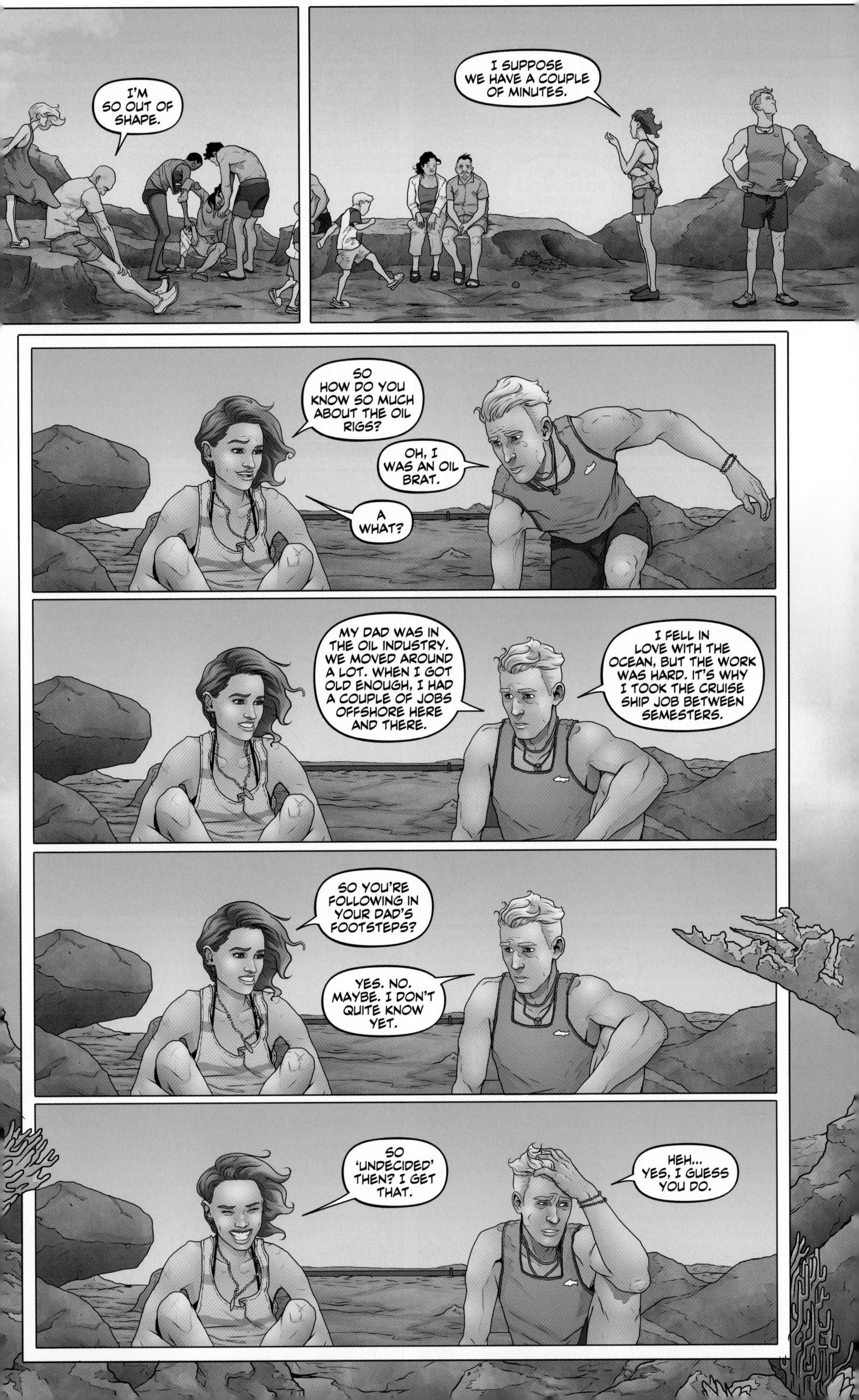
I'M SO OUT OF SHAPE.
I SUPPOSE WE HAVE A COUPLE OF MINUTES.
SO HOW DO YOU KNOW SO MUCH ABOUT THE OIL RIGS?
OH, I WAS AN OIL BRAT.
A WHAT?
MY DAD WAS IN THE OIL INDUSTRY. WE MOVED AROUND A LOT. WHEN I GOT OLD ENOUGH, I HAD A COUPLE OF JOBS OFFSHORE HERE AND THERE.
I FELL IN LOVE WITH THE OCEAN, BUT THE WORK WAS HARD. IT'S WHY I TOOK THE CRUISE SHIP JOB BETWEEN SEMESTERS.
SO YOU'RE FOLLOWING IN YOUR DAD'S FOOTSTEPS?
YES. NO. MAYBE. I DON'T QUITE KNOW YET.
SO 'UNDECIDED' THEN? I GET THAT.
HEH... YES, I GUESS YOU DO.

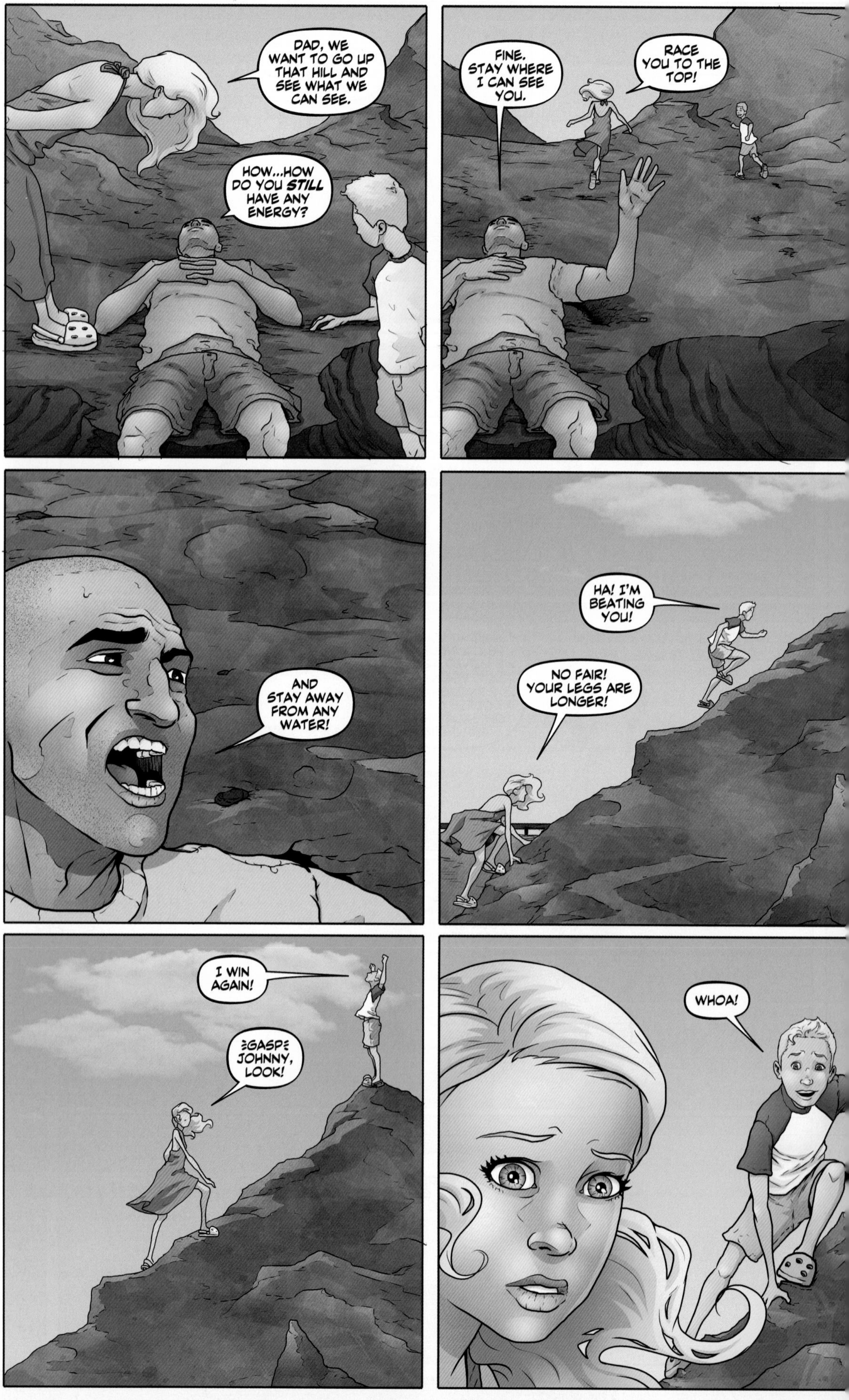
DAD, WE WANT TO GO UP THAT HILL AND SEE WHAT WE CAN SEE.
HOW...HOW DO YOU STILL HAVE ANY ENERGY?
FINE. STAY WHERE I CAN SEE YOU.
RACE YOU TO THE TOP!
AND STAY AWAY FROM ANY WATER!
HA! I'M BEATING YOU!
NO FAIR! YOUR LEGS ARE LONGER!
I WIN AGAIN!
=GASP= JOHNNY, LOOK!
WHOA!

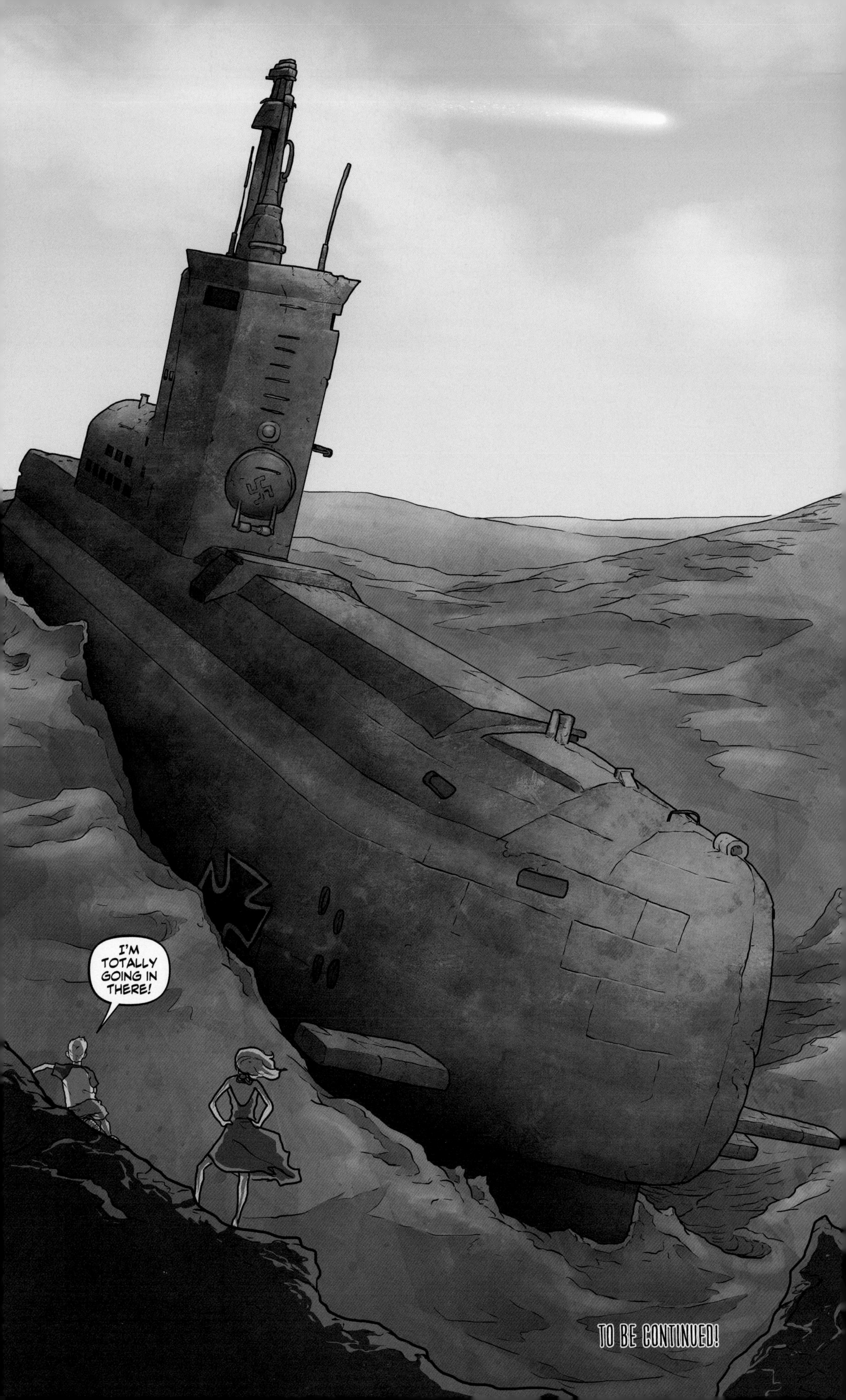
I'M TOTALLY GOING IN THERE!
TO BE CONTINUED!

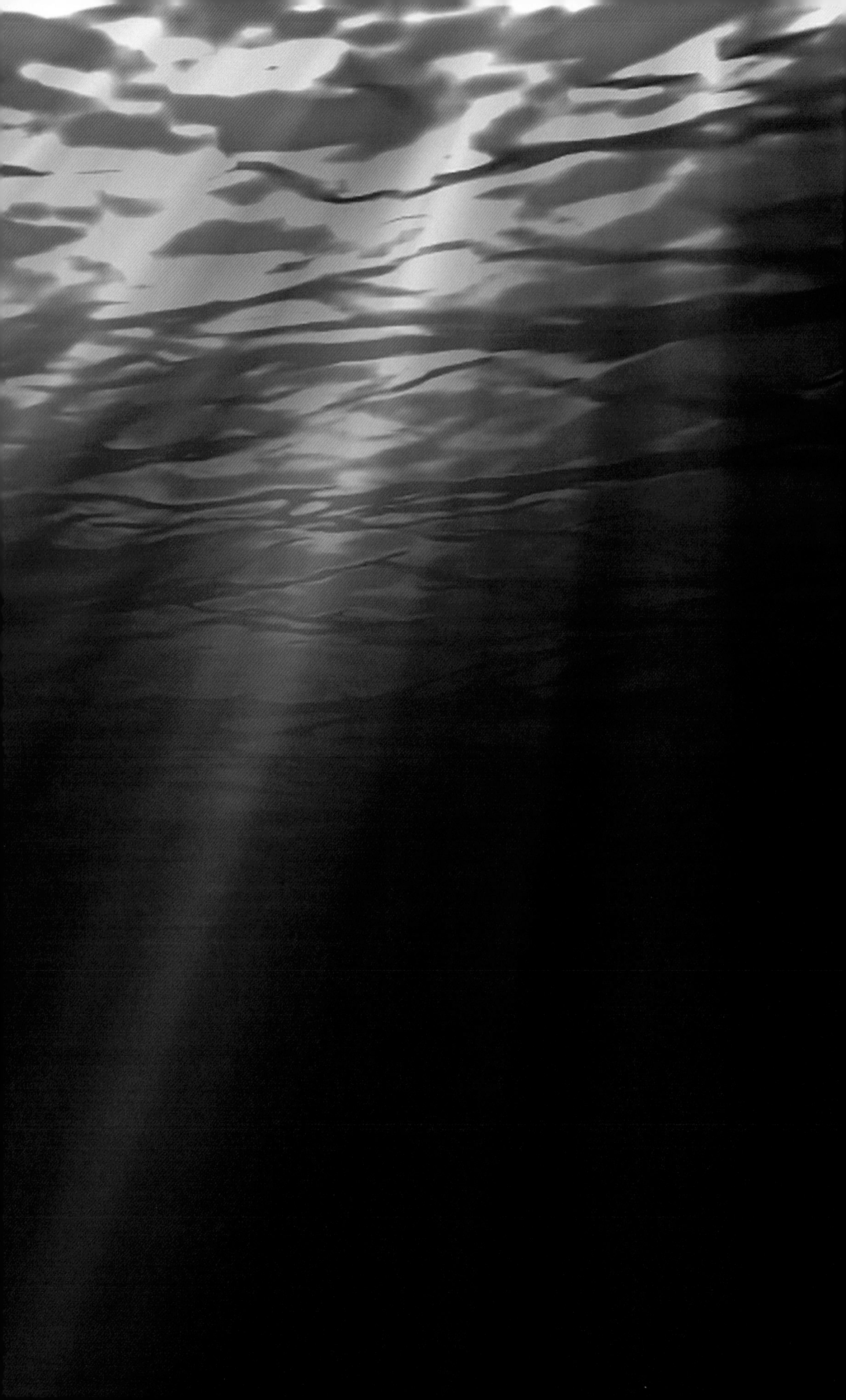

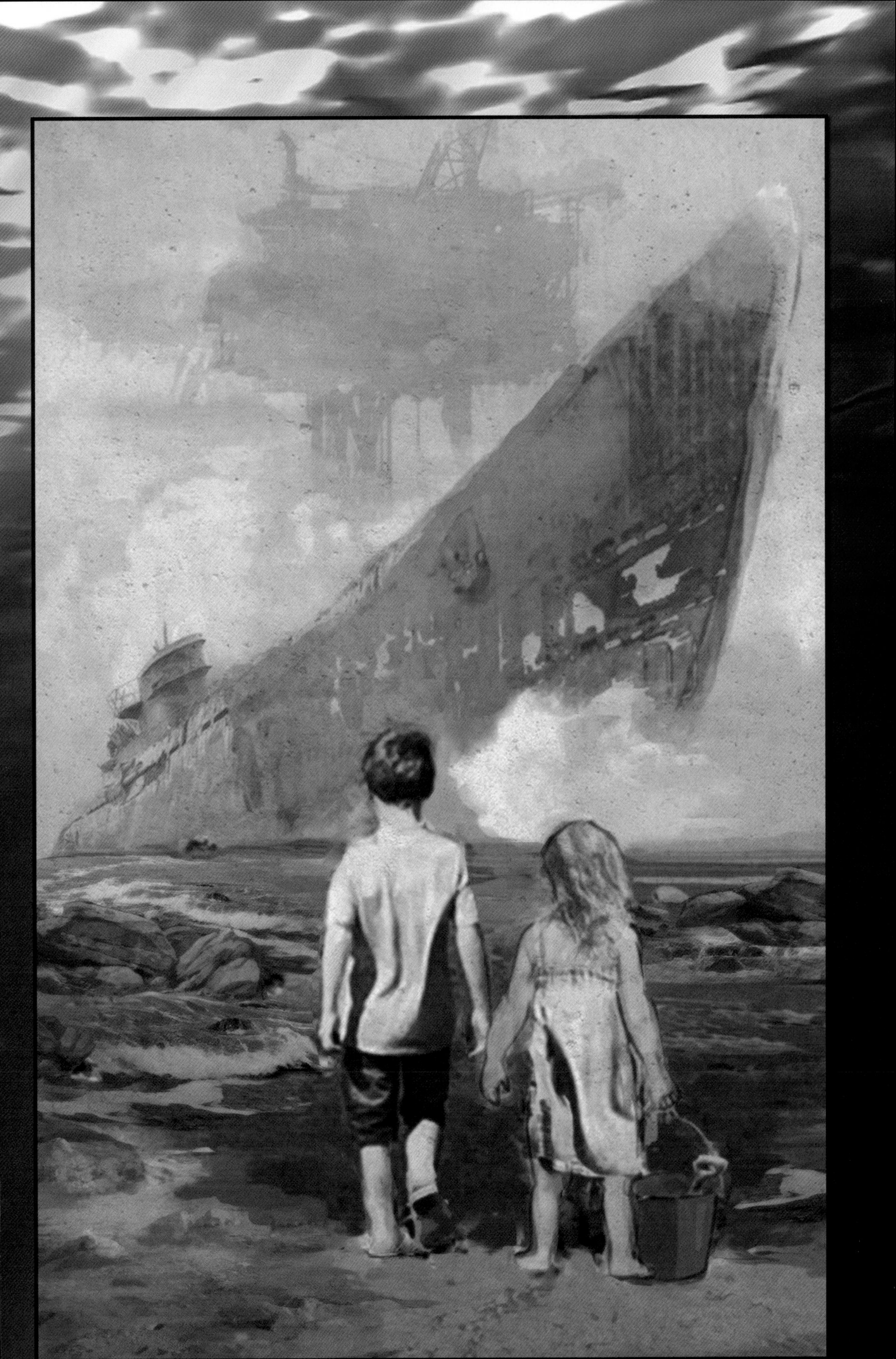

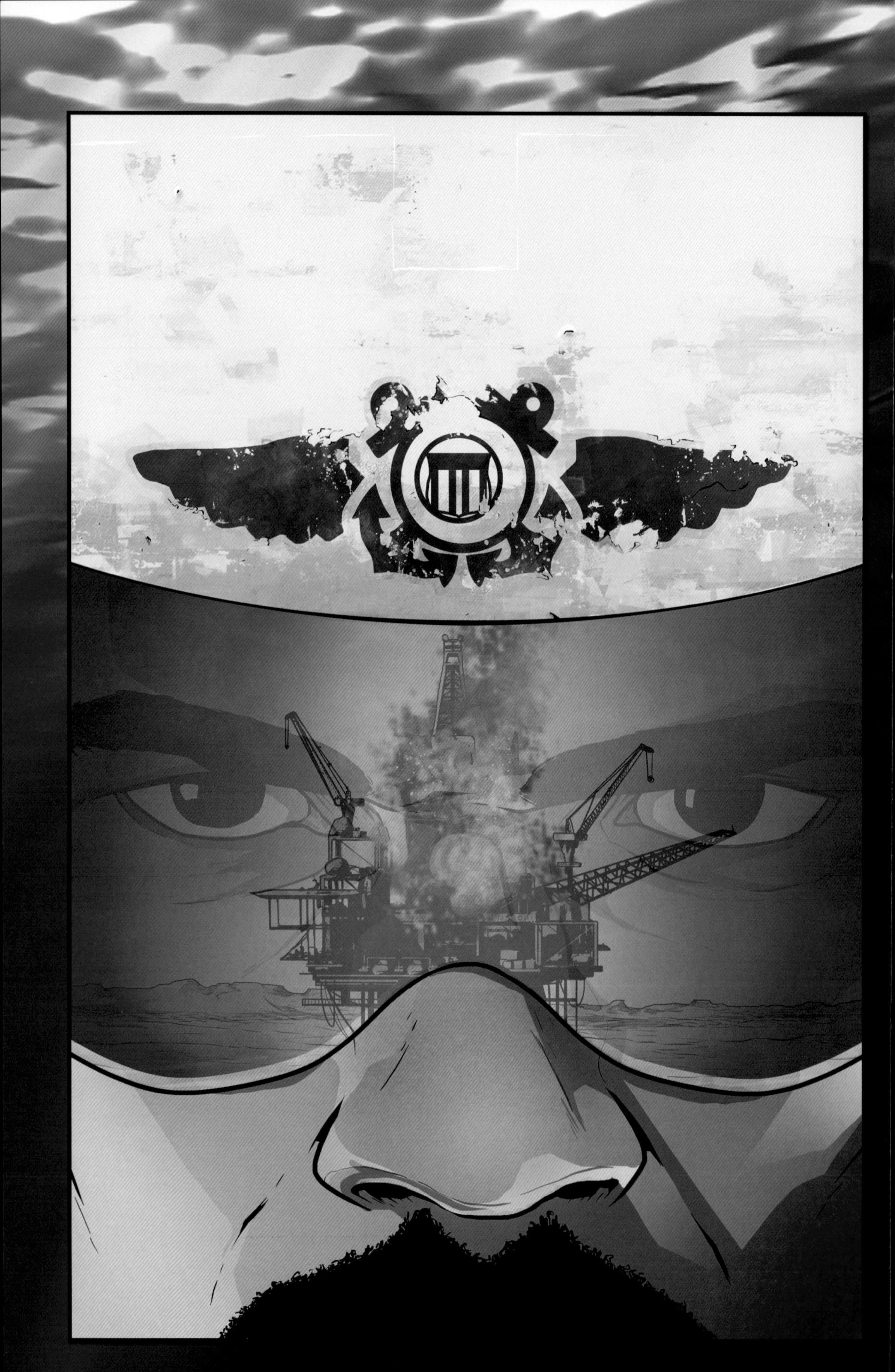

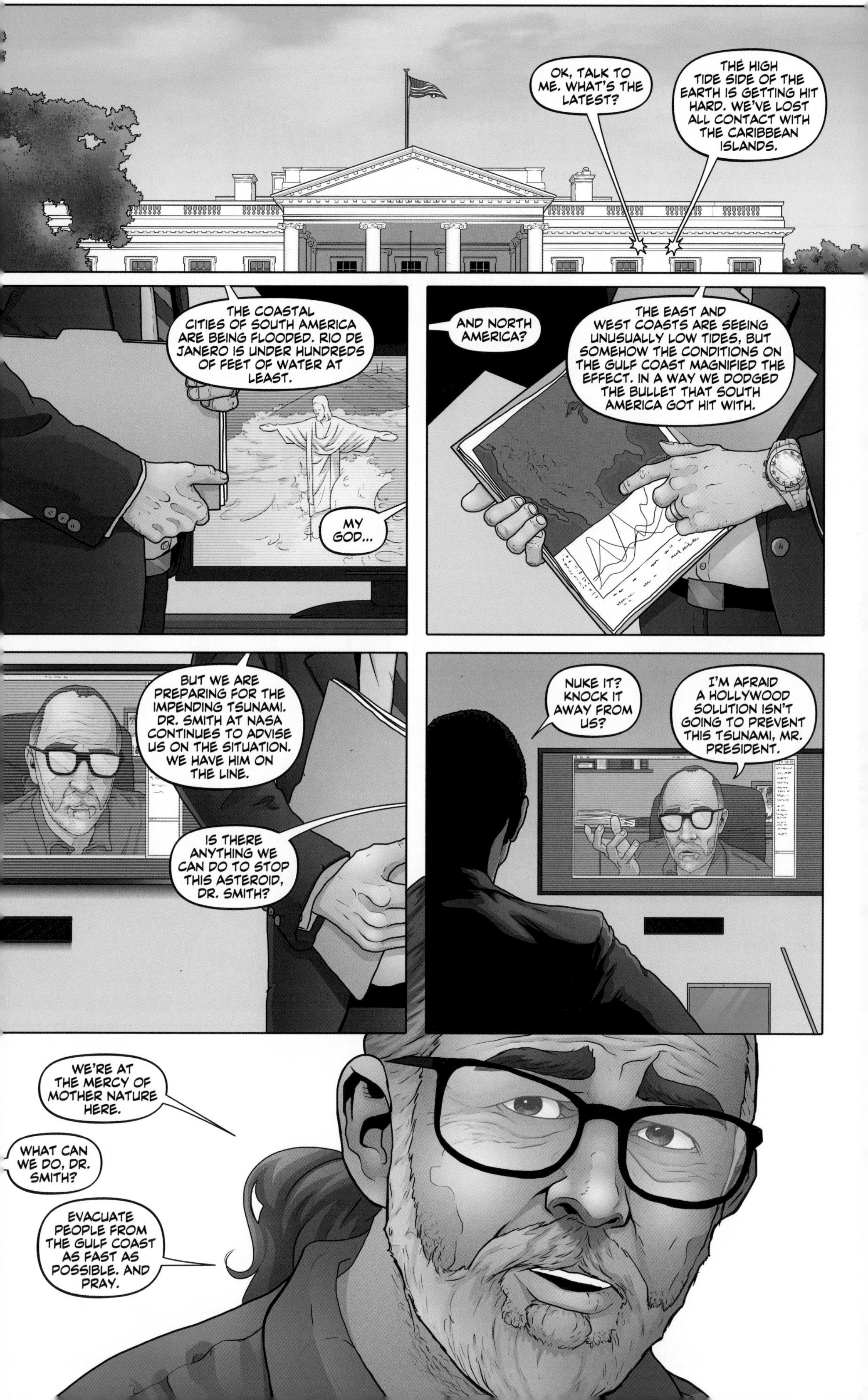
OK, TALK TO ME. WHAT'S THE LATEST?
THE HIGH TIDE SIDE OF THE EARTH IS GETTING HIT HARD. WE'VE LOST ALL CONTACT WITH THE CARIBBEAN ISLANDS.
THE COASTAL CITIES OF SOUTH AMERICA ARE BEING FLOODED. RIO DE JANERO IS UNDER HUNDREDS OF FEET OF WATER AT LEAST.
MY GOD...
AND NORTH AMERICA?
THE EAST AND WEST COASTS ARE SEEING UNUSUALLY LOW TIDES, BUT SOMEHOW THE CONDITIONS ON THE GULF COAST MAGNIFIED THE EFFECT. IN A WAY WE DODGED THE BULLET THAT SOUTH AMERICA GOT HIT WITH.
BUT WE ARE PREPARING FOR THE IMPENDING TSUNAMI. DR. SMITH AT NASA CONTINUES TO ADVISE US ON THE SITUATION. WE HAVE HIM ON THE LINE.
IS THERE ANYTHING WE CAN DO TO STOP THIS ASTEROID, DR. SMITH?
NUKE IT? KNOCK IT AWAY FROM US?
I'M AFRAID A HOLLYWOOD SOLUTION ISN'T GOING TO PREVENT THIS TSUNAMI, MR. PRESIDENT.
WE'RE AT THE MERCY OF MOTHER NATURE HERE.
WHAT CAN WE DO, DR. SMITH?
EVACUATE PEOPLE FROM THE GULF COAST AS FAST AS POSSIBLE. AND PRAY.

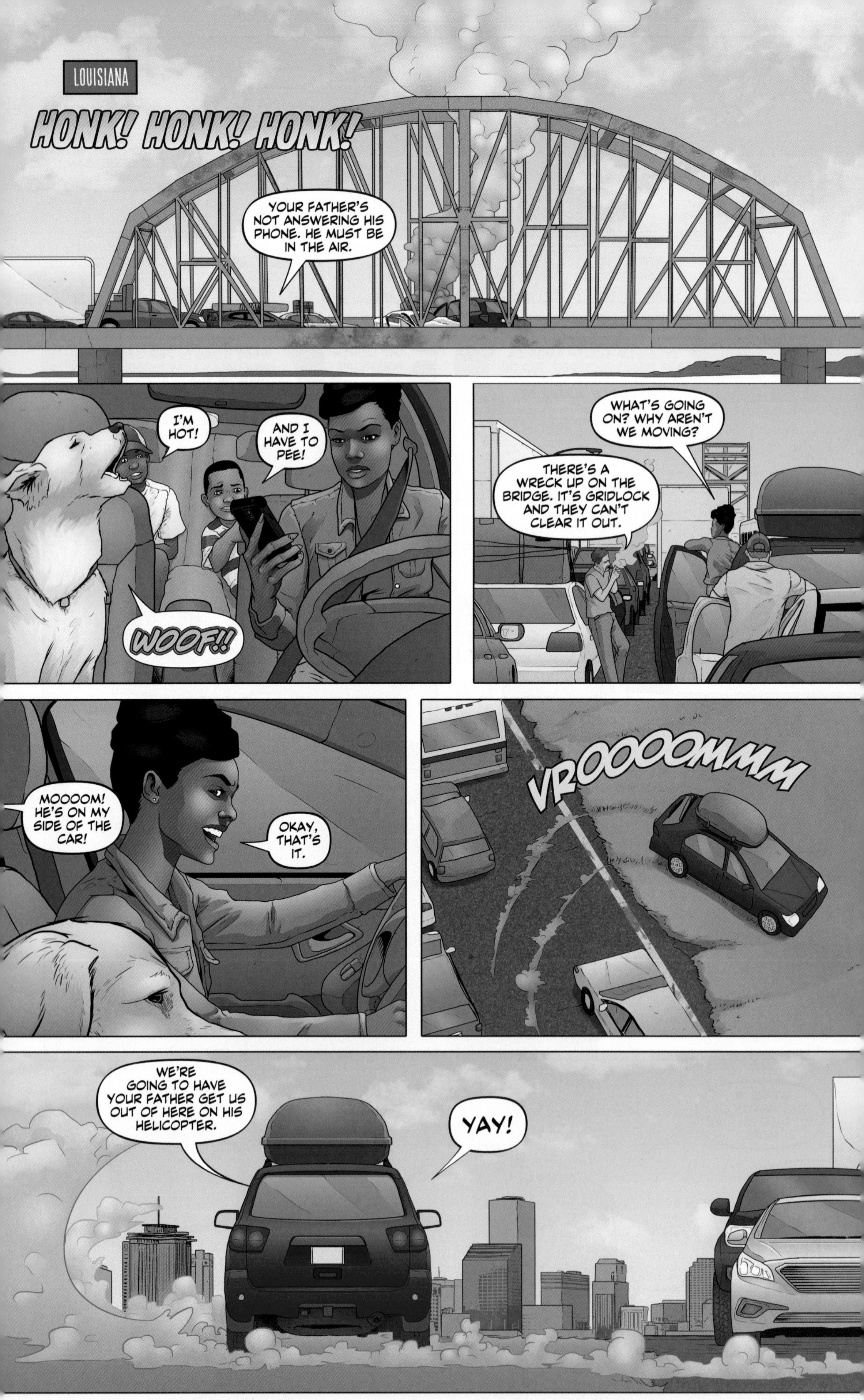
LOUISIANA
HONK! HONK! HONK!
YOUR FATHER'S NOT ANSWERING HIS PHONE. HE MUST BE IN THE AIR.
I'M HOT!
AND I HAVE TO PEE!
WOOF!!
WHAT'S GOING ON? WHY AREN'T WE MOVING?
THERE'S A WRECK UP ON THE BRIDGE. IT'S GRIDLOCK AND THEY CAN'T CLEAR IT OUT.
MOOOOM! HE'S ON MY SIDE OF THE CAR!
OKAY, THAT'S IT.
VROOOOOMMM
WE'RE GOING TO HAVE YOUR FATHER GET US OUT OF HERE ON HIS HELICOPTER.
YAY!

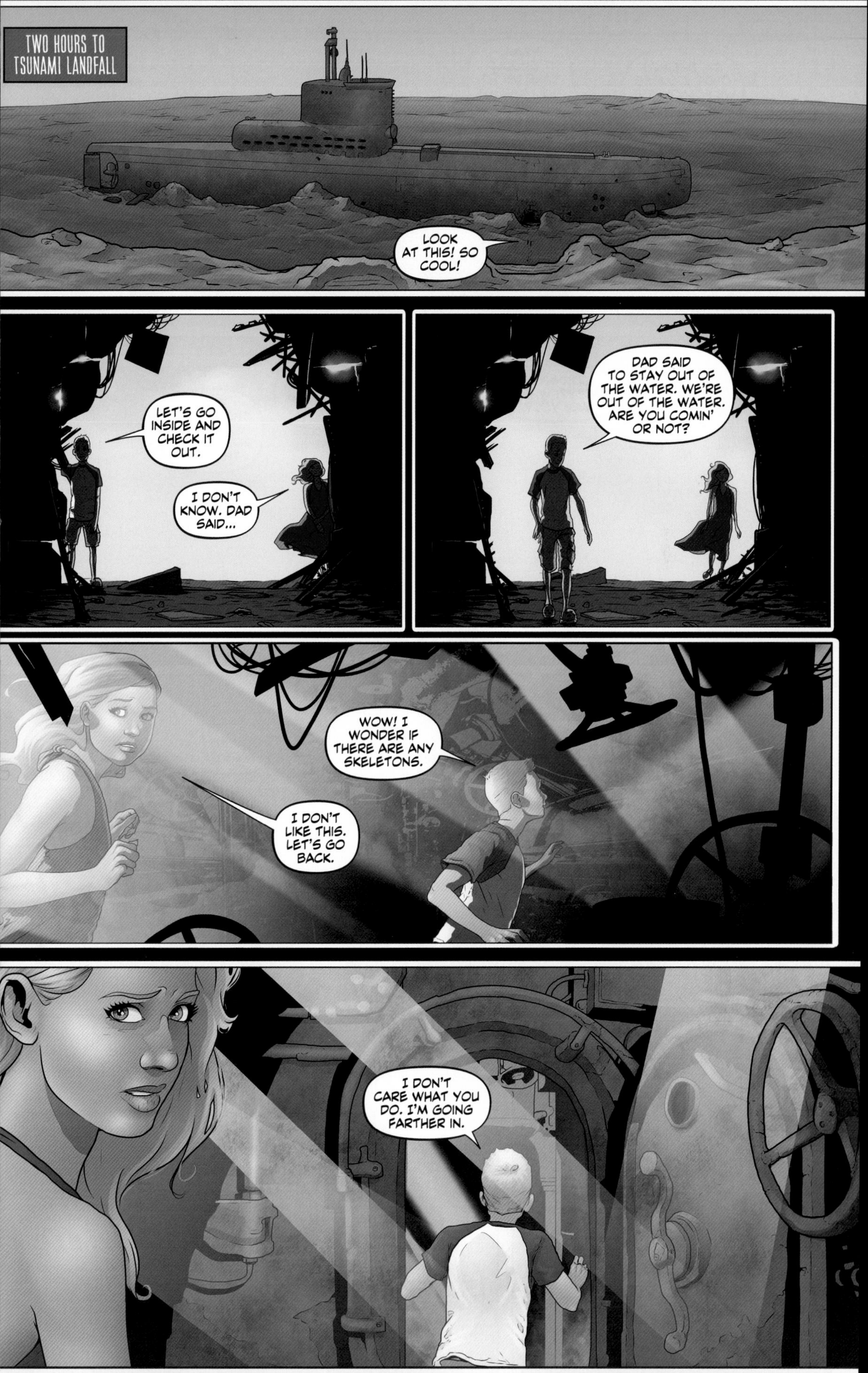
TWO HOURS TO TSUNAMI LANDFALL
LOOK AT THIS! SO COOL!
LET'S GO INSIDE AND CHECK IT OUT.
I DON'T KNOW. DAD SAID...
DAD SAID TO STAY OUT OF THE WATER. WE'RE OUT OF THE WATER. ARE YOU COMIN' OR NOT?
WOW! I WONDER IF THERE ARE ANY SKELETONS.
I DON'T LIKE THIS. LET'S GO BACK.
I DON'T CARE WHAT YOU DO. I'M GOING FARTHER IN.

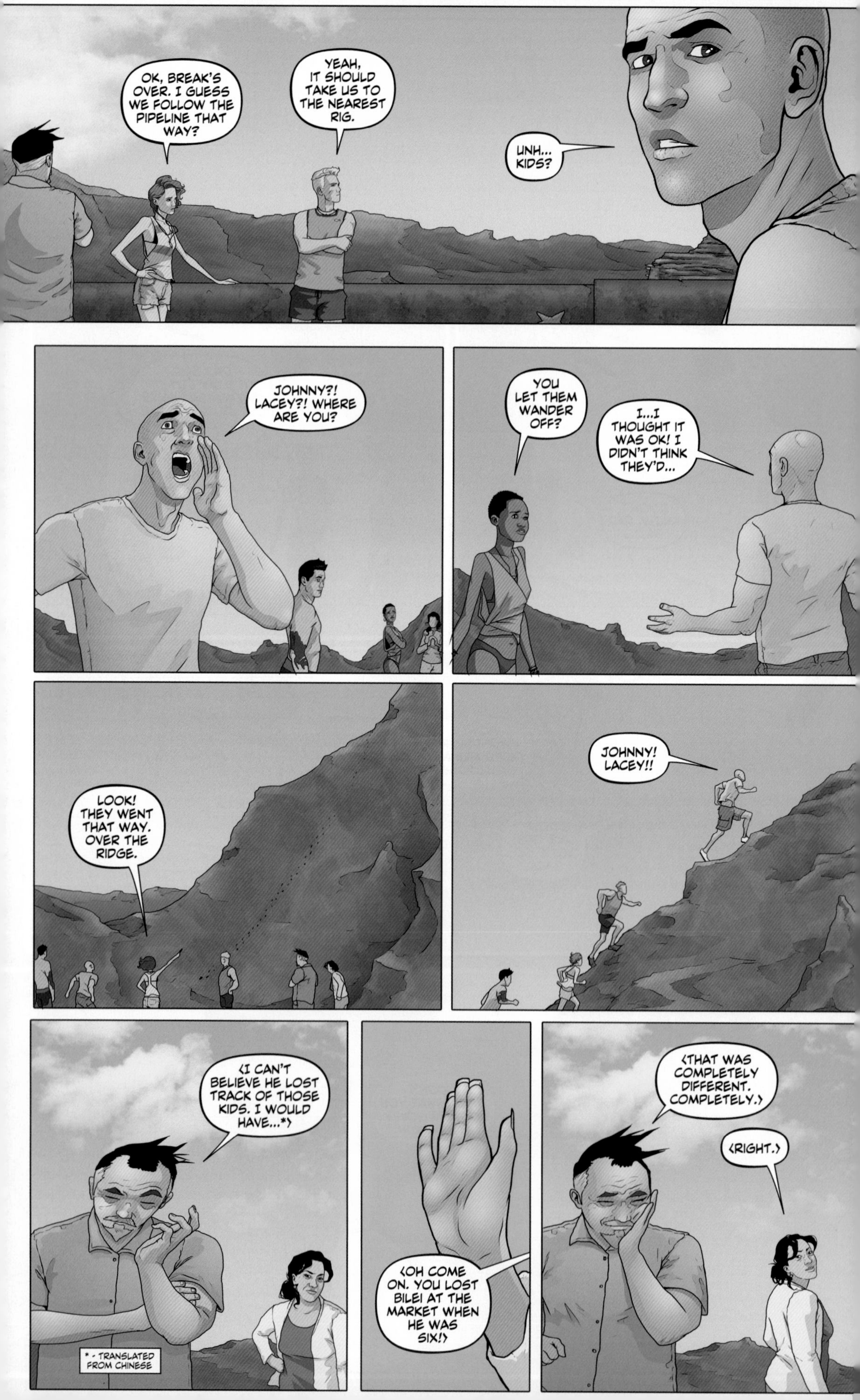
OK, BREAK'S OVER. I GUESS WE FOLLOW THE PIPELINE THAT WAY?
YEAH, IT SHOULD TAKE US TO THE NEAREST RIG.
UNH... KIDS?
JOHNNY?! LACEY?! WHERE ARE YOU?
YOU LET THEM WANDER OFF?
I...I THOUGHT IT WAS OK! I DIDN'T THINK THEY'D...
LOOK! THEY WENT THAT WAY. OVER THE RIDGE.
JOHNNY! LACEY!!
<I CAN'T BELIEVE HE LOST TRACK OF THOSE KIDS. I WOULD HAVE...*>
* - TRANSLATED FROM CHINESE
<OH COME ON. YOU LOST BILEI AT THE MARKET WHEN HE WAS SIX!>
<THAT WAS COMPLETELY DIFFERENT. COMPLETELY.>
<RIGHT.>

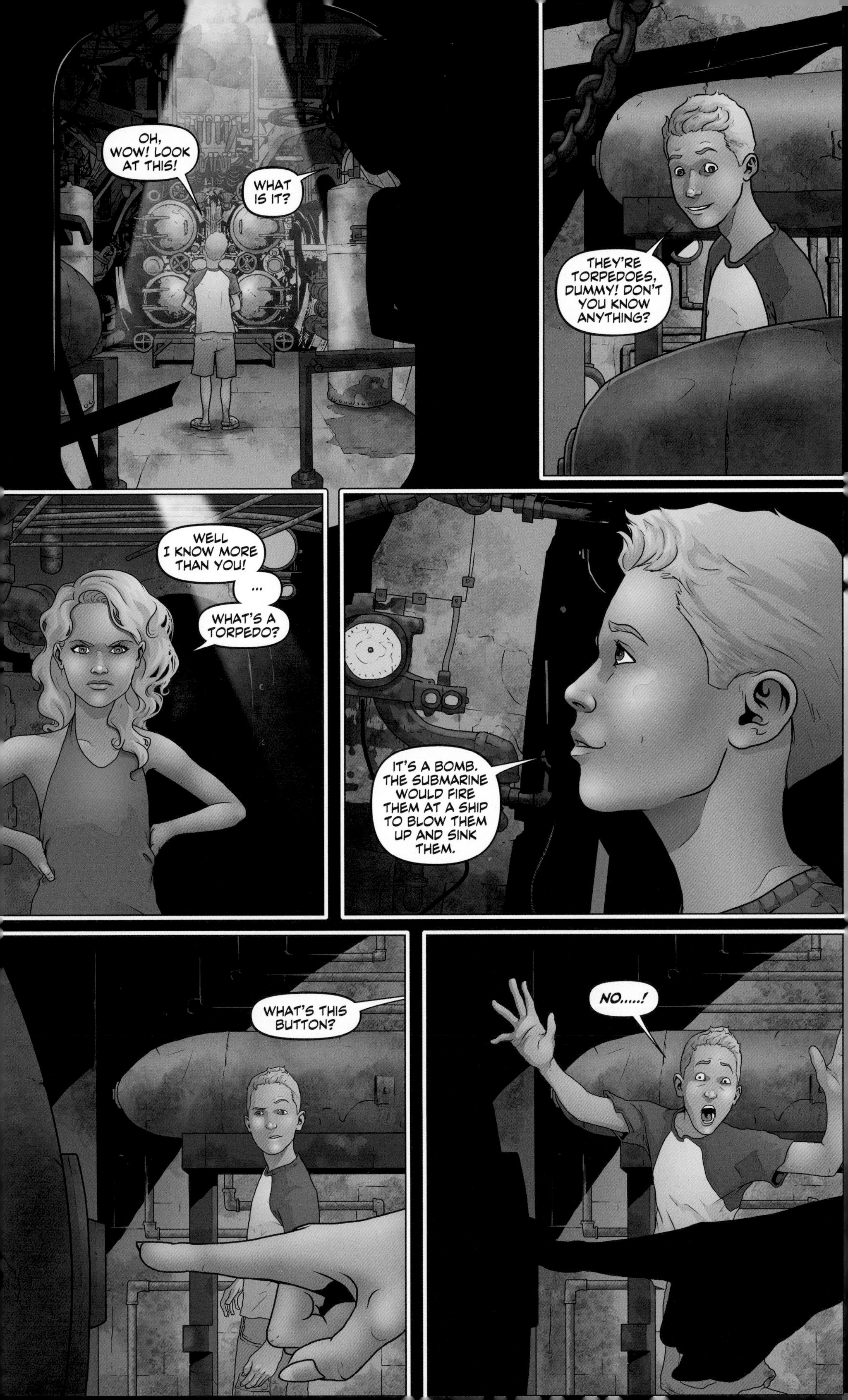
OH, WOW! LOOK AT THIS!
WHAT IS IT?
THEY'RE TORPEDOES, DUMMY! DON'T YOU KNOW ANYTHING?
WELL I KNOW MORE THAN YOU!
...
WHAT'S A TORPEDO?
IT'S A BOMB. THE SUBMARINE WOULD FIRE THEM AT A SHIP TO BLOW THEM UP AND SINK THEM.
WHAT'S THIS BUTTON?
NO.....!

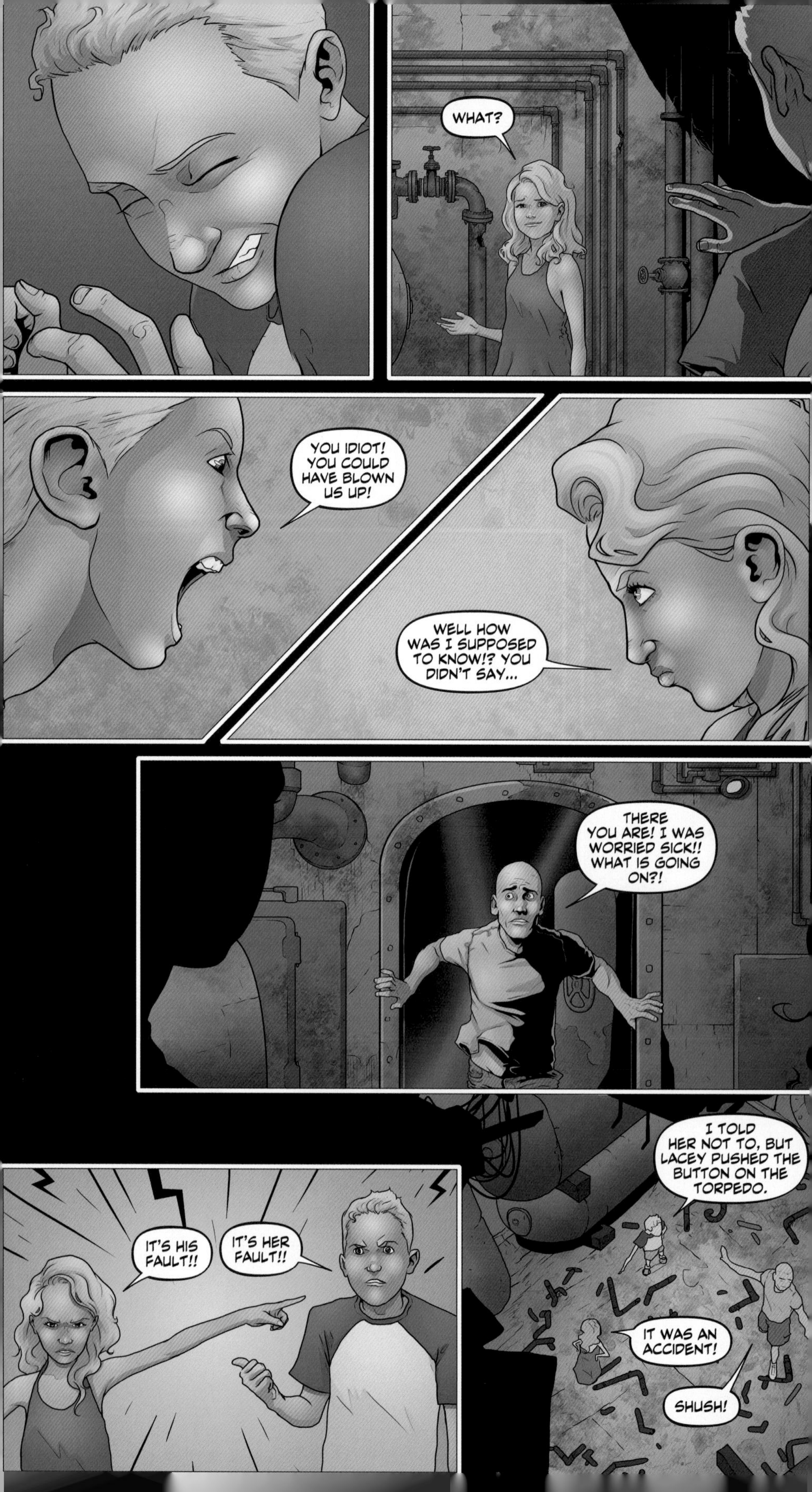
WHAT?
YOU IDIOT! YOU COULD HAVE BLOWN US UP!
WELL HOW WAS I SUPPOSED TO KNOW!? YOU DIDN'T SAY...
THERE YOU ARE! I WAS WORRIED SICK!! WHAT IS GOING ON?!
I TOLD HER NOT TO, BUT LACEY PUSHED THE BUTTON ON THE TORPEDO.
IT WAS AN ACCIDENT!
SHUSH!
IT'S HIS FAULT!!
IT'S HER FAULT!!

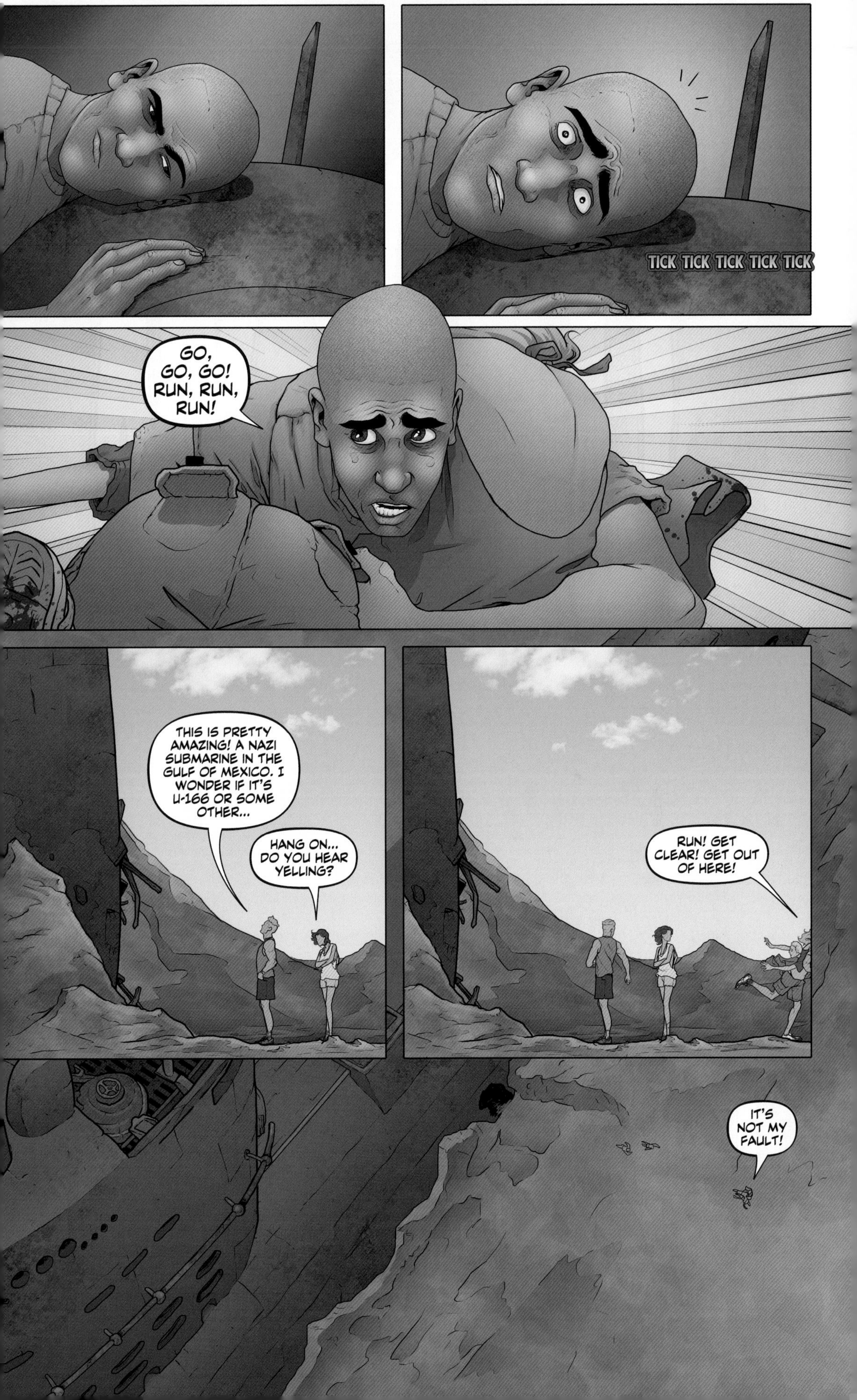
TICK TICK TICK TICK TICK
GO, GO, GO! RUN, RUN, RUN!
THIS IS PRETTY AMAZING! A NAZI SUBMARINE IN THE GULF OF MEXICO. I WONDER IF IT'S U-166 OR SOME OTHER...
HANG ON... DO YOU HEAR YELLING?
RUN! GET CLEAR! GET OUT OF HERE!
IT'S NOT MY FAULT!

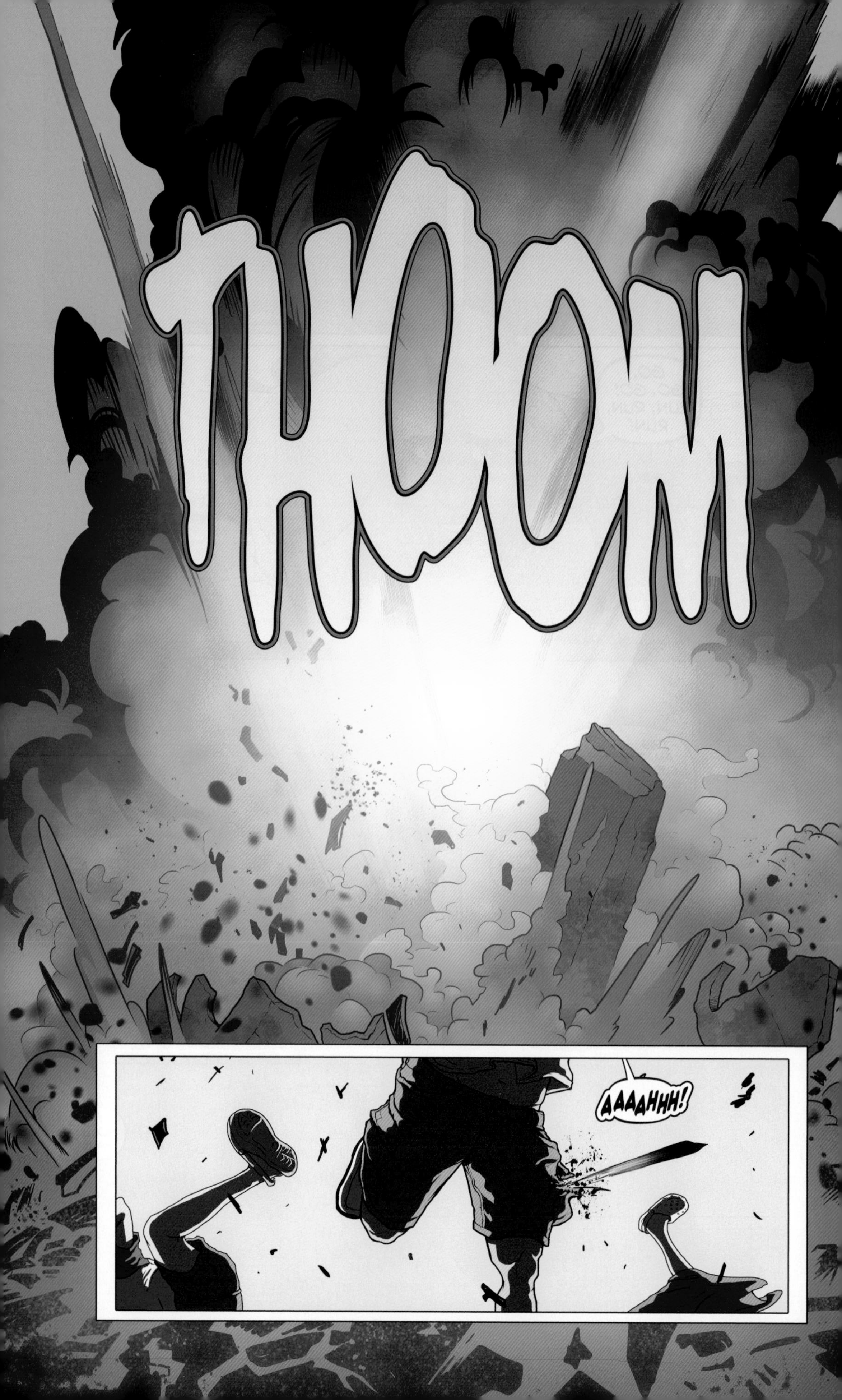
THOOM
AAAAHHH!

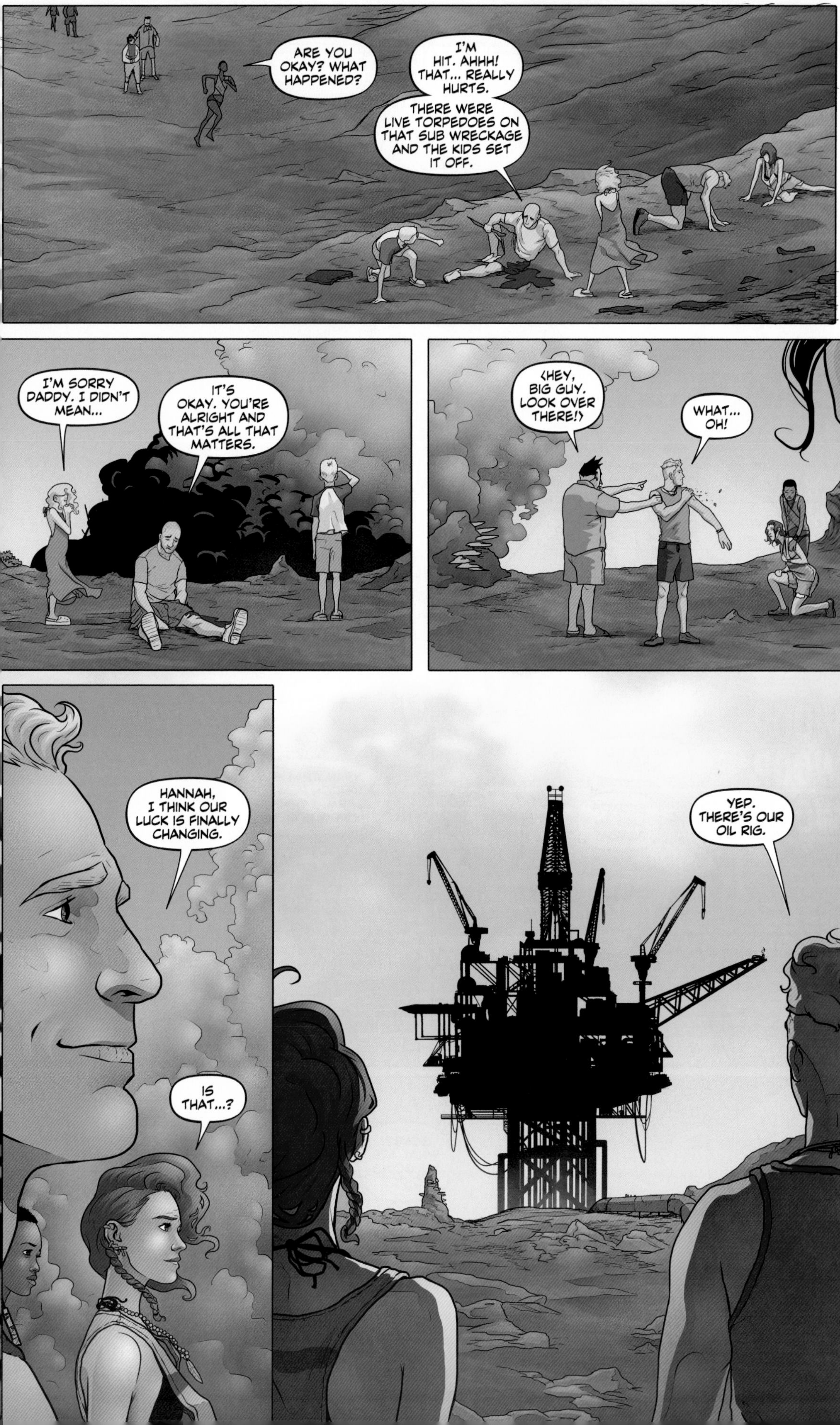
ARE YOU OKAY? WHAT HAPPENED?
I'M HIT. AHHH! THAT... REALLY HURTS.
THERE WERE LIVE TORPEDOES ON THAT SUB WRECKAGE AND THE KIDS SET IT OFF.
I'M SORRY DADDY. I DIDN'T MEAN...
IT'S OKAY. YOU'RE ALRIGHT AND THAT'S ALL THAT MATTERS.
‹HEY, BIG GUY. LOOK OVER THERE!›
WHAT... OH!
HANNAH, I THINK OUR LUCK IS FINALLY CHANGING.
IS THAT...?
YEP. THERE'S OUR OIL RIG.

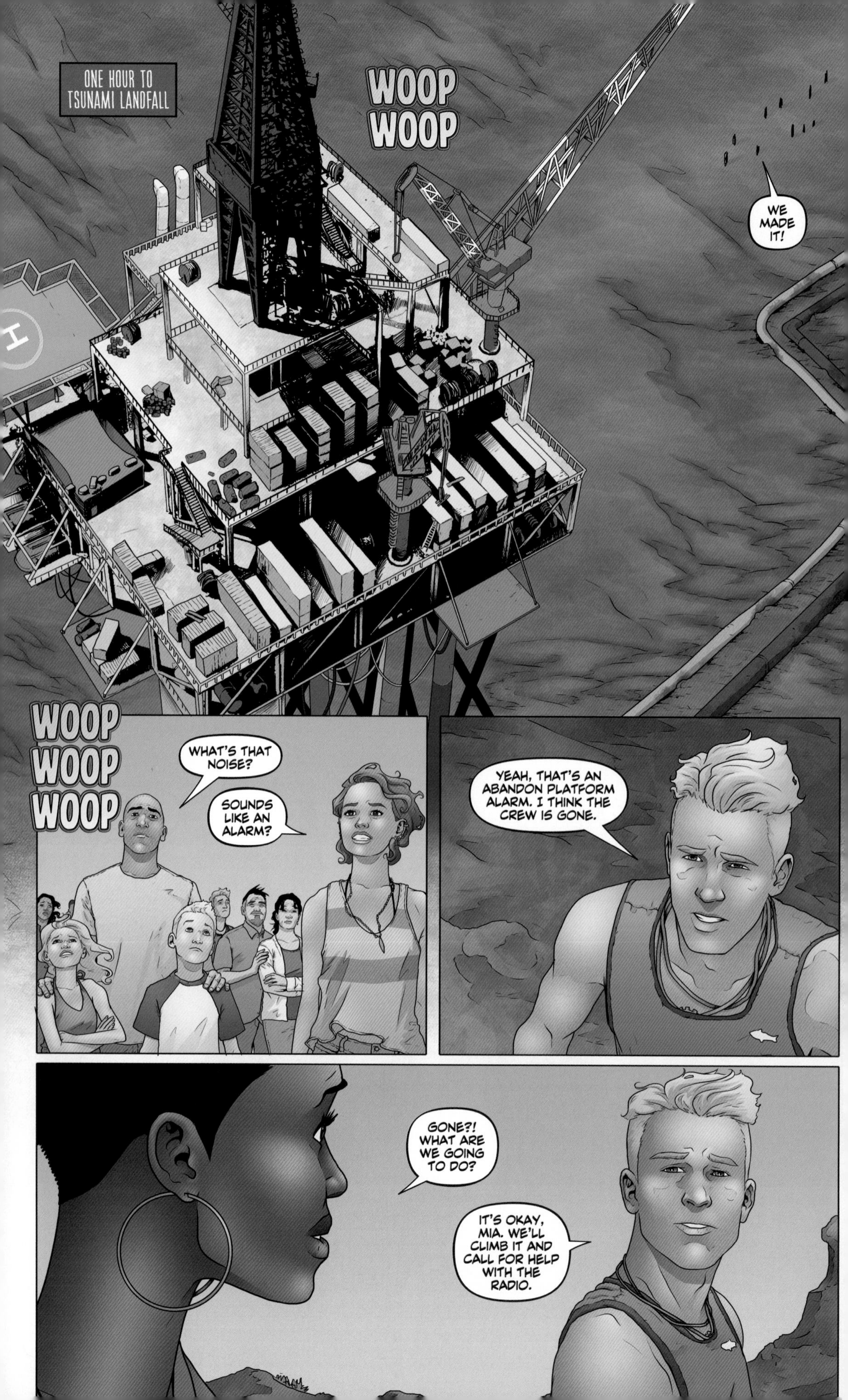
ONE HOUR TO TSUNAMI LANDFALL
WOOP WOOP
WE MADE IT!
WOOP WOOP WOOP
WHAT'S THAT NOISE?
SOUNDS LIKE AN ALARM?
YEAH, THAT'S AN ABANDON PLATFORM ALARM. I THINK THE CREW IS GONE.
GONE?! WHAT ARE WE GOING TO DO?
IT'S OKAY, MIA. WE'LL CLIMB IT AND CALL FOR HELP WITH THE RADIO.

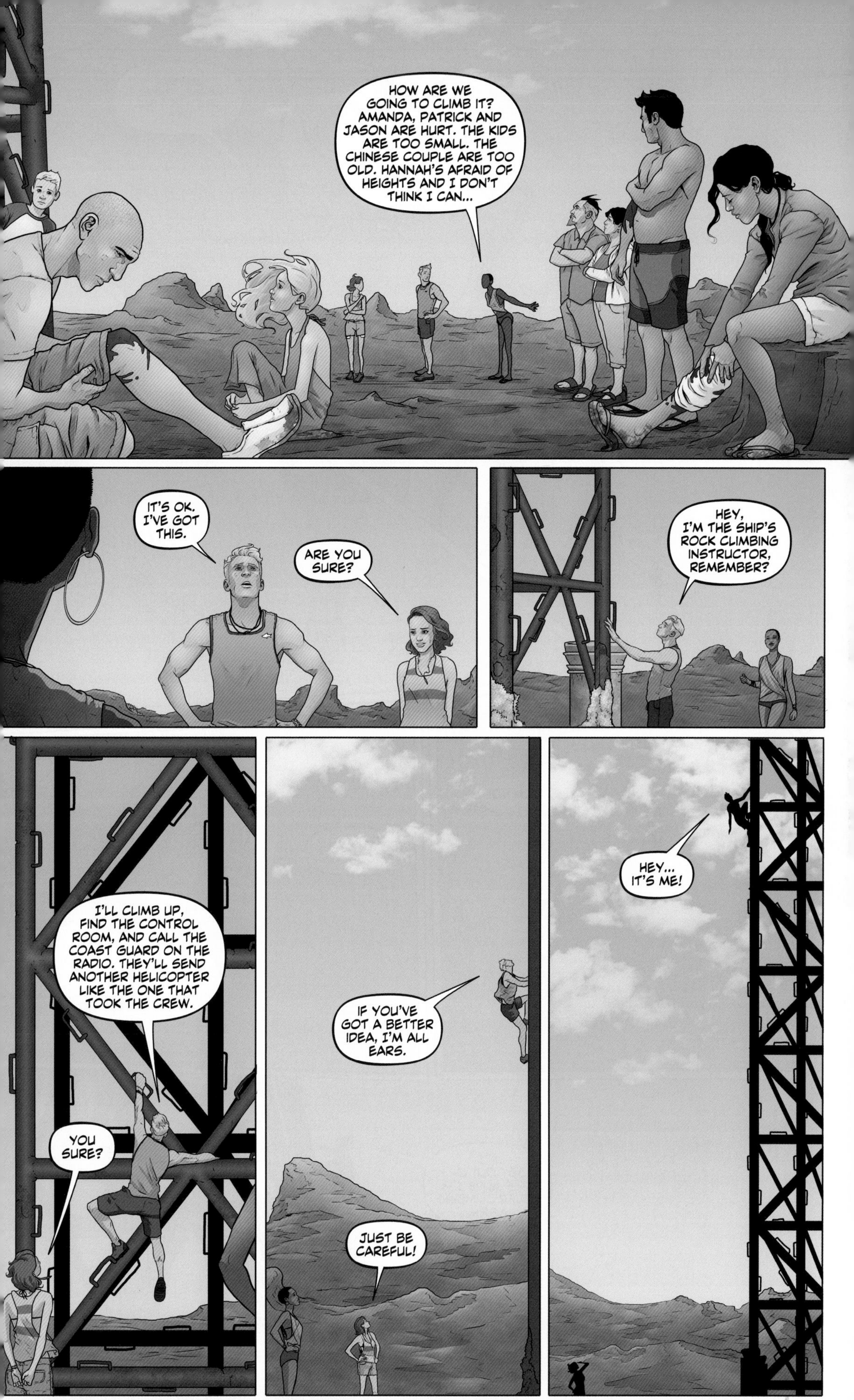
HOW ARE WE GOING TO CLIMB IT? AMANDA, PATRICK AND JASON ARE HURT. THE KIDS ARE TOO SMALL. THE CHINESE COUPLE ARE TOO OLD. HANNAH'S AFRAID OF HEIGHTS AND I DON'T THINK I CAN...
IT'S OK. I'VE GOT THIS.
ARE YOU SURE?
HEY, I'M THE SHIP'S ROCK CLIMBING INSTRUCTOR, REMEMBER?
I'LL CLIMB UP, FIND THE CONTROL ROOM, AND CALL THE COAST GUARD ON THE RADIO. THEY'LL SEND ANOTHER HELICOPTER LIKE THE ONE THAT TOOK THE CREW.
YOU SURE?
IF YOU'VE GOT A BETTER IDEA, I'M ALL EARS.
JUST BE CAREFUL!
HEY... IT'S ME!

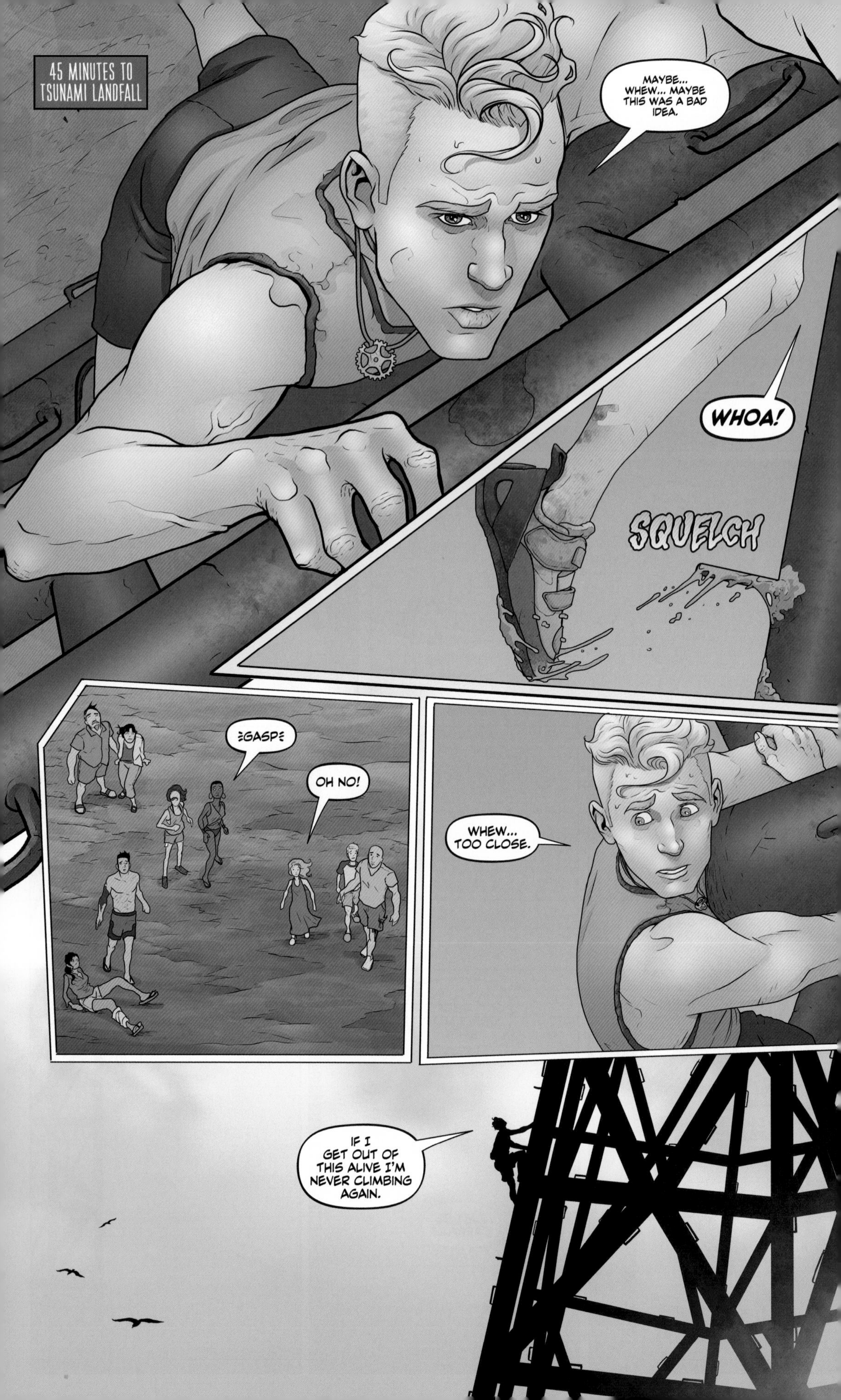
45 MINUTES TO TSUNAMI LANDFALL
MAYBE... WHEW... MAYBE THIS WAS A BAD IDEA.
WHOA!
SQUELCH
GASP
OH NO!
WHEW... TOO CLOSE.
IF I GET OUT OF THIS ALIVE I'M NEVER CLIMBING AGAIN.

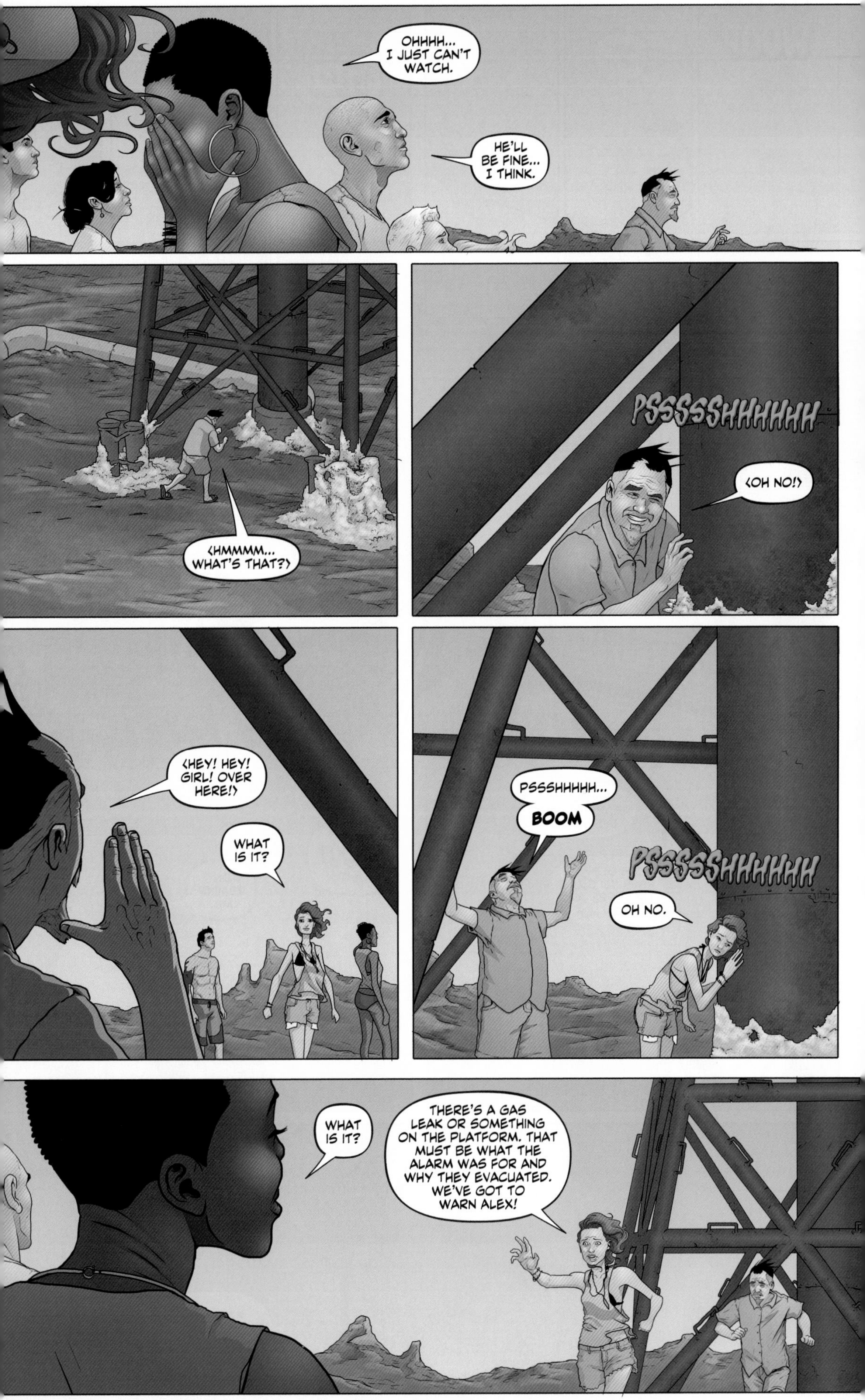
OHHHH... I JUST CAN'T WATCH.
HE'LL BE FINE... I THINK.
‹HMMMM... WHAT'S THAT?›
PSSSSSHHHHHH
‹OH NO!›
‹HEY! HEY! GIRL! OVER HERE!›
WHAT IS IT?
PSSSHHHHH...
BOOM
PSSSSSHHHHHH
OH NO.
WHAT IS IT?
THERE'S A GAS LEAK OR SOMETHING ON THE PLATFORM. THAT MUST BE WHAT THE ALARM WAS FOR AND WHY THEY EVACUATED. WE'VE GOT TO WARN ALEX!

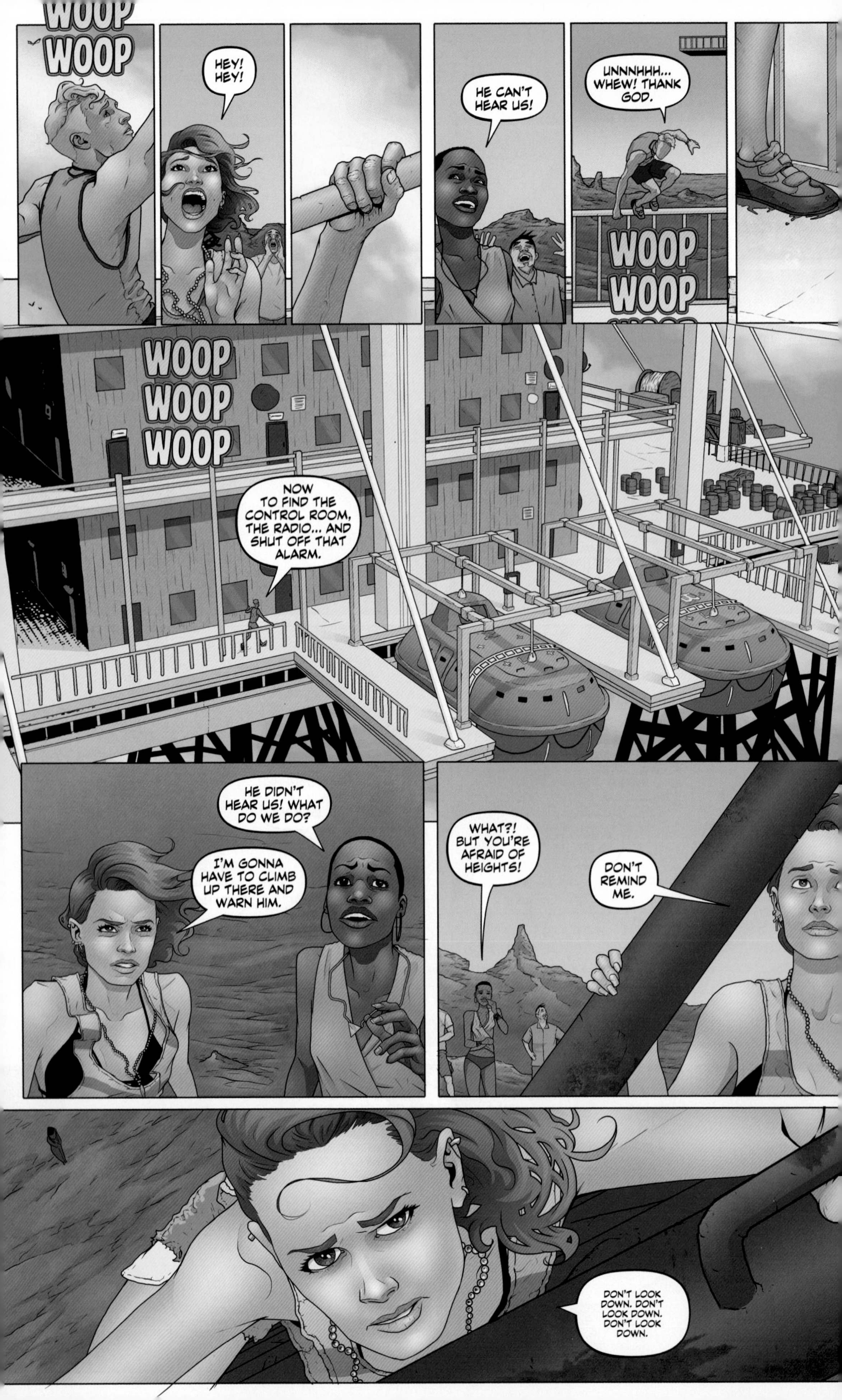
WOOP
WOOP
HEY! HEY!
HE CAN'T HEAR US!
UNNNHHH... WHEW! THANK GOD.
WOOP
WOOP
WOOP
WOOP
WOOP
NOW TO FIND THE CONTROL ROOM, THE RADIO... AND SHUT OFF THAT ALARM.
HE DIDN'T HEAR US! WHAT DO WE DO?
I'M GONNA HAVE TO CLIMB UP THERE AND WARN HIM.
WHAT?! BUT YOU'RE AFRAID OF HEIGHTS!
DON'T REMIND ME.
DON'T LOOK DOWN. DON'T LOOK DOWN. DON'T LOOK DOWN.

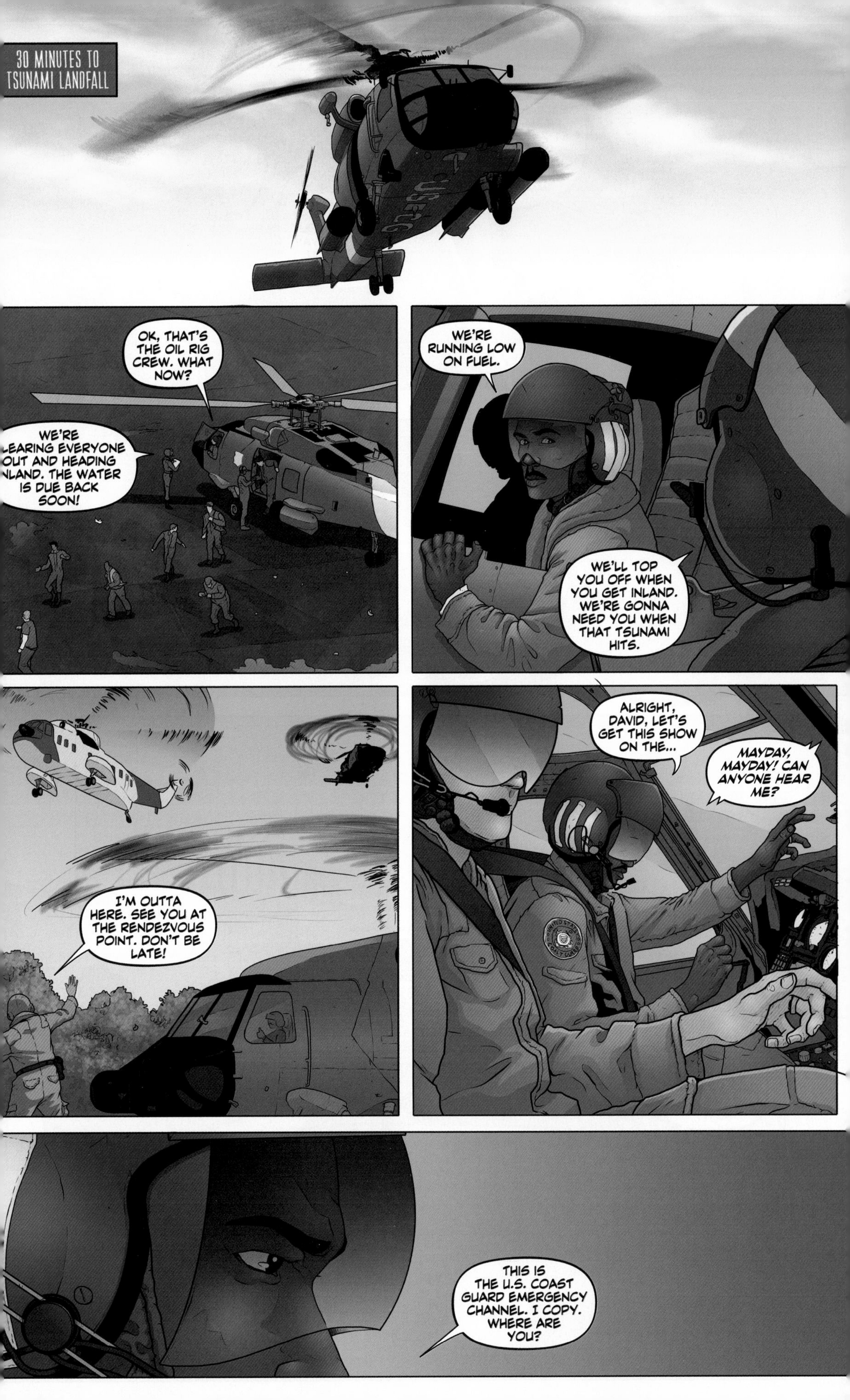
30 MINUTES TO TSUNAMI LANDFALL
USCG
OK, THAT'S THE OIL RIG CREW. WHAT NOW?
WE'RE LEARING EVERYONE OUT AND HEADING NLAND. THE WATER IS DUE BACK SOON!
WE'RE RUNNING LOW ON FUEL.
WE'LL TOP YOU OFF WHEN YOU GET INLAND. WE'RE GONNA NEED YOU WHEN THAT TSUNAMI HITS.
I'M OUTTA HERE. SEE YOU AT THE RENDEZVOUS POINT. DON'T BE LATE!
ALRIGHT, DAVID, LET'S GET THIS SHOW ON THE...
MAYDAY, MAYDAY! CAN ANYONE HEAR ME?
THIS IS THE U.S. COAST GUARD EMERGENCY CHANNEL. I COPY. WHERE ARE YOU?

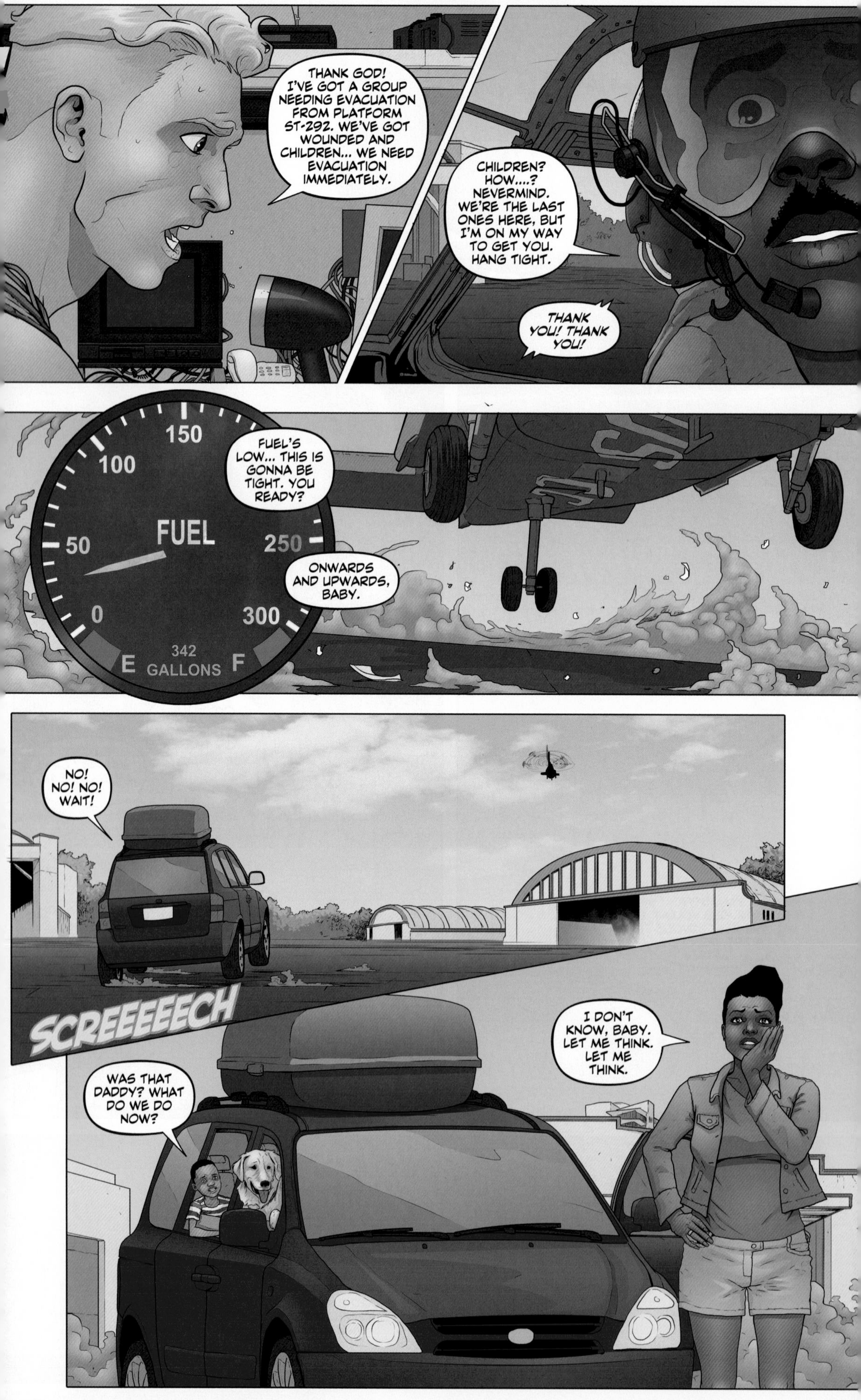
THANK GOD! I'VE GOT A GROUP NEEDING EVACUATION FROM PLATFORM ST-292. WE'VE GOT WOUNDED AND CHILDREN... WE NEED EVACUATION IMMEDIATELY.
CHILDREN? HOW....? NEVERMIND. WE'RE THE LAST ONES HERE, BUT I'M ON MY WAY TO GET YOU. HANG TIGHT.
THANK YOU! THANK YOU!
150
100
50
FUEL
250
0
300
342
E
GALLONS
F
FUEL'S LOW... THIS IS GONNA BE TIGHT. YOU READY?
ONWARDS AND UPWARDS, BABY.
NO! NO! NO! WAIT!
SCREEEEECH
WAS THAT DADDY? WHAT DO WE DO NOW?
I DON'T KNOW, BABY. LET ME THINK. LET ME THINK.

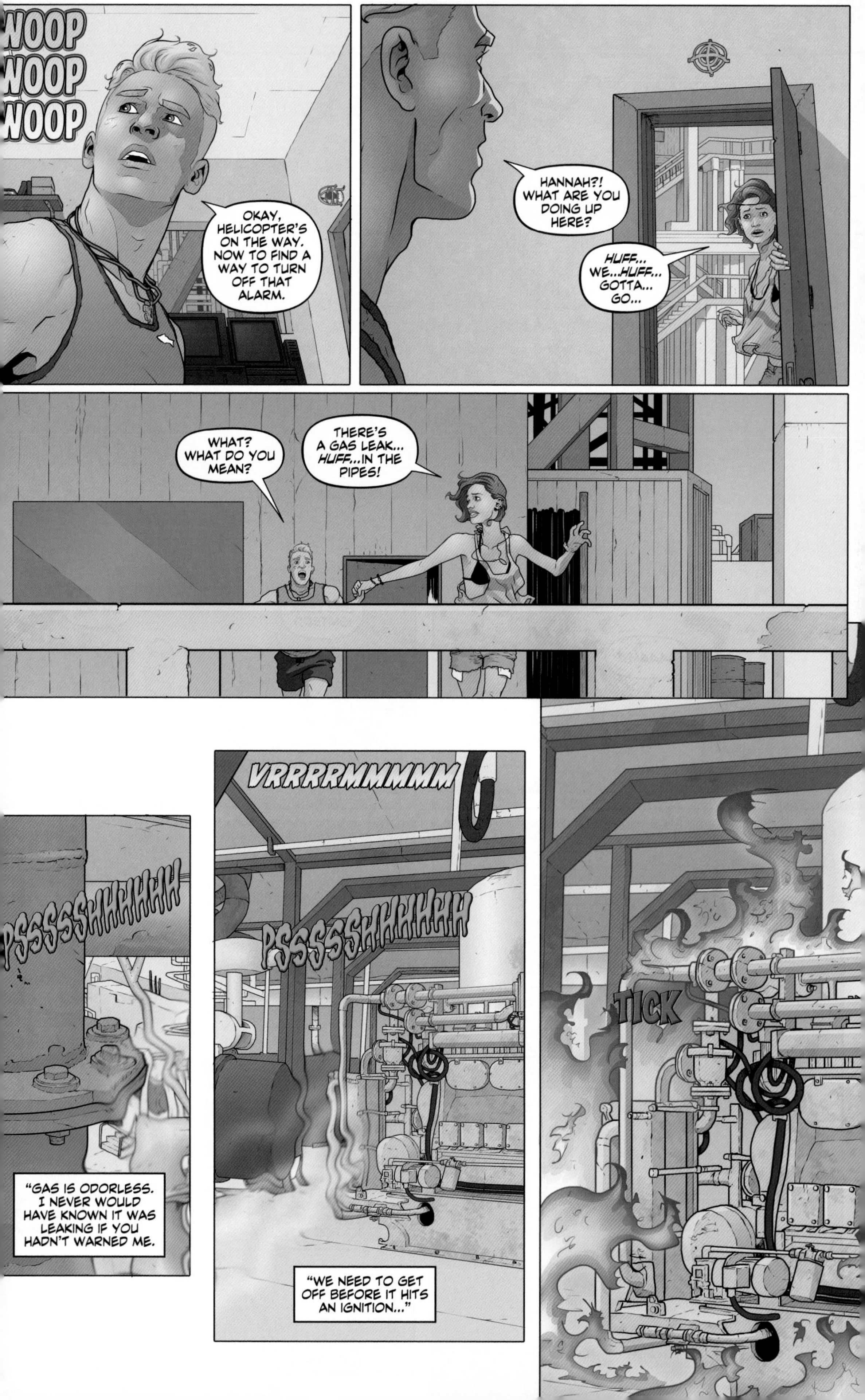
WOOP
WOOP
WOOP
OKAY, HELICOPTER'S ON THE WAY. NOW TO FIND A WAY TO TURN OFF THAT ALARM.
HANNAH?! WHAT ARE YOU DOING UP HERE?
HUFF... WE...HUFF... GOTTA... GO...
WHAT? WHAT DO YOU MEAN?
THERE'S A GAS LEAK... HUFF...IN THE PIPES!
PSSSSSHHHHHH
"GAS IS ODORLESS. I NEVER WOULD HAVE KNOWN IT WAS LEAKING IF YOU HADN'T WARNED ME.
VRRRRMMMMM
PSSSSSHHHHHH
"WE NEED TO GET OFF BEFORE IT HITS AN IGNITION..."
TICK

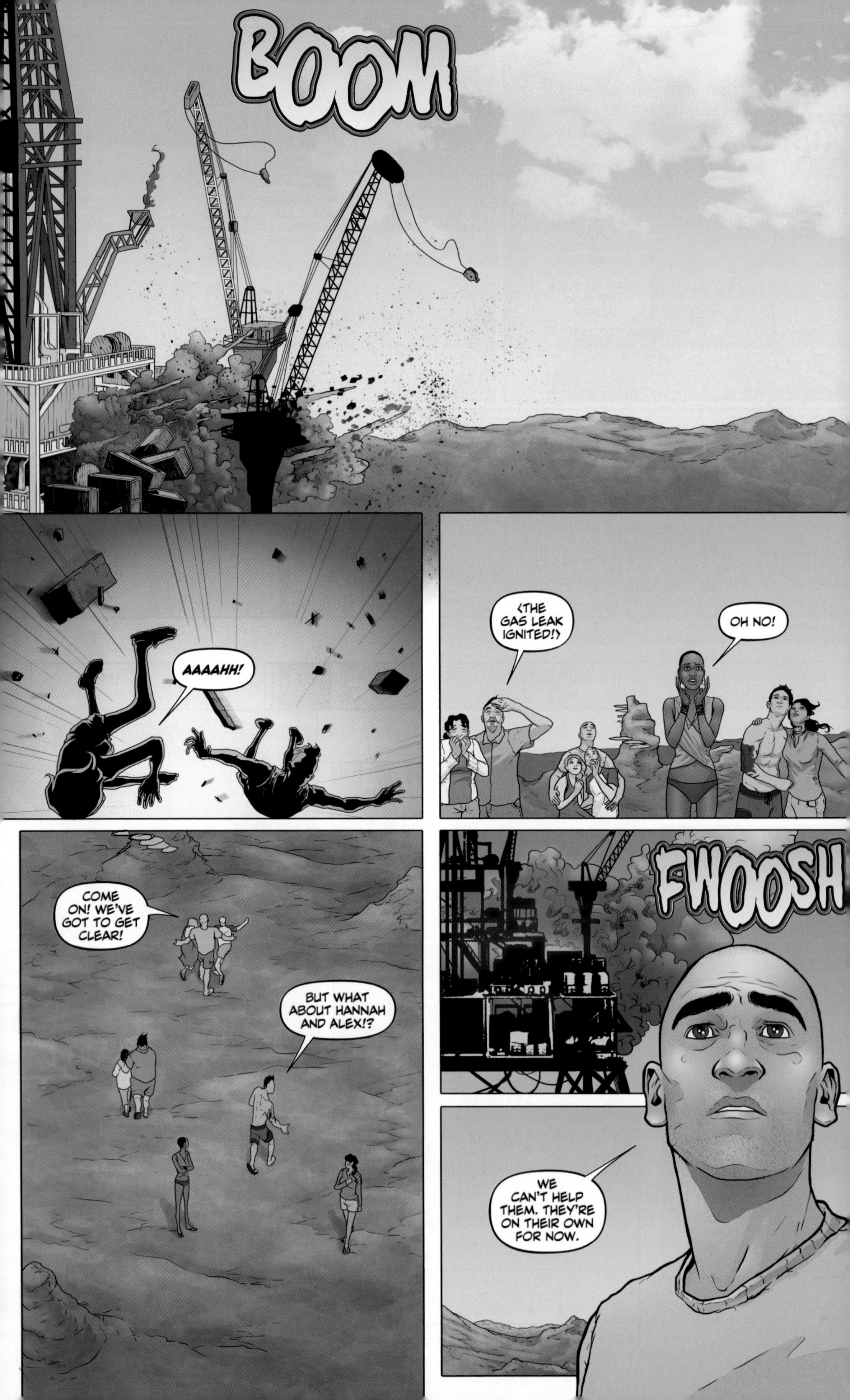
BOOM
AAAAHH!
‹THE GAS LEAK IGNITED!›
OH NO!
COME ON! WE'VE GOT TO GET CLEAR!
BUT WHAT ABOUT HANNAH AND ALEX!?
FWOOSH
WE CAN'T HELP THEM. THEY'RE ON THEIR OWN FOR NOW.

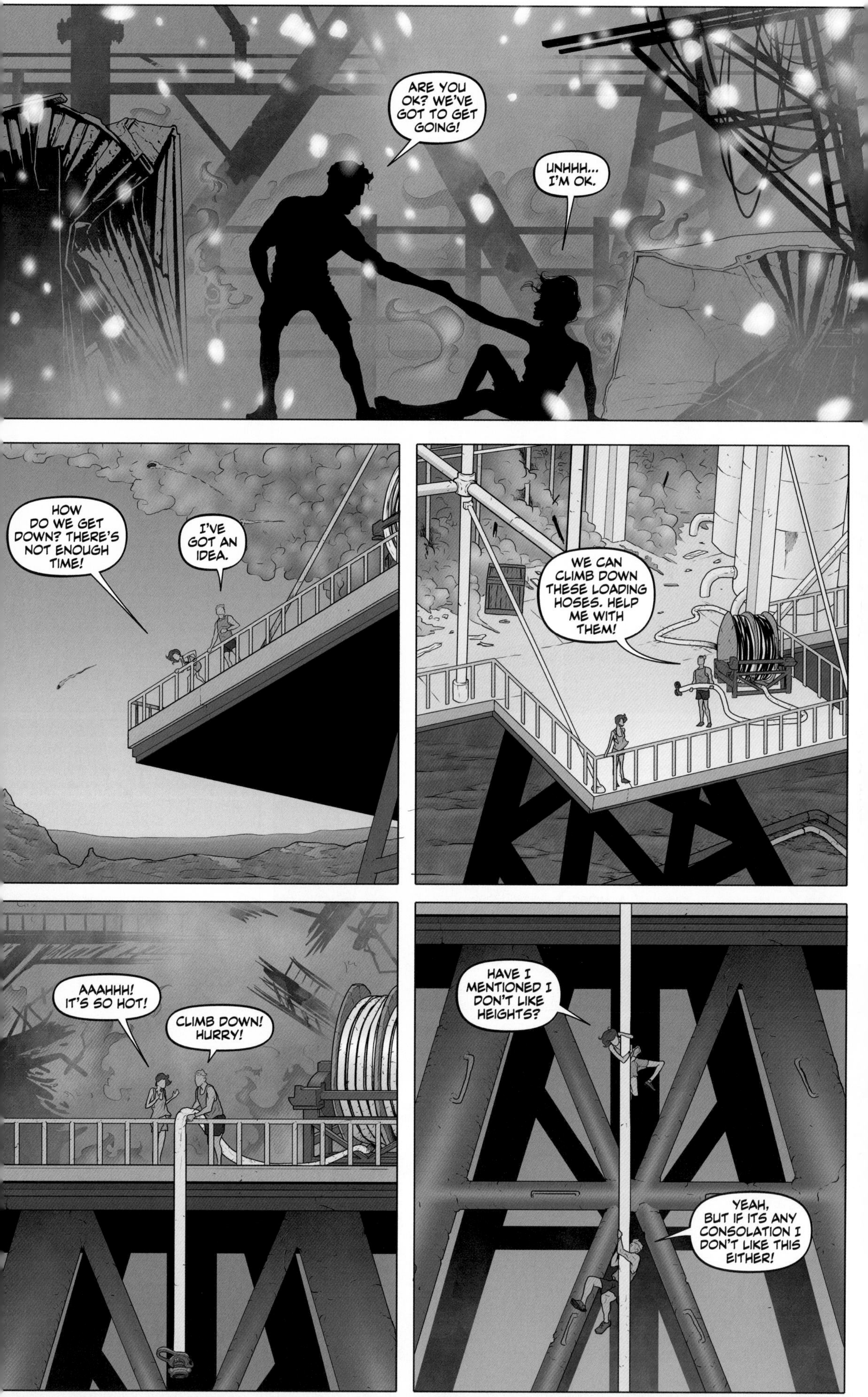
ARE YOU OK? WE'VE GOT TO GET GOING!
UNHHH... I'M OK.
HOW DO WE GET DOWN? THERE'S NOT ENOUGH TIME!
I'VE GOT AN IDEA.
WE CAN CLIMB DOWN THESE LOADING HOSES. HELP ME WITH THEM!
AAAHHH! IT'S SO HOT!
CLIMB DOWN! HURRY!
HAVE I MENTIONED I DON'T LIKE HEIGHTS?
YEAH, BUT IF ITS ANY CONSOLATION I DON'T LIKE THIS EITHER!

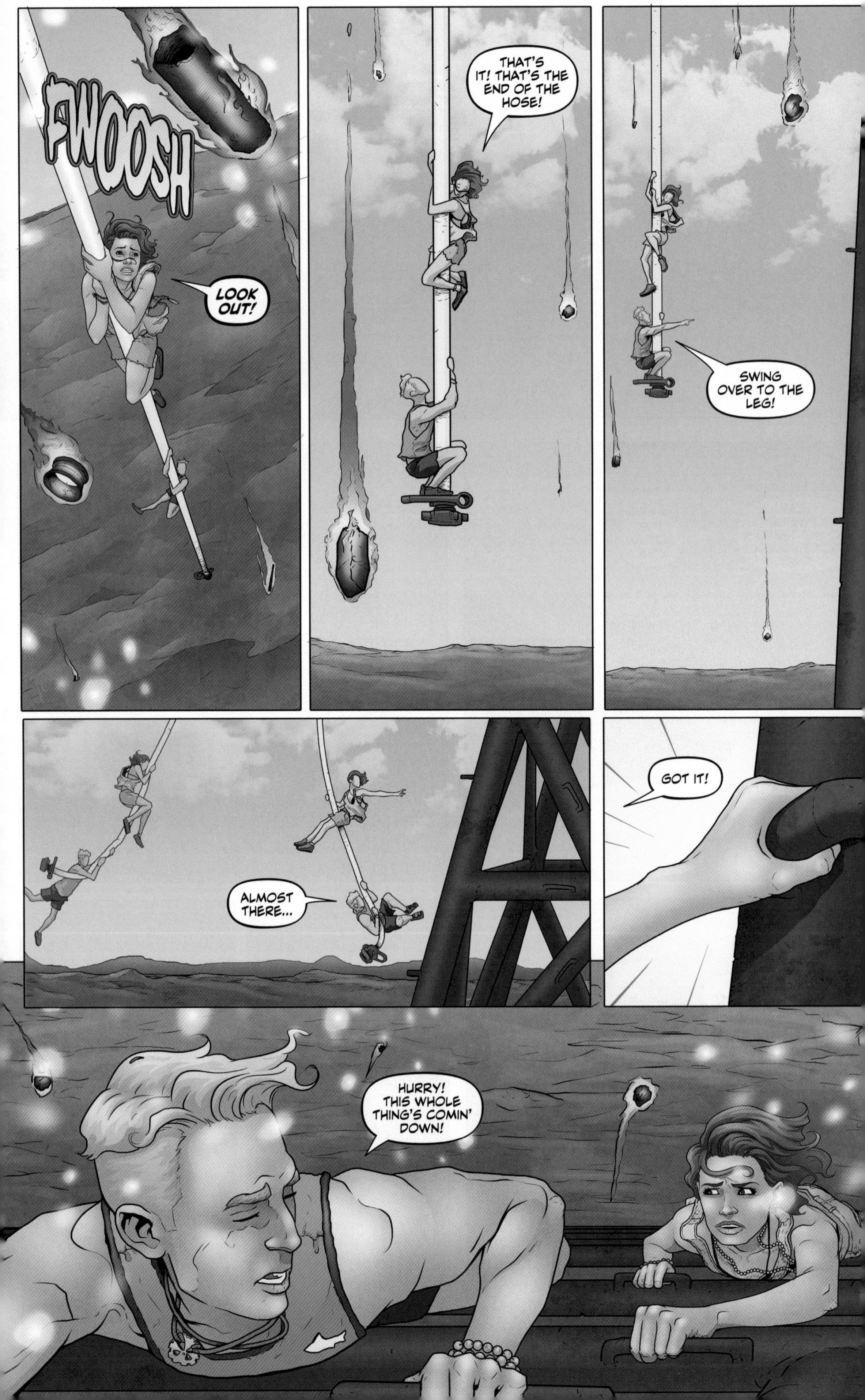
FWOOSH
LOOK OUT!
THAT'S IT! THAT'S THE END OF THE HOSE!
SWING OVER TO THE LEG!
ALMOST THERE...
GOT IT!
HURRY! THIS WHOLE THING'S COMIN' DOWN!

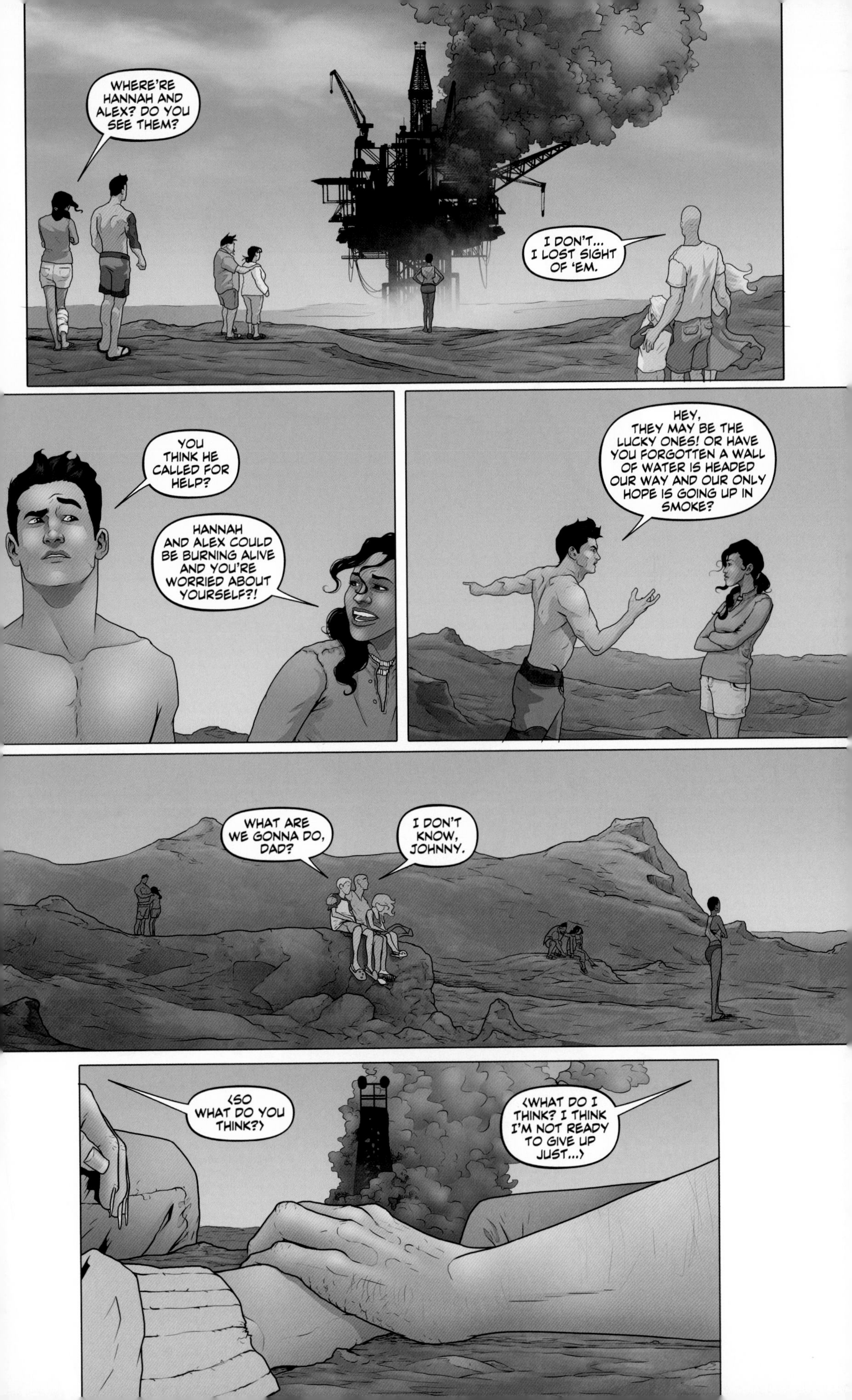
WHERE'RE HANNAH AND ALEX? DO YOU SEE THEM?
I DON'T... I LOST SIGHT OF 'EM.
YOU THINK HE CALLED FOR HELP?
HANNAH AND ALEX COULD BE BURNING ALIVE AND YOU'RE WORRIED ABOUT YOURSELF?!
HEY, THEY MAY BE THE LUCKY ONES! OR HAVE YOU FORGOTTEN A WALL OF WATER IS HEADED OUR WAY AND OUR ONLY HOPE IS GOING UP IN SMOKE?
WHAT ARE WE GONNA DO, DAD?
I DON'T KNOW, JOHNNY.
‹SO WHAT DO YOU THINK?›
‹WHAT DO I THINK? I THINK I'M NOT READY TO GIVE UP JUST...›

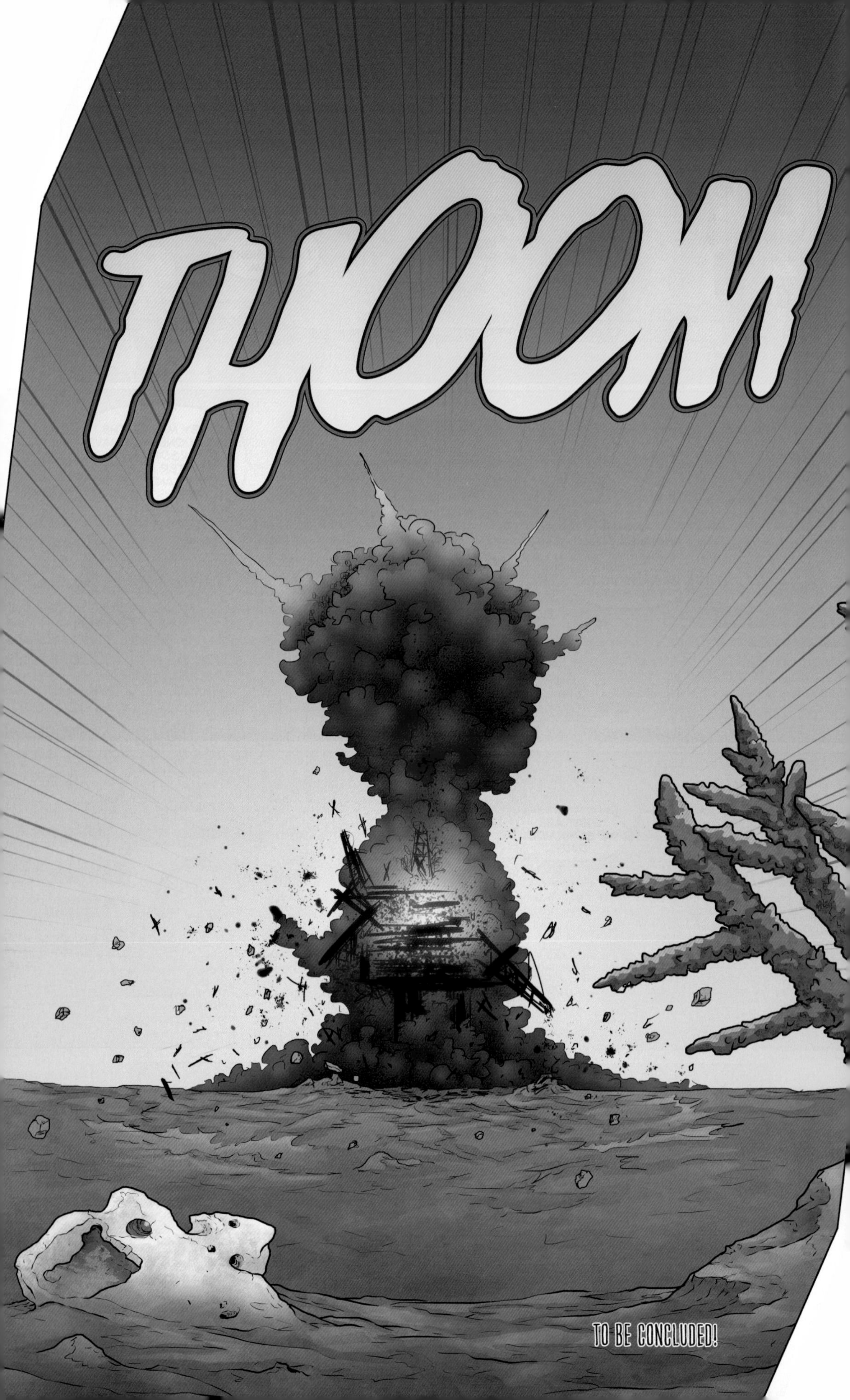
THOOM
TO BE CONCLUDED!

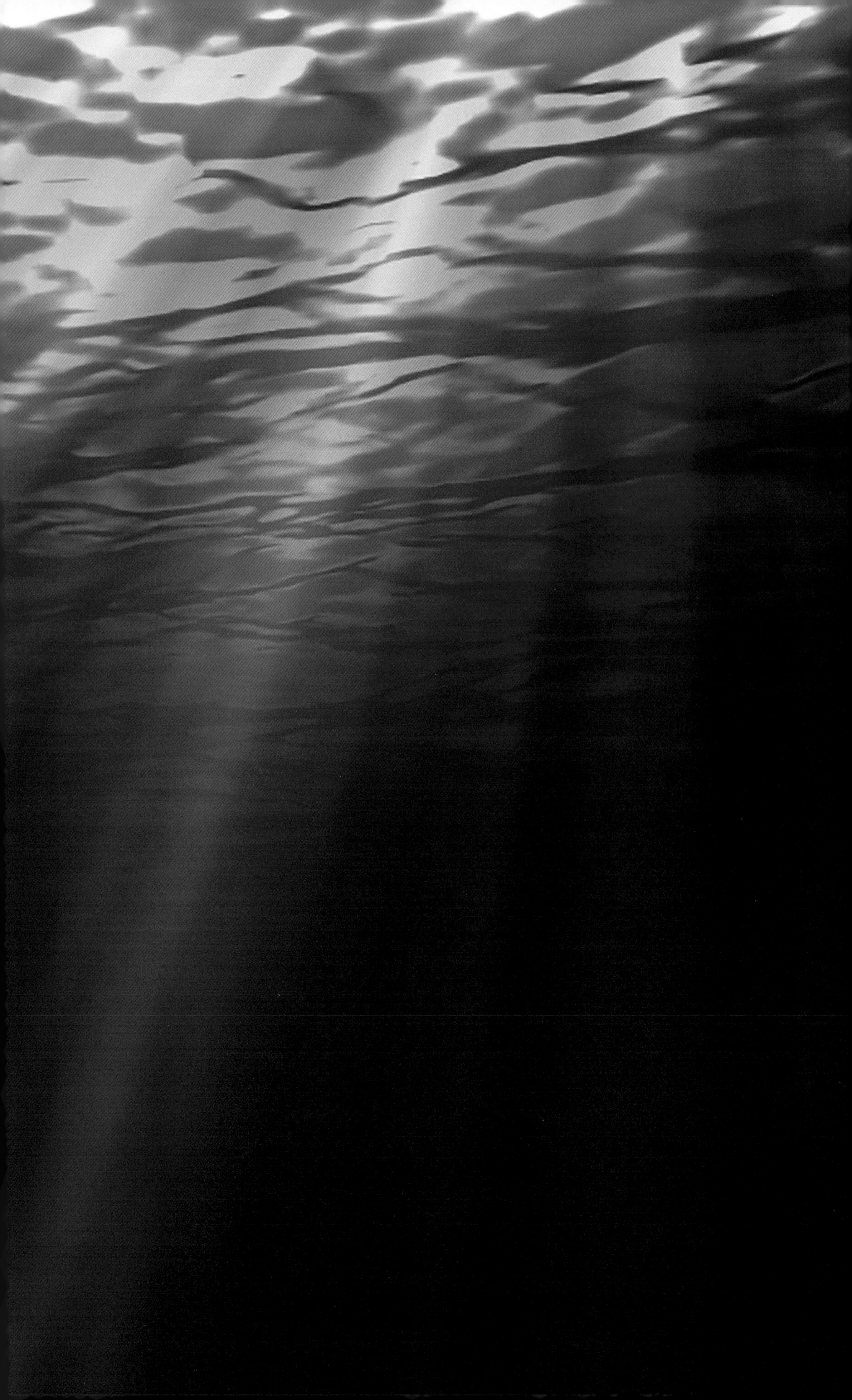

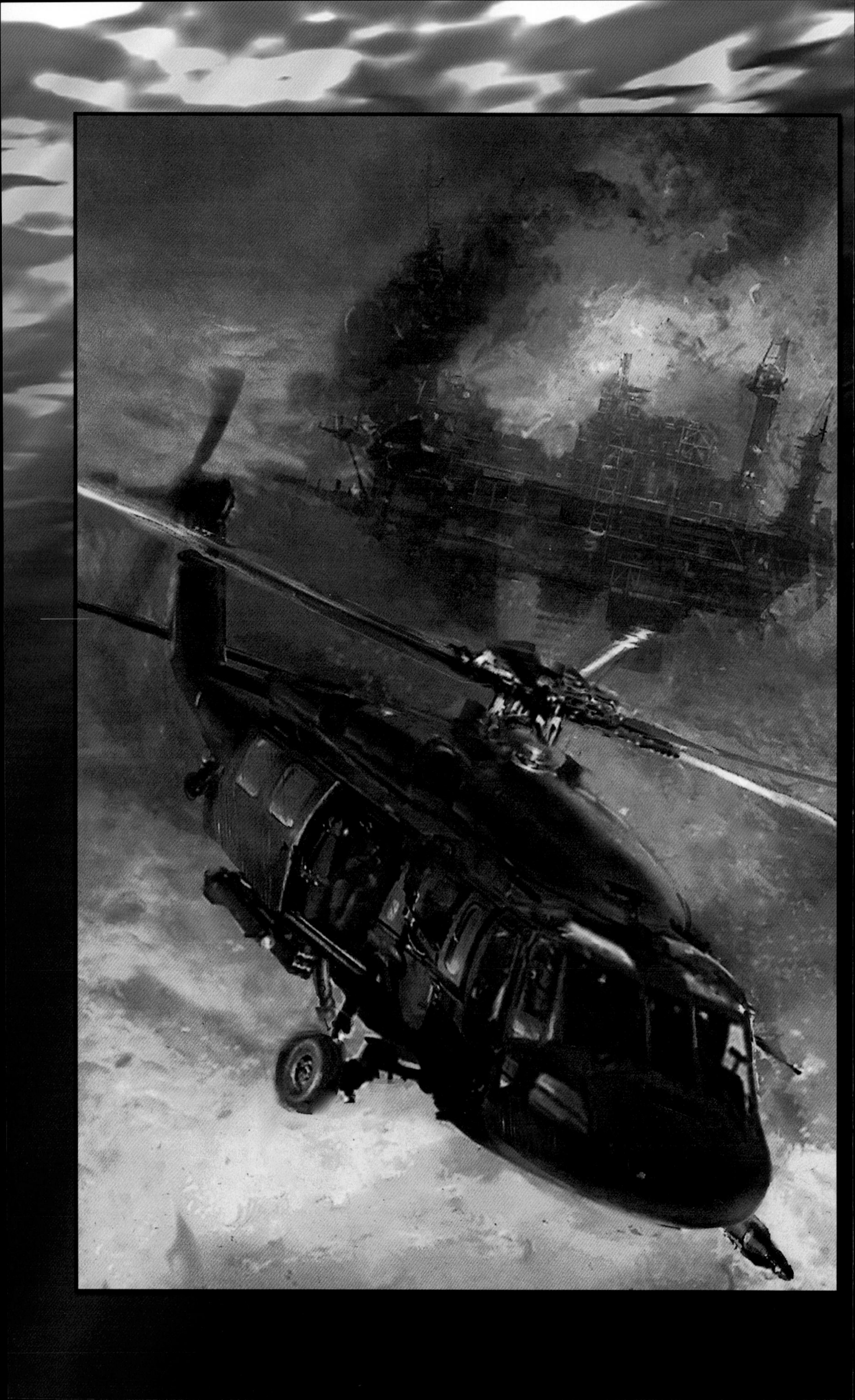

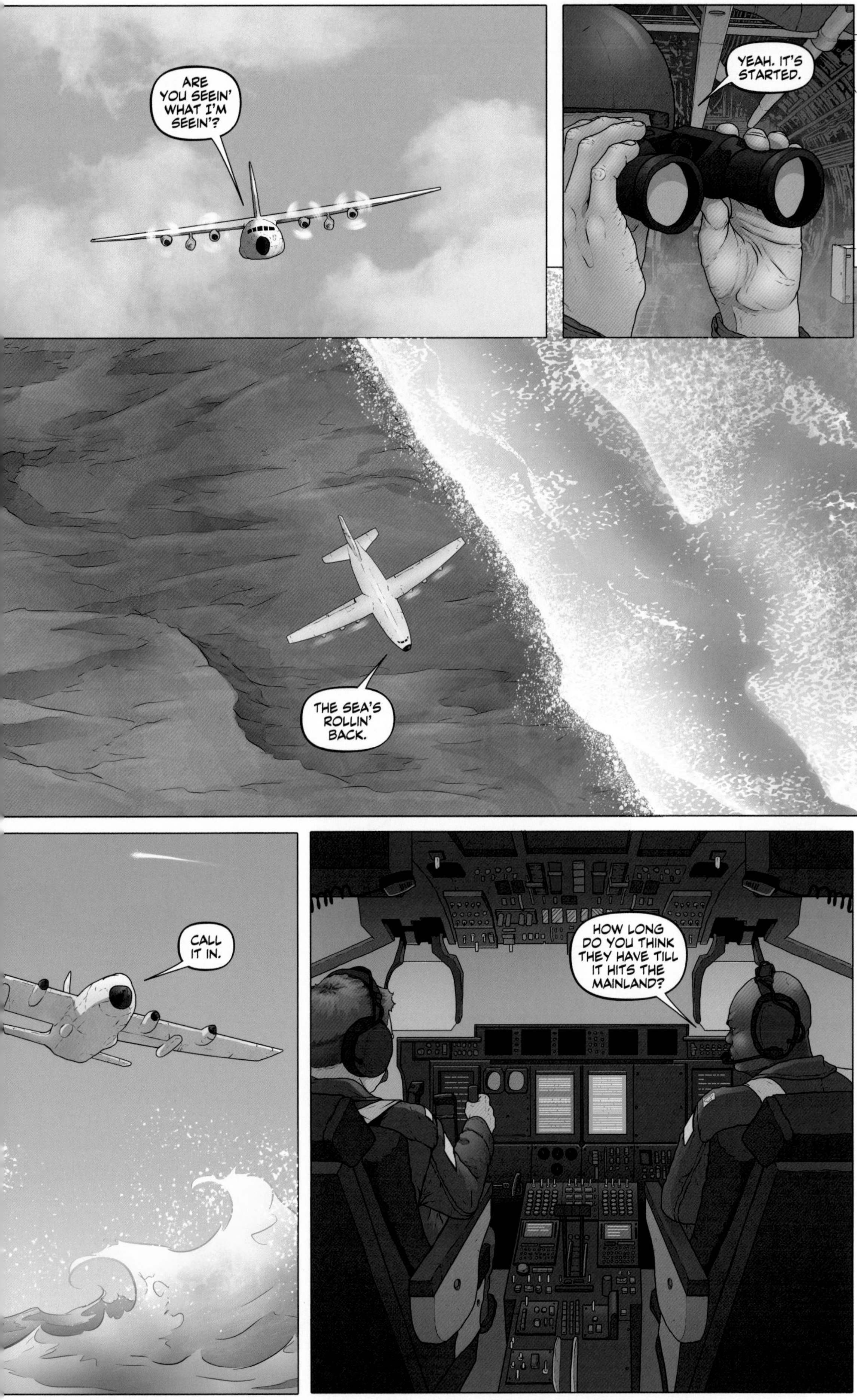
ARE YOU SEEIN' WHAT I'M SEEIN'?
YEAH. IT'S STARTED.
THE SEA'S ROLLIN' BACK.
CALL IT IN.
HOW LONG DO YOU THINK THEY HAVE TILL IT HITS THE MAINLAND?

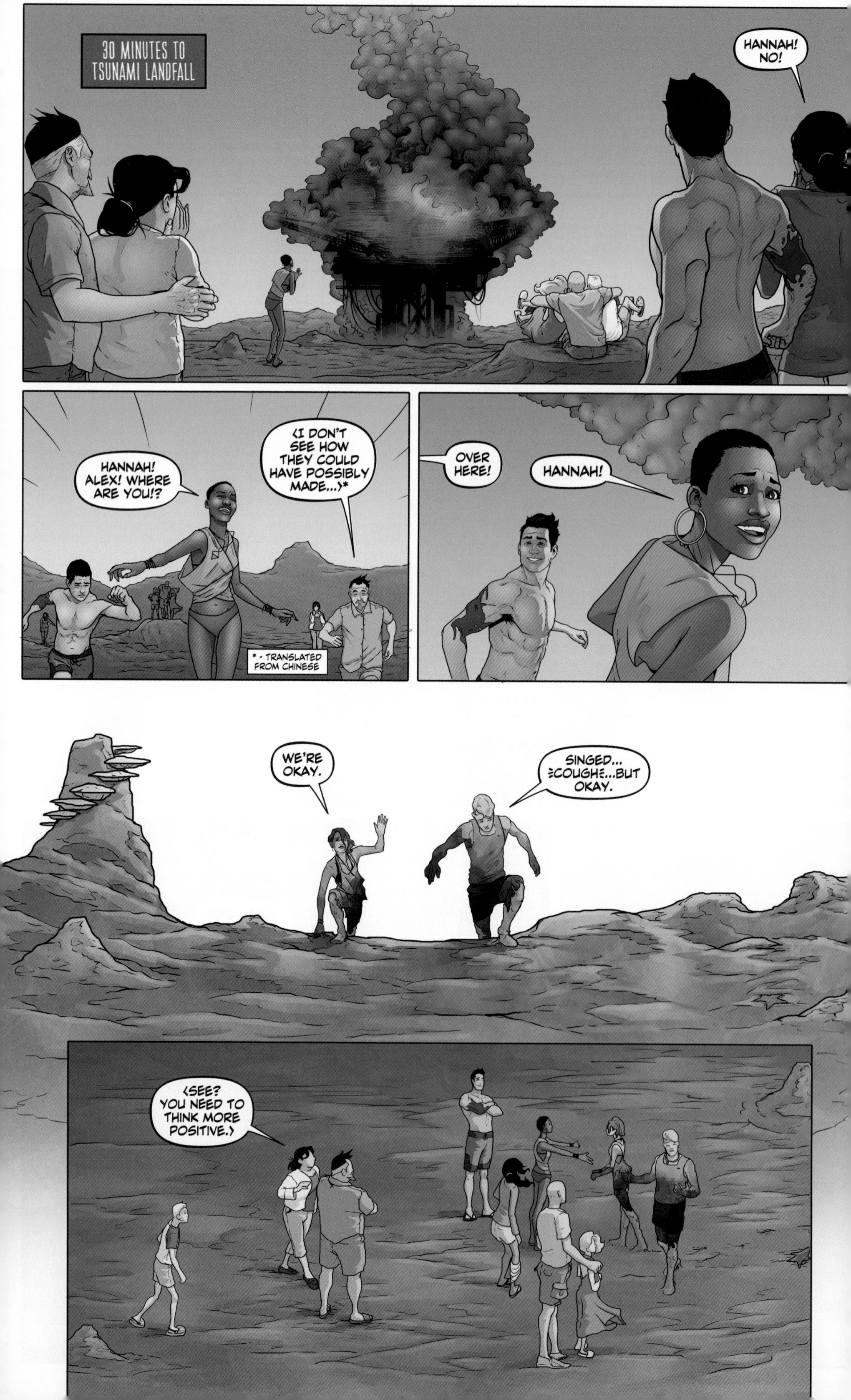
30 MINUTES TO TSUNAMI LANDFALL
HANNAH! NO!
HANNAH! ALEX! WHERE ARE YOU!?
‹I DON'T SEE HOW THEY COULD HAVE POSSIBLY MADE...›*
* - TRANSLATED FROM CHINESE
OVER HERE!
HANNAH!
WE'RE OKAY.
SINGED... ≈COUGH≈...BUT OKAY.
‹SEE? YOU NEED TO THINK MORE POSITIVE.›

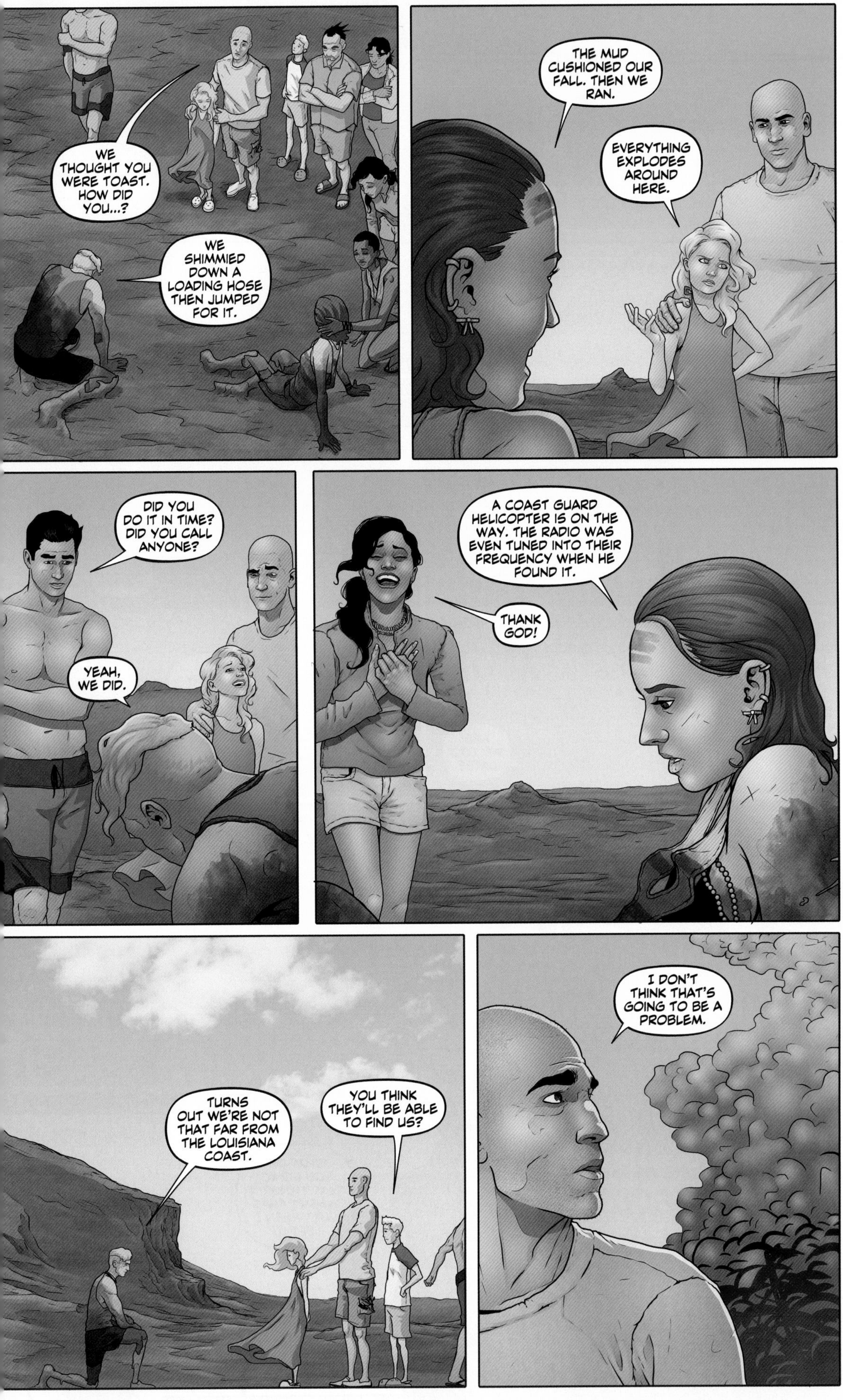
WE THOUGHT YOU WERE TOAST. HOW DID YOU...?
WE SHIMMIED DOWN A LOADING HOSE THEN JUMPED FOR IT.
THE MUD CUSHIONED OUR FALL. THEN WE RAN.
EVERYTHING EXPLODES AROUND HERE.
DID YOU DO IT IN TIME? DID YOU CALL ANYONE?
YEAH, WE DID.
A COAST GUARD HELICOPTER IS ON THE WAY. THE RADIO WAS EVEN TUNED INTO THEIR FREQUENCY WHEN HE FOUND IT.
THANK GOD!
TURNS OUT WE'RE NOT THAT FAR FROM THE LOUISIANA COAST.
YOU THINK THEY'LL BE ABLE TO FIND US?
I DON'T THINK THAT'S GOING TO BE A PROBLEM.

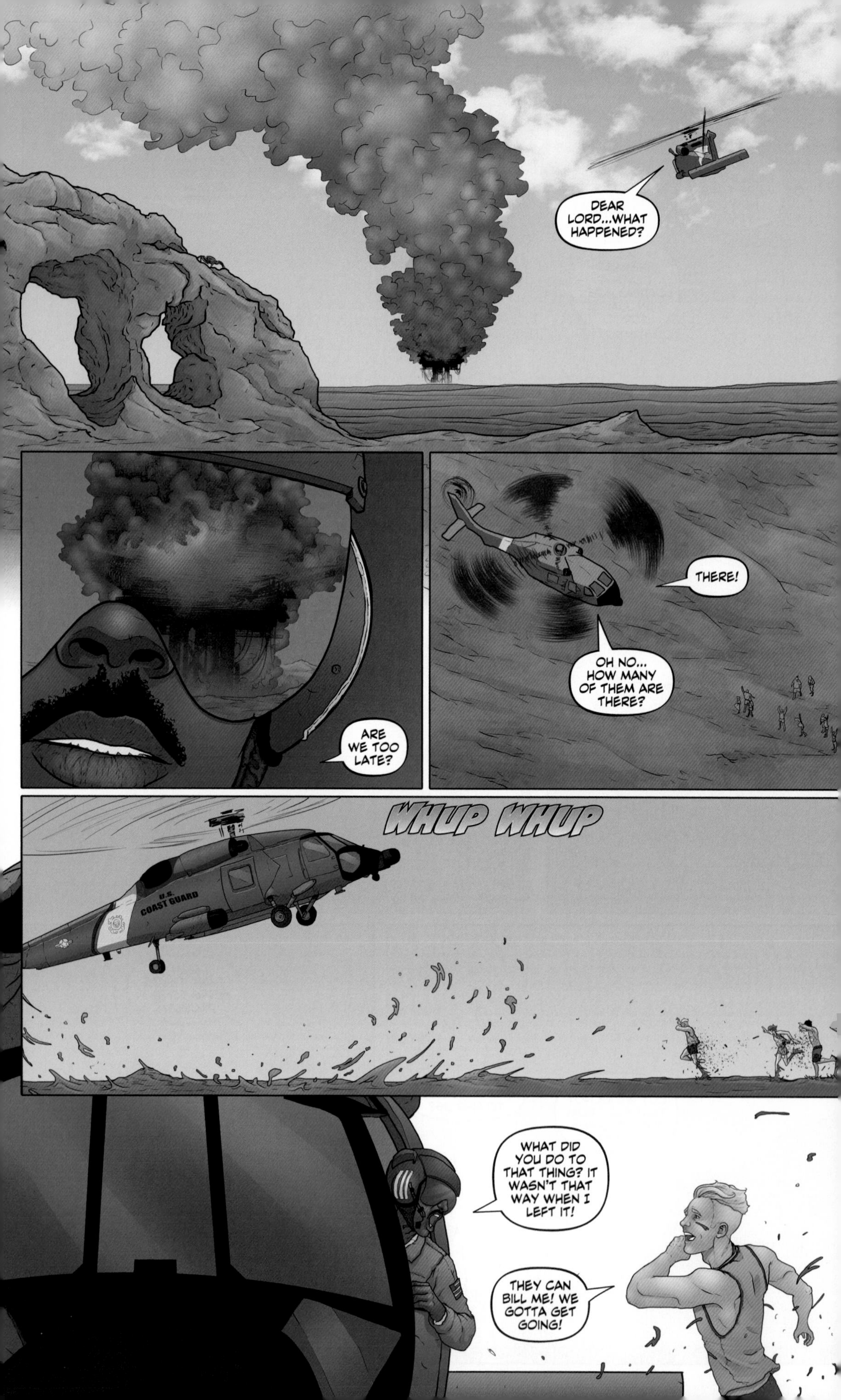
DEAR LORD...WHAT HAPPENED?
ARE WE TOO LATE?
THERE!
OH NO... HOW MANY OF THEM ARE THERE?
WHUP WHUP
U.S. COAST GUARD
WHAT DID YOU DO TO THAT THING? IT WASN'T THAT WAY WHEN I LEFT IT!
THEY CAN BILL ME! WE GOTTA GET GOING!

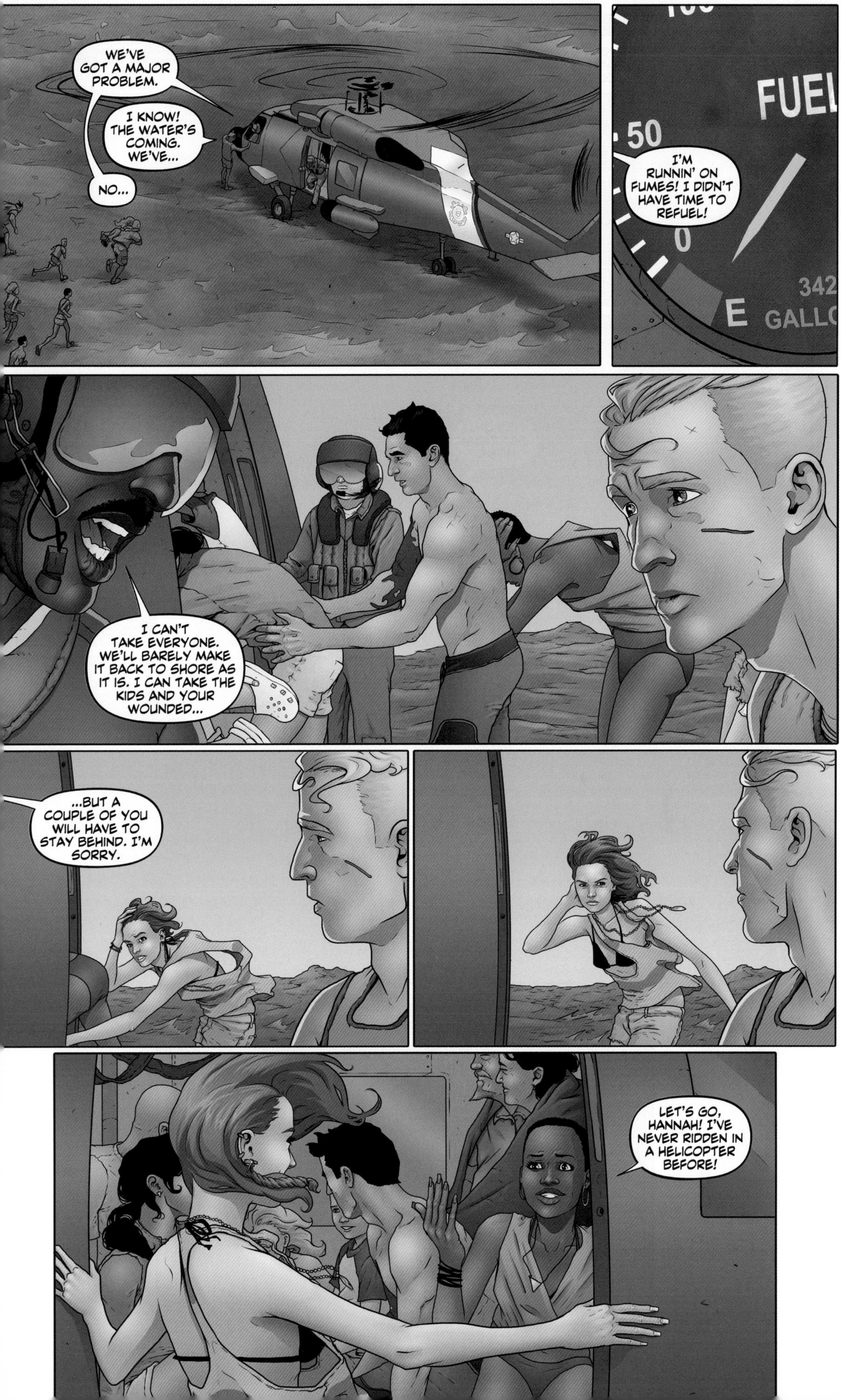
WE'VE GOT A MAJOR PROBLEM.
I KNOW! THE WATER'S COMING. WE'VE...
NO...
100
FUEL
50
I'M RUNNIN' ON FUMES! I DIDN'T HAVE TIME TO REFUEL!
0
E
342
GALLO
I CAN'T TAKE EVERYONE. WE'LL BARELY MAKE IT BACK TO SHORE AS IT IS. I CAN TAKE THE KIDS AND YOUR WOUNDED...
...BUT A COUPLE OF YOU WILL HAVE TO STAY BEHIND. I'M SORRY.
LET'S GO, HANNAH! I'VE NEVER RIDDEN IN A HELICOPTER BEFORE!

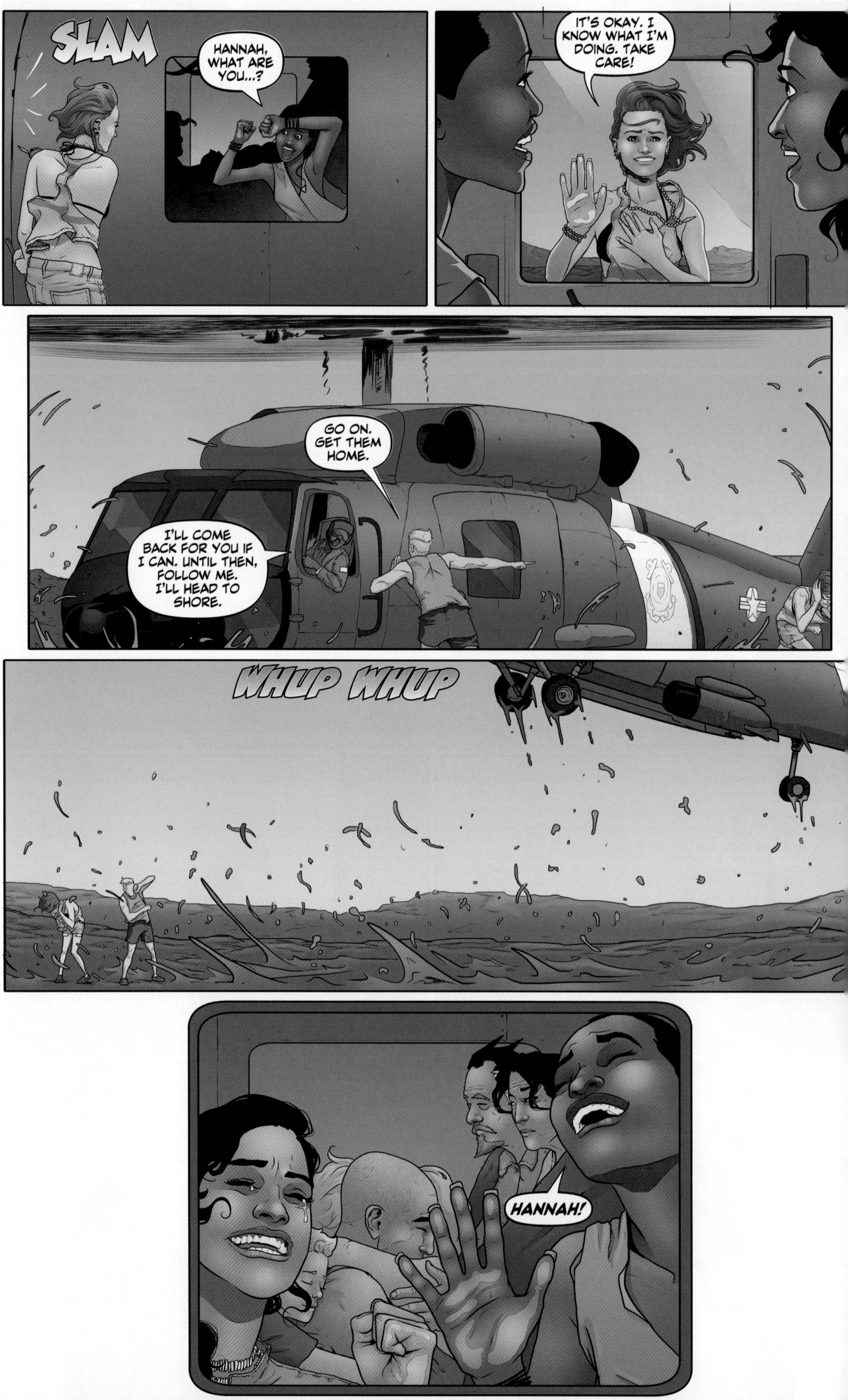
SLAM
HANNAH, WHAT ARE YOU...?
IT'S OKAY. I KNOW WHAT I'M DOING. TAKE CARE!
GO ON. GET THEM HOME.
I'LL COME BACK FOR YOU IF I CAN. UNTIL THEN, FOLLOW ME. I'LL HEAD TO SHORE.
WHUP WHUP
HANNAH!

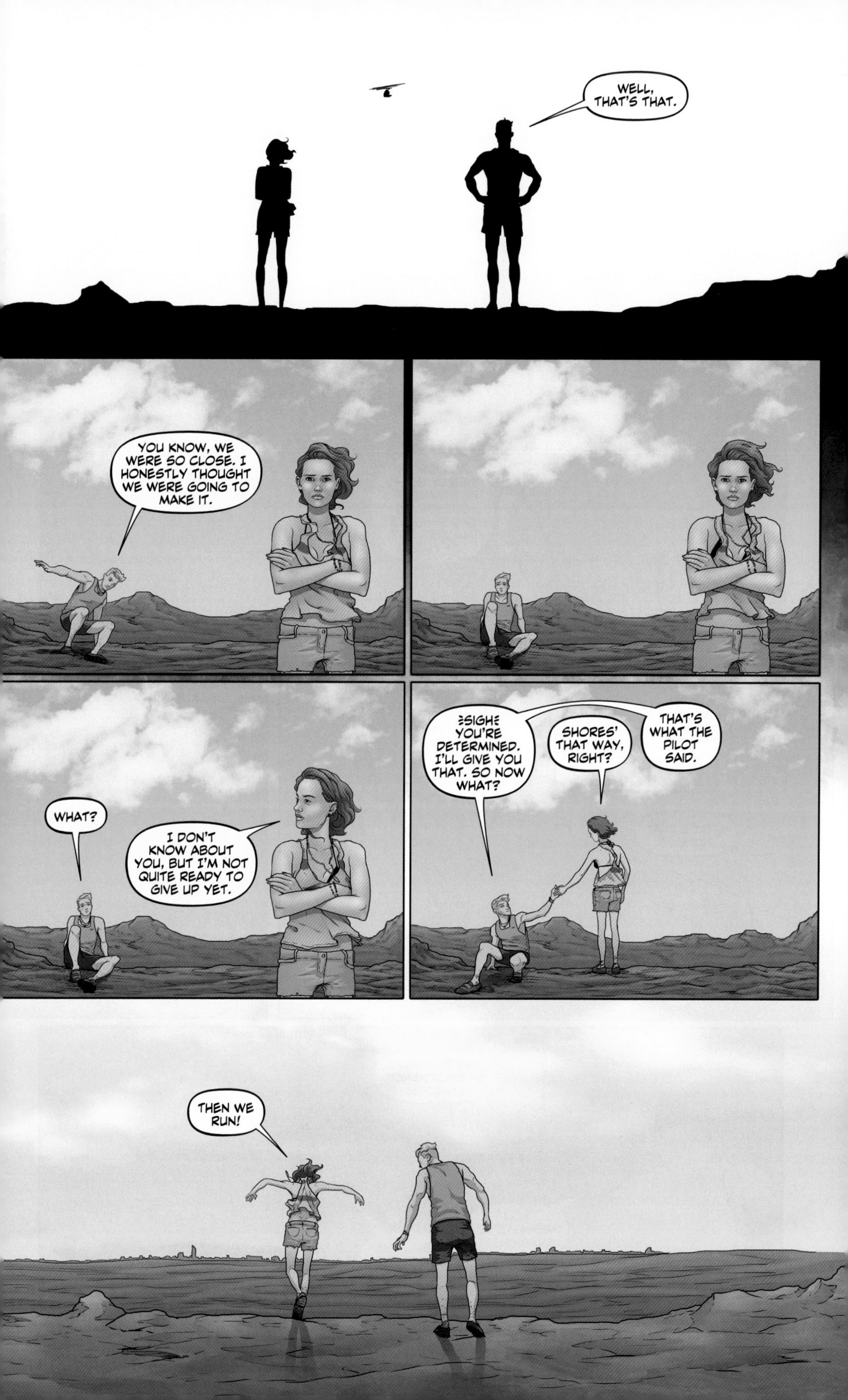
WELL, THAT'S THAT.
YOU KNOW, WE WERE SO CLOSE. I HONESTLY THOUGHT WE WERE GOING TO MAKE IT.
WHAT?
I DON'T KNOW ABOUT YOU, BUT I'M NOT QUITE READY TO GIVE UP YET.
≡SIGH≡ YOU'RE DETERMINED. I'LL GIVE YOU THAT. SO NOW WHAT?
SHORES' THAT WAY, RIGHT?
THAT'S WHAT THE PILOT SAID.
THEN WE RUN!

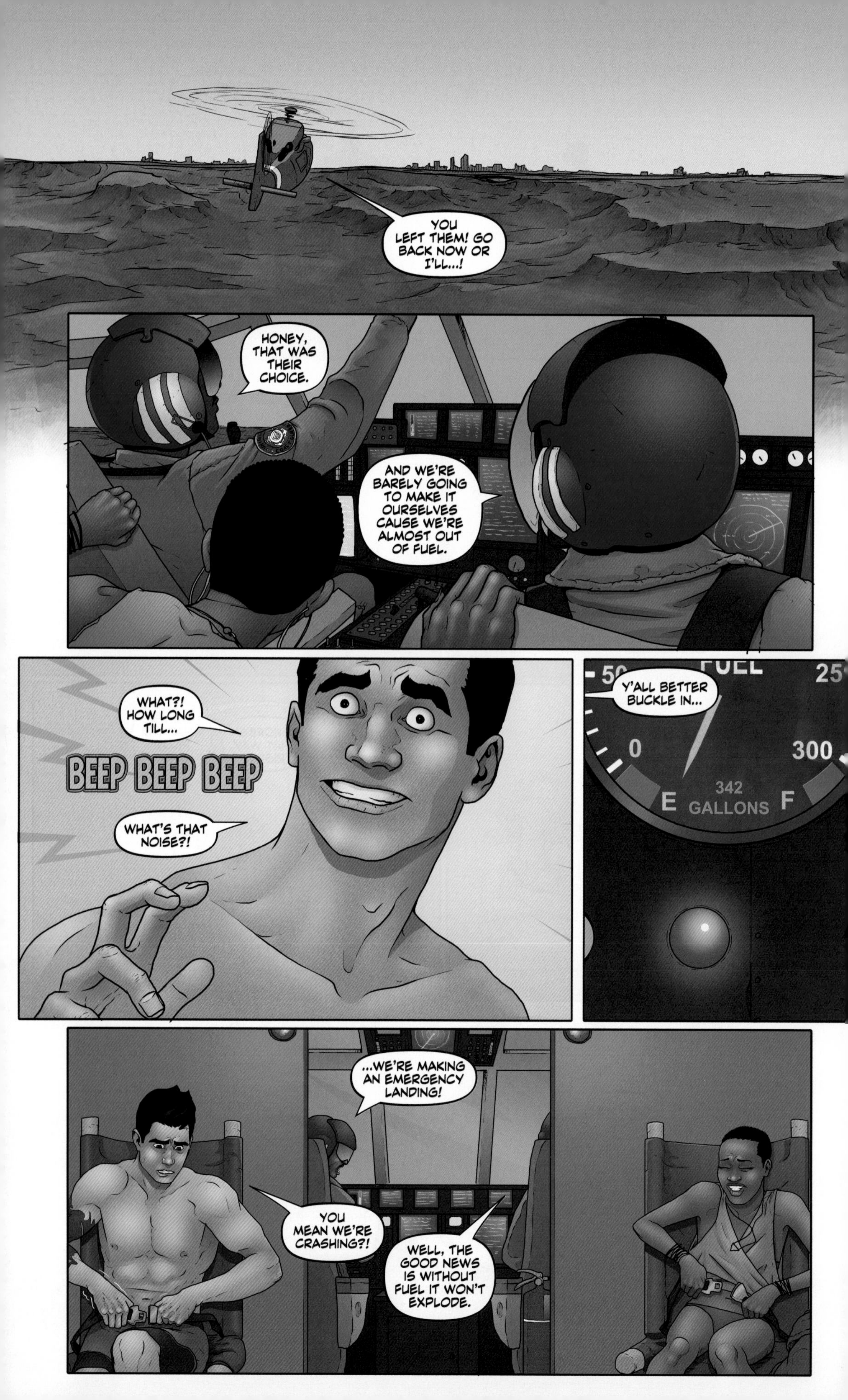
YOU LEFT THEM! GO BACK NOW OR I'LL...!
HONEY, THAT WAS THEIR CHOICE.
AND WE'RE BARELY GOING TO MAKE IT OURSELVES CAUSE WE'RE ALMOST OUT OF FUEL.
WHAT?! HOW LONG TILL...
BEEP BEEP BEEP
WHAT'S THAT NOISE?!
Y'ALL BETTER BUCKLE IN...
FUEL
50
25
0
300
E
342
GALLONS
F
...WE'RE MAKING AN EMERGENCY LANDING!
YOU MEAN WE'RE CRASHING?!
WELL, THE GOOD NEWS IS WITHOUT FUEL IT WON'T EXPLODE.

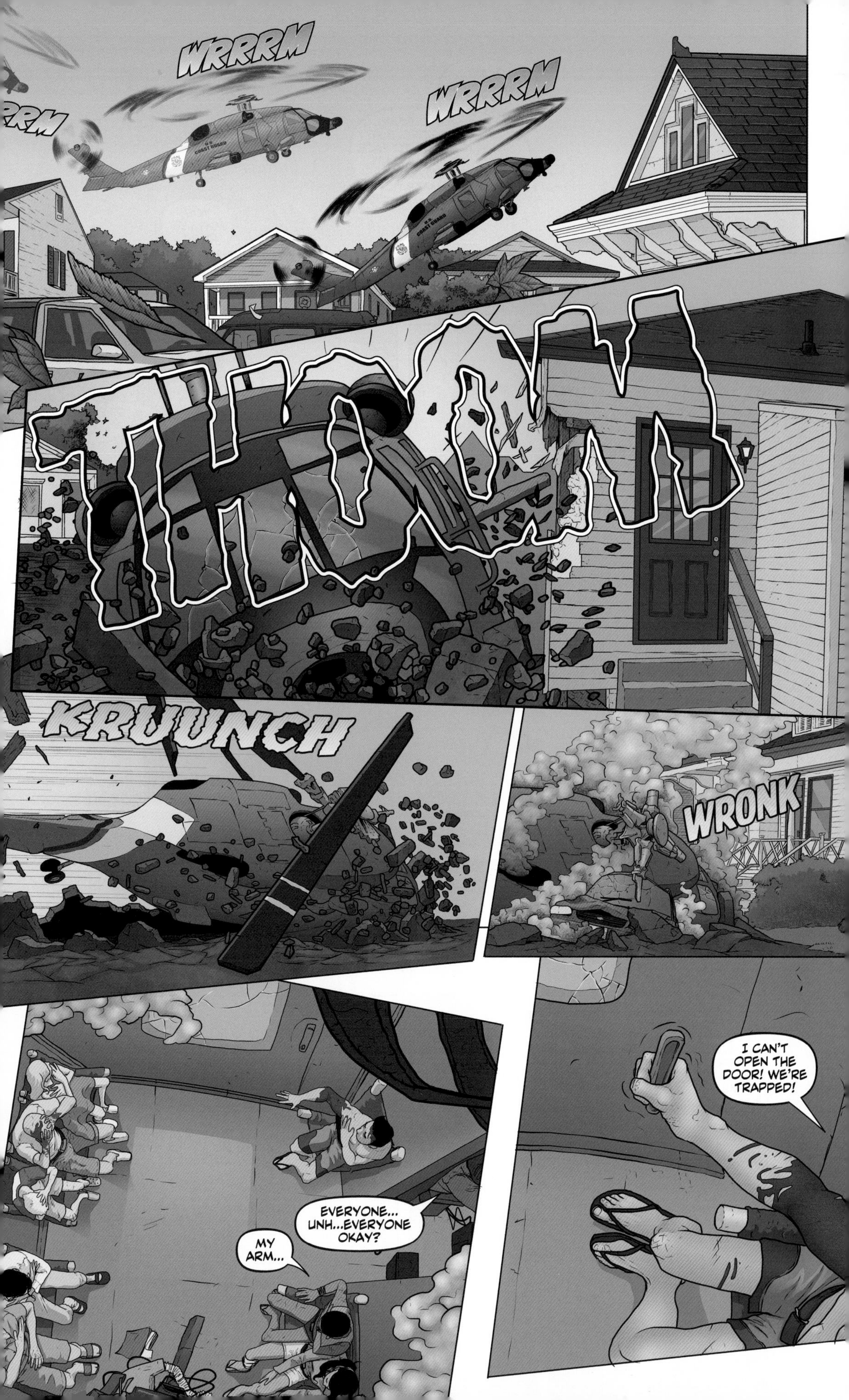
WRRRM
RRM
WRRRM
U.S. COAST GUARD
U.S. COAST GUARD
THOOM
KRUUNCH
WRONK
EVERYONE... UNH...EVERYONE OKAY?
MY ARM...
I CAN'T OPEN THE DOOR! WE'RE TRAPPED!

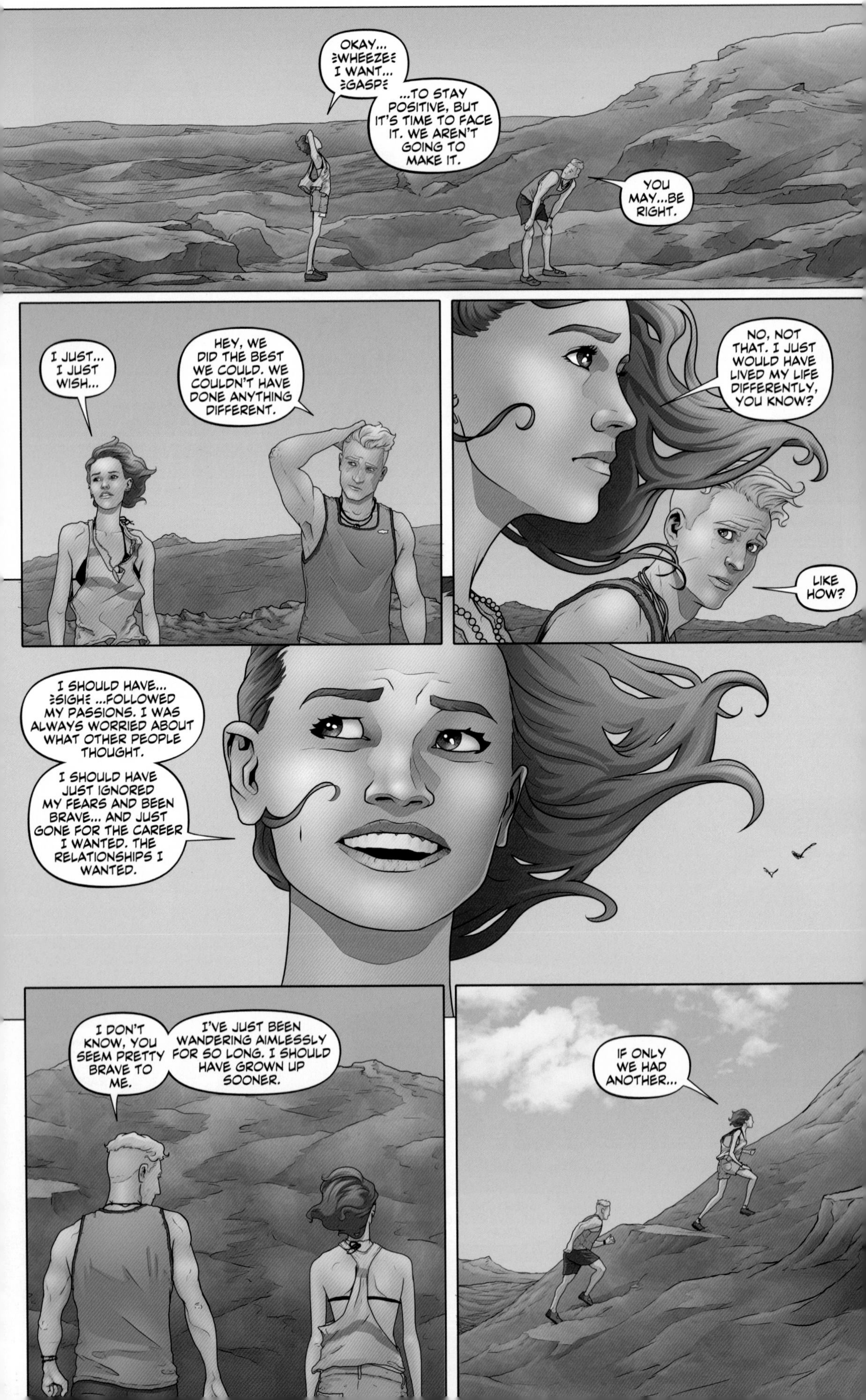
OKAY... ≡WHEEZE≡ I WANT... ≡GASP≡
...TO STAY POSITIVE, BUT IT'S TIME TO FACE IT. WE AREN'T GOING TO MAKE IT.
YOU MAY...BE RIGHT.
I JUST... I JUST WISH...
HEY, WE DID THE BEST WE COULD. WE COULDN'T HAVE DONE ANYTHING DIFFERENT.
NO, NOT THAT. I JUST WOULD HAVE LIVED MY LIFE DIFFERENTLY, YOU KNOW?
LIKE HOW?
I SHOULD HAVE... ≡SIGH≡ ...FOLLOWED MY PASSIONS. I WAS ALWAYS WORRIED ABOUT WHAT OTHER PEOPLE THOUGHT.
I SHOULD HAVE JUST IGNORED MY FEARS AND BEEN BRAVE... AND JUST GONE FOR THE CAREER I WANTED. THE RELATIONSHIPS I WANTED.
I DON'T KNOW, YOU SEEM PRETTY BRAVE TO ME.
I'VE JUST BEEN WANDERING AIMLESSLY FOR SO LONG. I SHOULD HAVE GROWN UP SOONER.
IF ONLY WE HAD ANOTHER...

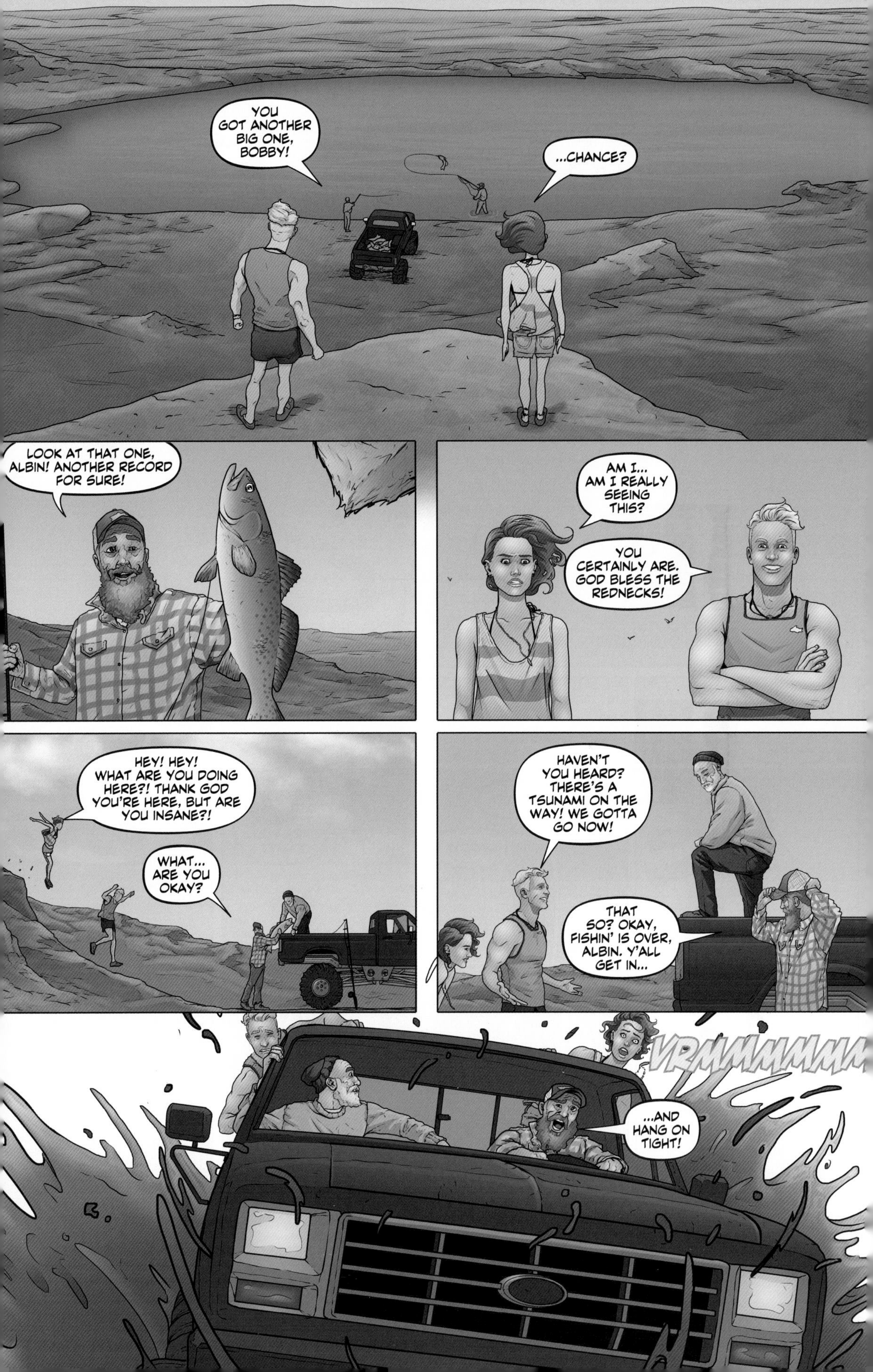
YOU GOT ANOTHER BIG ONE, BOBBY!
...CHANCE?
LOOK AT THAT ONE, ALBIN! ANOTHER RECORD FOR SURE!
AM I... AM I REALLY SEEING THIS?
YOU CERTAINLY ARE. GOD BLESS THE REDNECKS!
HEY! HEY! WHAT ARE YOU DOING HERE?! THANK GOD YOU'RE HERE, BUT ARE YOU INSANE?!
WHAT... ARE YOU OKAY?
HAVEN'T YOU HEARD? THERE'S A TSUNAMI ON THE WAY! WE GOTTA GO NOW!
THAT SO? OKAY, FISHIN' IS OVER, ALBIN. Y'ALL GET IN...
VRMMMMMM
...AND HANG ON TIGHT!

WE GOTTA GET OUT OF HERE! THE DOOR IS JAMMED!
WHAT?!
NOW EVERYONE CALM DOWN! DON'T PANIC!
WHOOOOSH
THE CAR'S ON FIRE!
OKAY... MAYBE NOW PANIC.
CRACK
WHA...?
COME ON! GET OUT QUICKLY!
WHOEVER YOU ARE, I'M GLAD YOU'RE...
CATHY?!
DADDY!
WE SAW YOUR HELICOPTER GO DOWN AND CAME TO HELP. ARE YOU OKAY?
YOU'RE SUPPOSED TO BE MILES AWAY AT HIGH GROUND BY NOW! WHAT HAPPENED?
THERE WAS A WRECK AT THE BRIDGE AND WE COULDN'T EVACUATE! I THOUGHT WE COULD COME BACK HERE AND FLY OUT WITH YOU. NOW... WELL... WHAT DO WE DO?

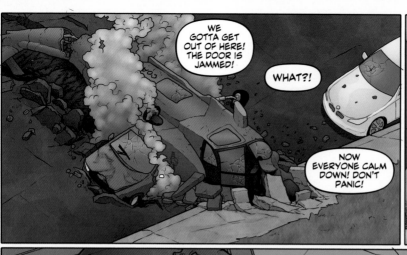

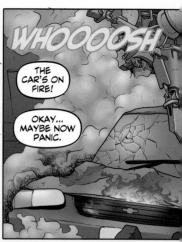

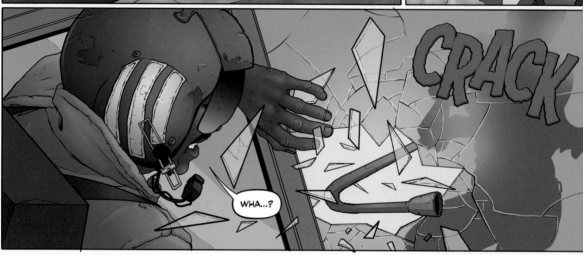

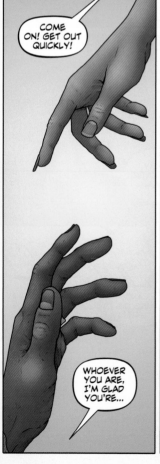

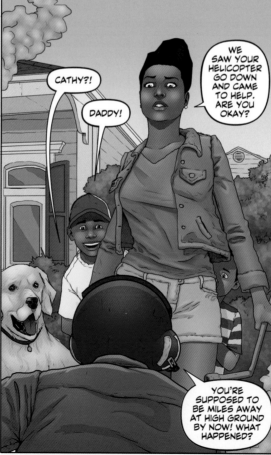

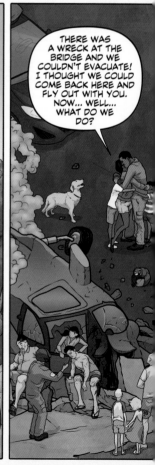

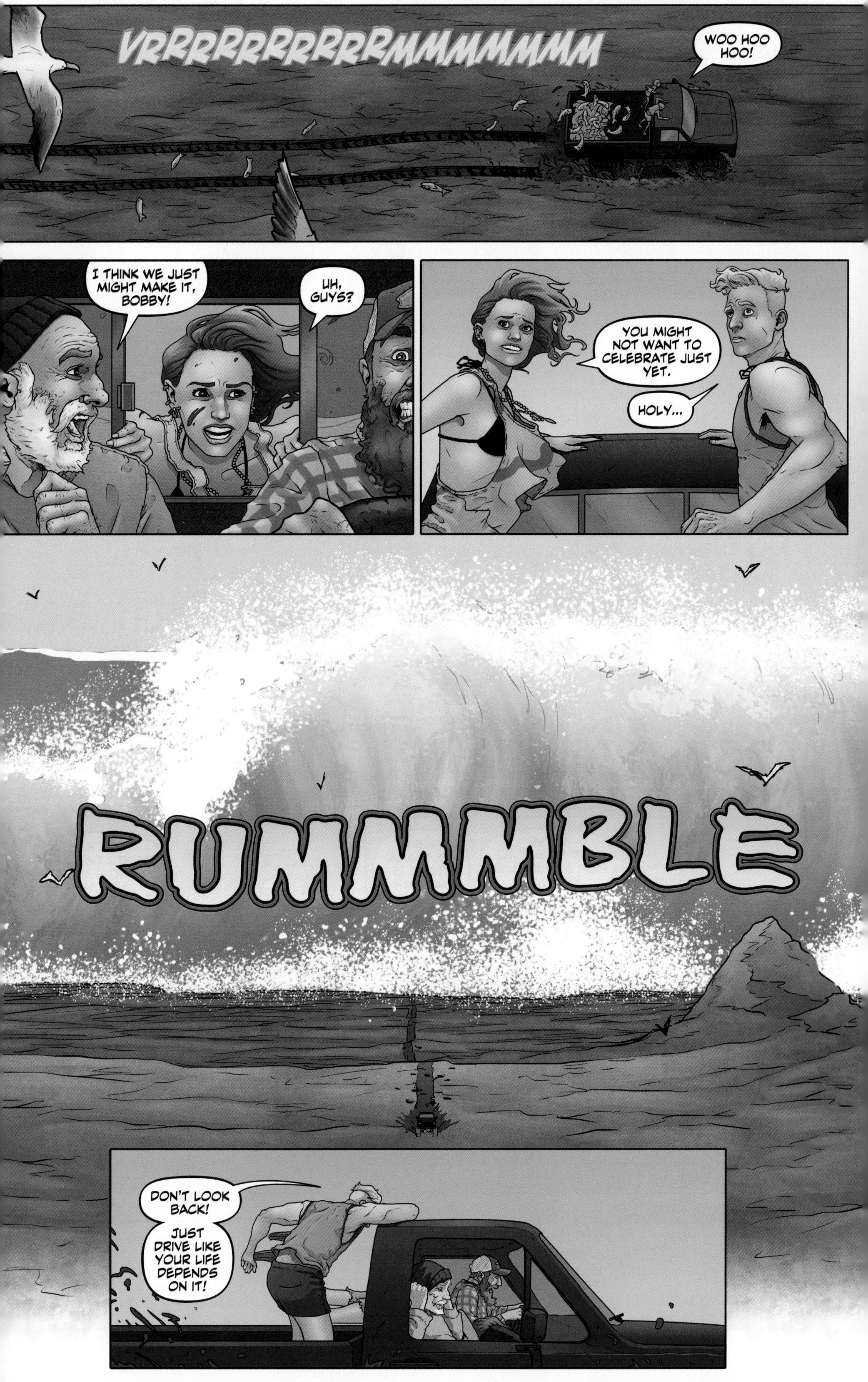
VRRRRRRRRRRMMMMMMM
WOO HOO HOO!
I THINK WE JUST MIGHT MAKE IT, BOBBY!
UH, GUYS?
YOU MIGHT NOT WANT TO CELEBRATE JUST YET.
HOLY...
RUMMMBLE
DON'T LOOK BACK!
JUST DRIVE LIKE YOUR LIFE DEPENDS ON IT!

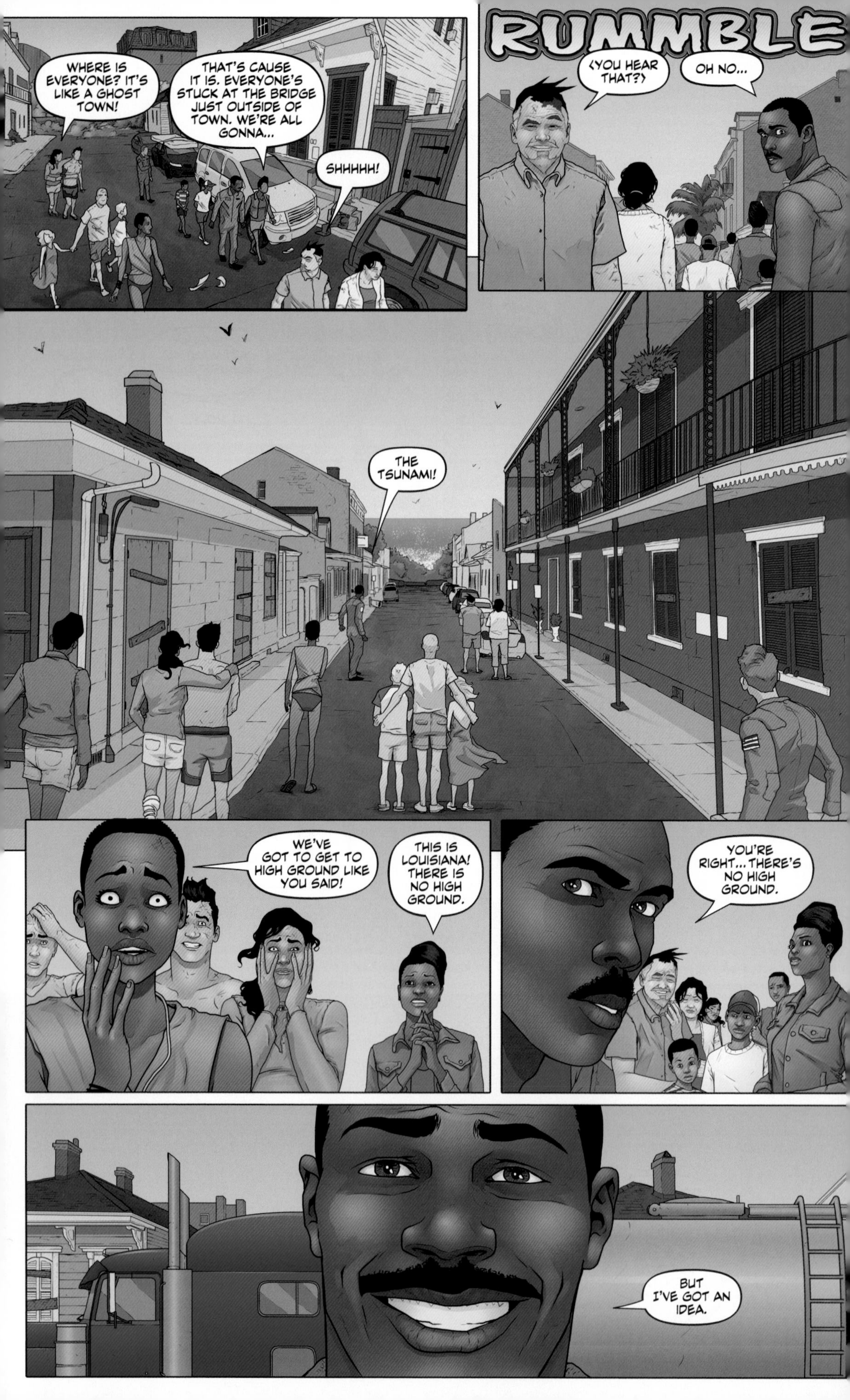
WHERE IS EVERYONE? IT'S LIKE A GHOST TOWN!
THAT'S CAUSE IT IS. EVERYONE'S STUCK AT THE BRIDGE JUST OUTSIDE OF TOWN. WE'RE ALL GONNA...
SHHHHH!
RUMMBLE
‹YOU HEAR THAT?›
OH NO...
THE TSUNAMI!
WE'VE GOT TO GET TO HIGH GROUND LIKE YOU SAID!
THIS IS LOUISIANA! THERE IS NO HIGH GROUND.
YOU'RE RIGHT... THERE'S NO HIGH GROUND.
BUT I'VE GOT AN IDEA.

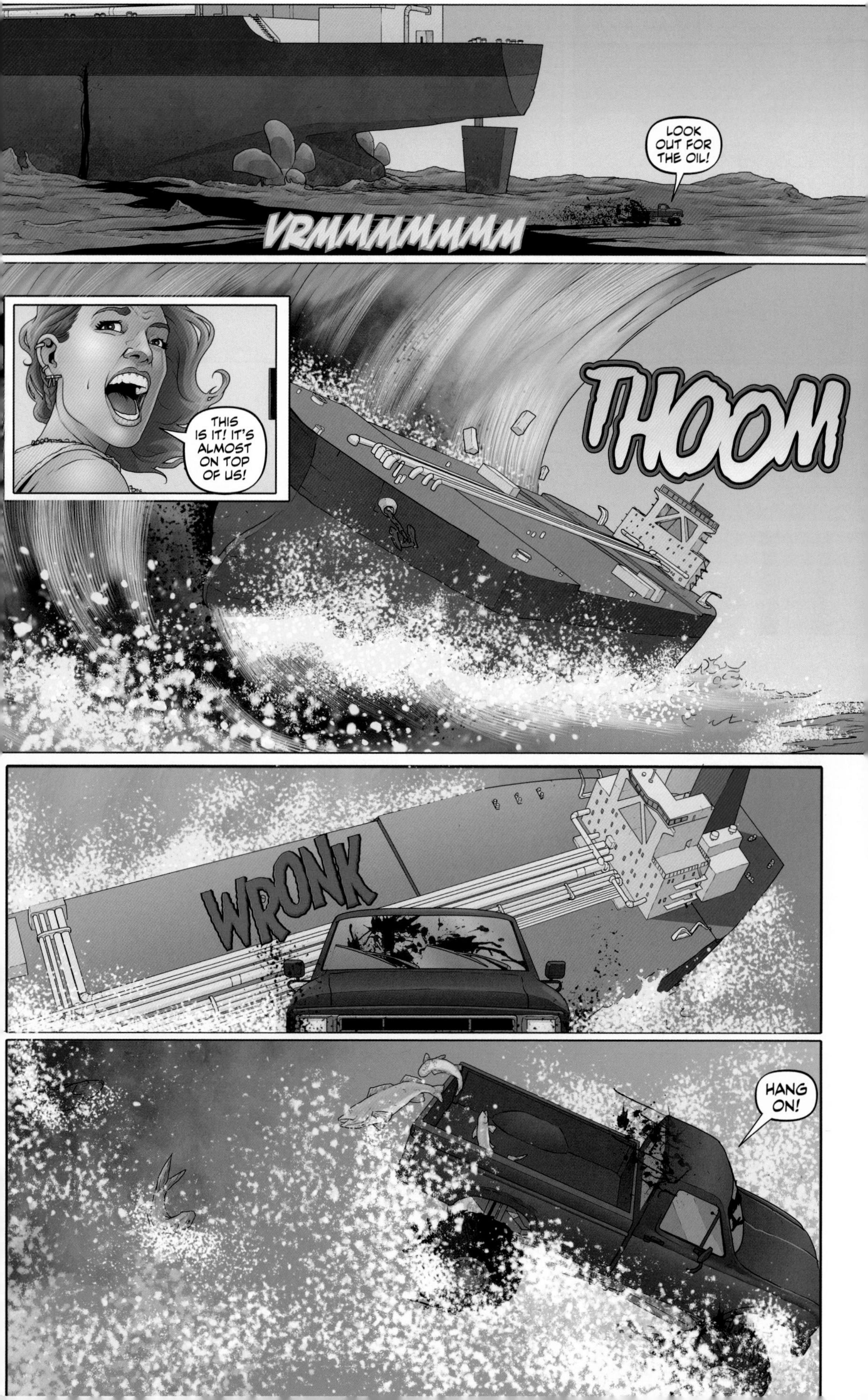
LOOK OUT FOR THE OIL!
VRMMMMMMMM
THIS IS IT! IT'S ALMOST ON TOP OF US!
THOOM
WRONK
HANG ON!

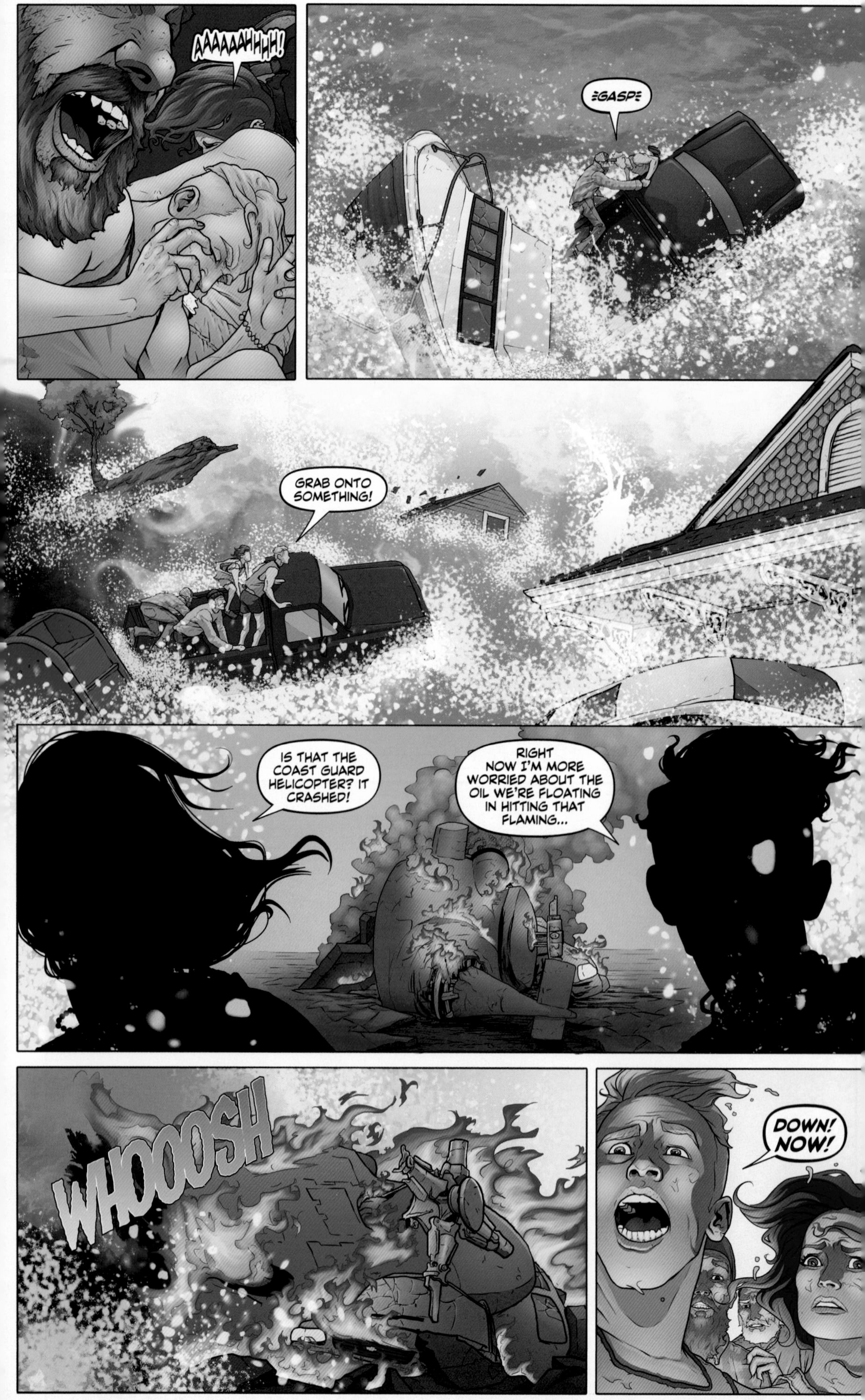
AAAAAAHHHH!
GASP
GRAB ONTO SOMETHING!
IS THAT THE COAST GUARD HELICOPTER? IT CRASHED!
RIGHT NOW I'M MORE WORRIED ABOUT THE OIL WE'RE FLOATING IN HITTING THAT FLAMING...
WHOOOSH
DOWN! NOW!

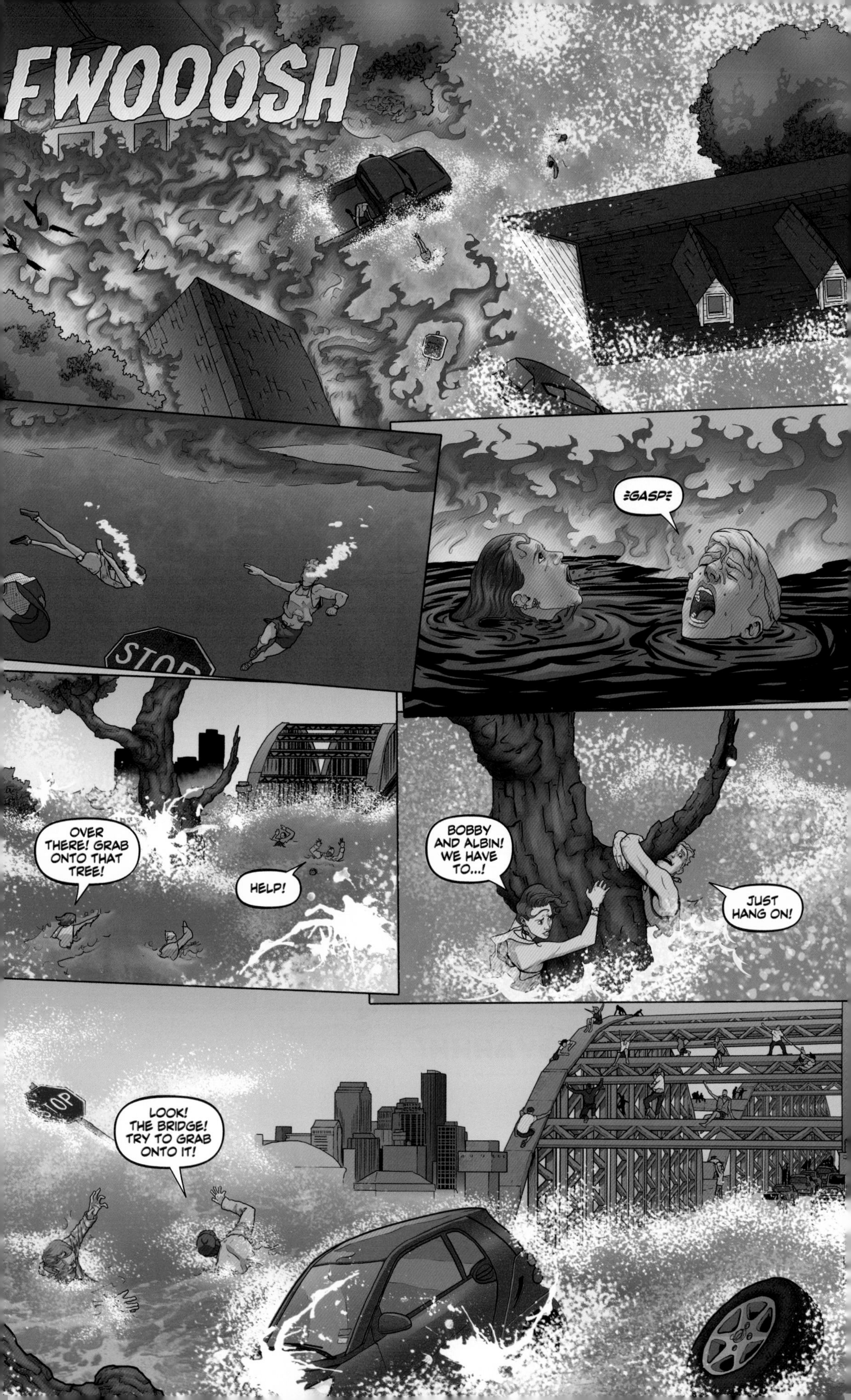
FWOOOSH
STOP
GASP
OVER THERE! GRAB ONTO THAT TREE!
HELP!
BOBBY AND ALBIN! WE HAVE TO...!
JUST HANG ON!
LOOK! THE BRIDGE! TRY TO GRAB ONTO IT!

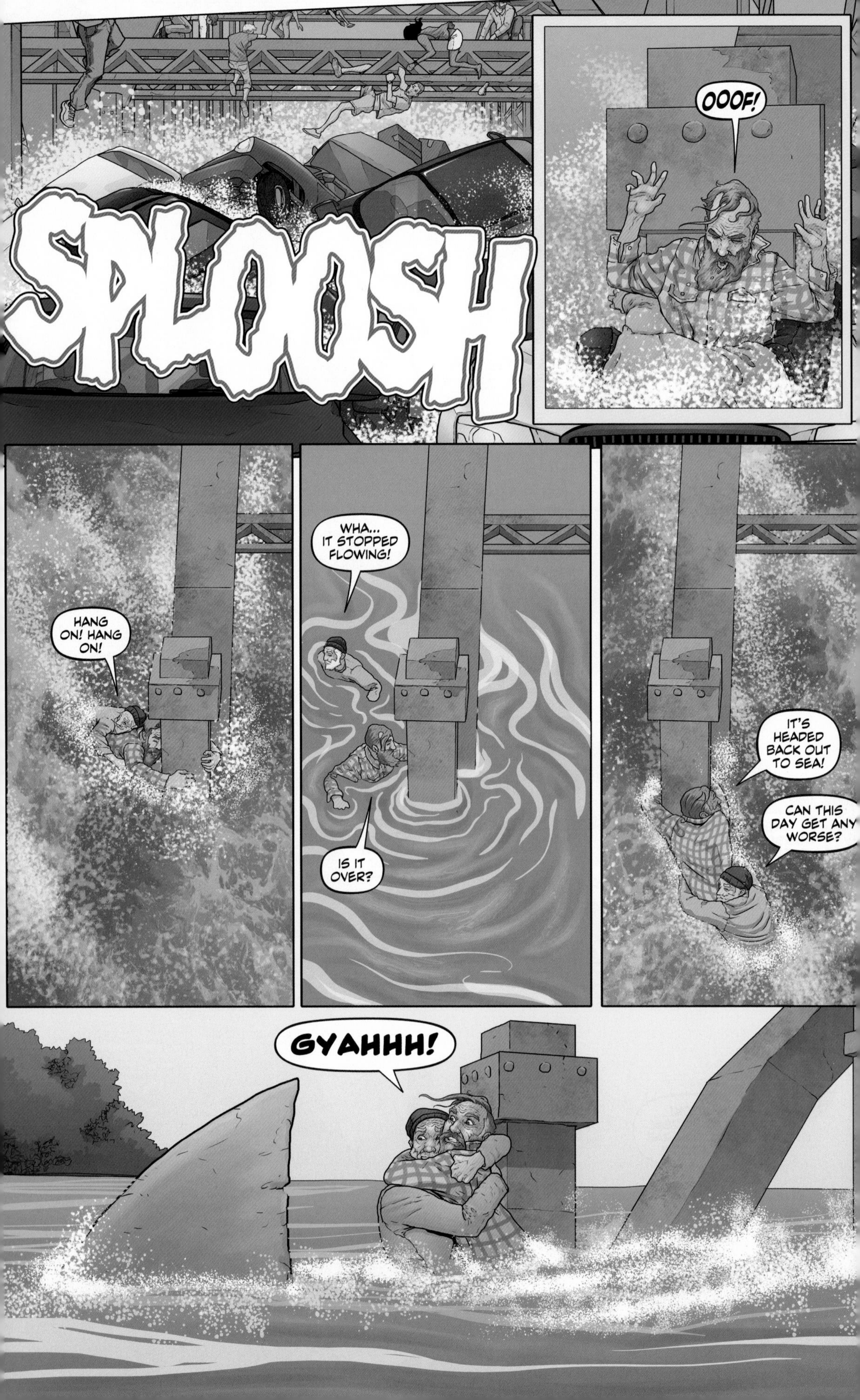
SPLOOSH
OOOF!
HANG ON! HANG ON!
WHA... IT STOPPED FLOWING!
IS IT OVER?
IT'S HEADED BACK OUT TO SEA!
CAN THIS DAY GET ANY WORSE?
GYAHHH!

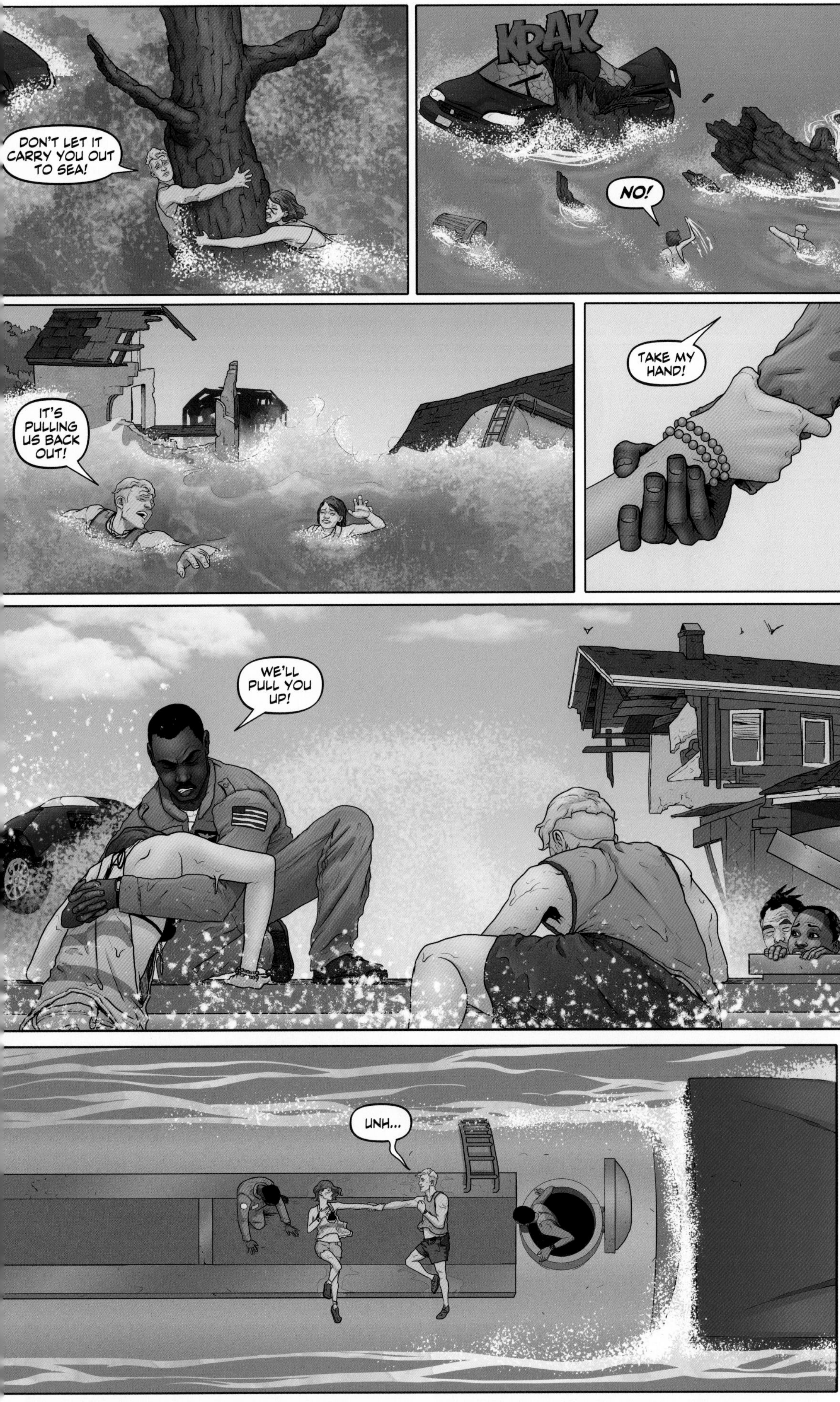
DON'T LET IT CARRY YOU OUT TO SEA!
KRAK
NO!
IT'S PULLING US BACK OUT!
TAKE MY HAND!
WE'LL PULL YOU UP!
UNH...

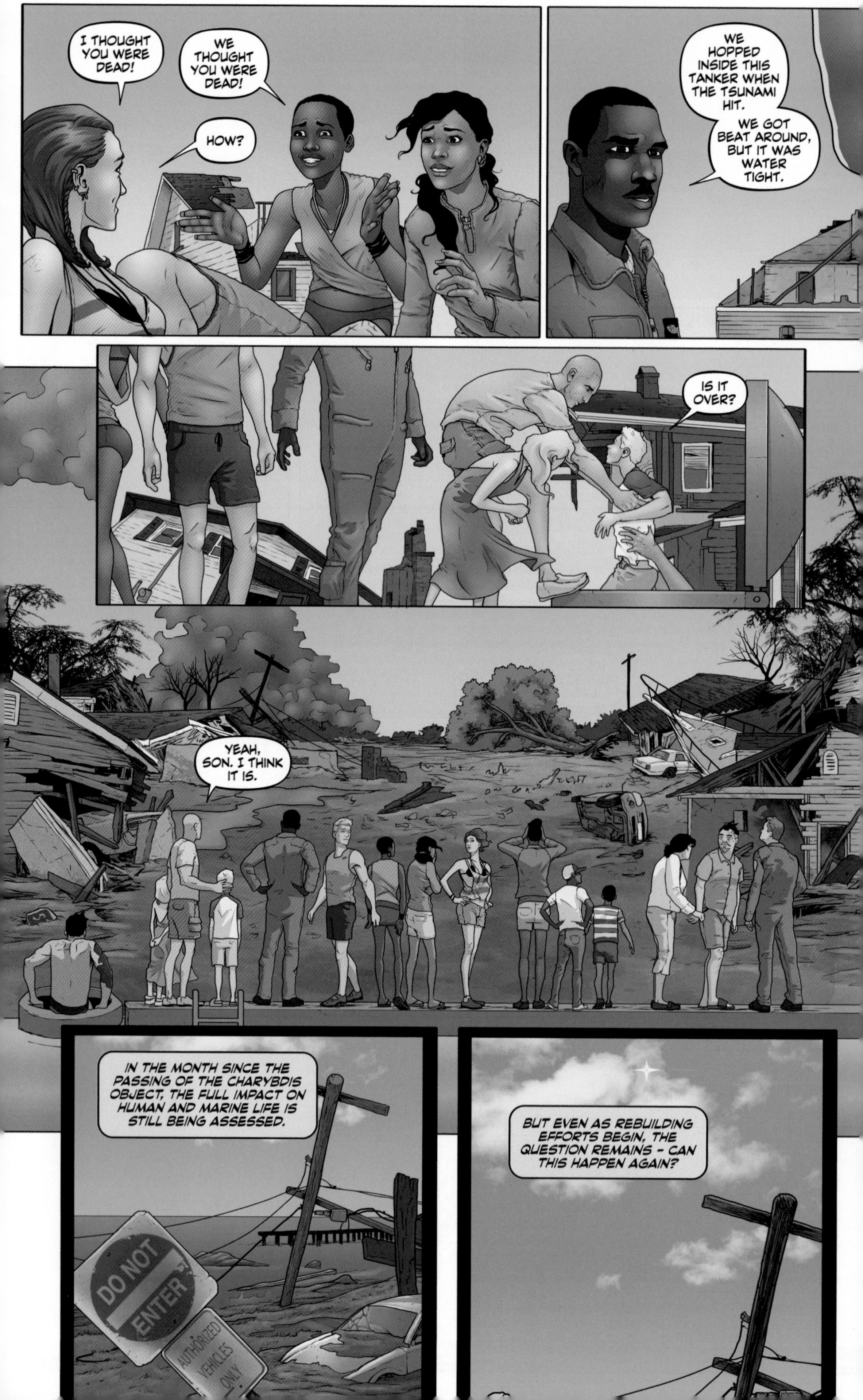
I THOUGHT YOU WERE DEAD!
WE THOUGHT YOU WERE DEAD!
HOW?
WE HOPPED INSIDE THIS TANKER WHEN THE TSUNAMI HIT.
WE GOT BEAT AROUND, BUT IT WAS WATER TIGHT.
IS IT OVER?
YEAH, SON. I THINK IT IS.
IN THE MONTH SINCE THE PASSING OF THE CHARYBDIS OBJECT, THE FULL IMPACT ON HUMAN AND MARINE LIFE IS STILL BEING ASSESSED.
DO NOT ENTER
AUTHORIZED VEHICLES ONLY
BUT EVEN AS REBUILDING EFFORTS BEGIN, THE QUESTION REMAINS - CAN THIS HAPPEN AGAIN?

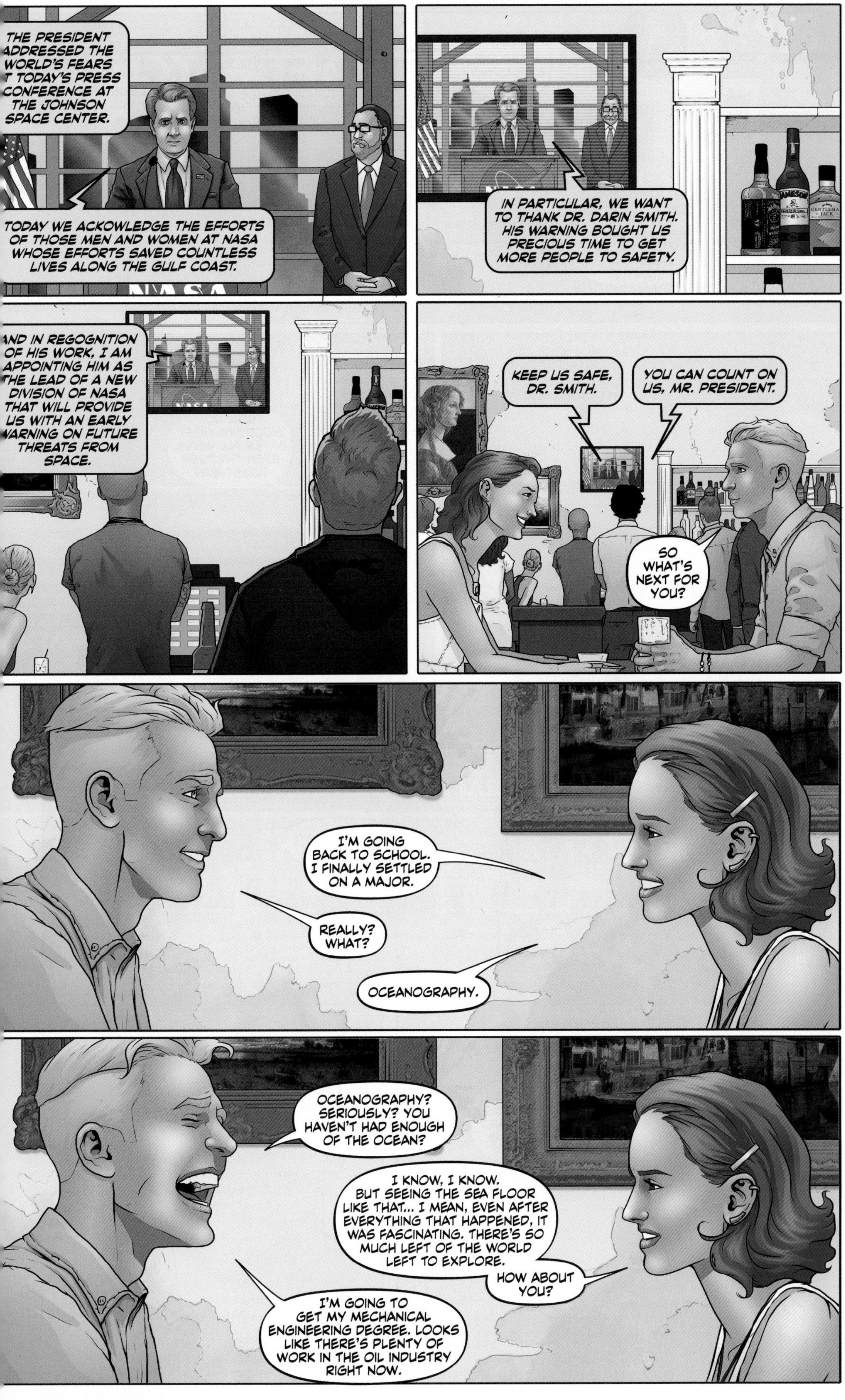
THE PRESIDENT ADDRESSED THE WORLD'S FEARS AT TODAY'S PRESS CONFERENCE AT THE JOHNSON SPACE CENTER.
TODAY WE ACKOWLEDGE THE EFFORTS OF THOSE MEN AND WOMEN AT NASA WHOSE EFFORTS SAVED COUNTLESS LIVES ALONG THE GULF COAST.
IN PARTICULAR, WE WANT TO THANK DR. DARIN SMITH. HIS WARNING BOUGHT US PRECIOUS TIME TO GET MORE PEOPLE TO SAFETY.
AND IN REGOGNITION OF HIS WORK, I AM APPOINTING HIM AS THE LEAD OF A NEW DIVISION OF NASA THAT WILL PROVIDE US WITH AN EARLY WARNING ON FUTURE THREATS FROM SPACE.
KEEP US SAFE, DR. SMITH.
YOU CAN COUNT ON US, MR. PRESIDENT.
SO WHAT'S NEXT FOR YOU?
I'M GOING BACK TO SCHOOL. I FINALLY SETTLED ON A MAJOR.
REALLY? WHAT?
OCEANOGRAPHY.
OCEANOGRAPHY? SERIOUSLY? YOU HAVEN'T HAD ENOUGH OF THE OCEAN?
I KNOW, I KNOW. BUT SEEING THE SEA FLOOR LIKE THAT... I MEAN, EVEN AFTER EVERYTHING THAT HAPPENED, IT WAS FASCINATING. THERE'S SO MUCH LEFT OF THE WORLD LEFT TO EXPLORE.
HOW ABOUT YOU?
I'M GOING TO GET MY MECHANICAL ENGINEERING DEGREE. LOOKS LIKE THERE'S PLENTY OF WORK IN THE OIL INDUSTRY RIGHT NOW.

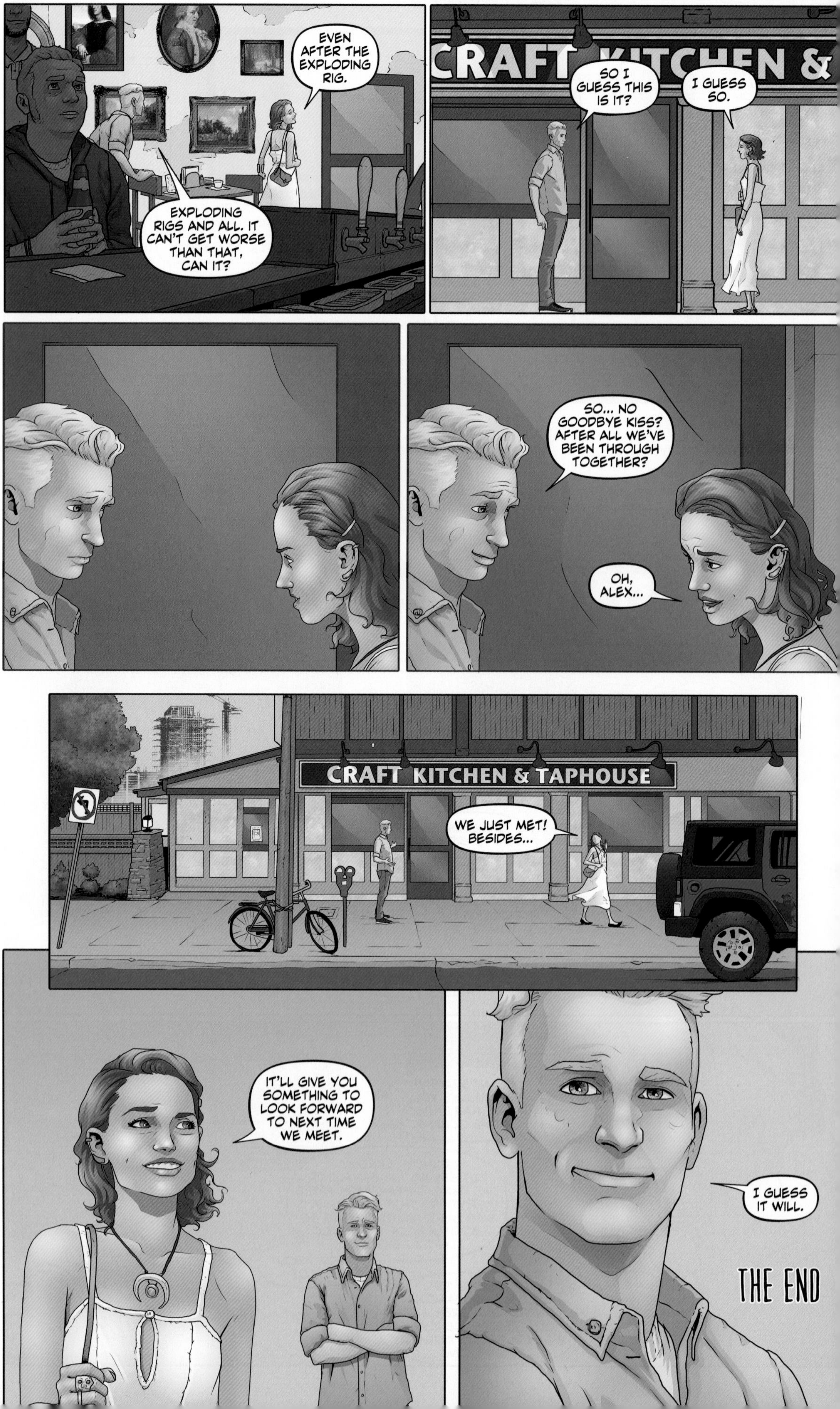
EVEN AFTER THE EXPLODING RIG.
EXPLODING RIGS AND ALL. IT CAN'T GET WORSE THAN THAT, CAN IT?
CRAFT KITCHEN &
SO I GUESS THIS IS IT?
I GUESS SO.
SO... NO GOODBYE KISS? AFTER ALL WE'VE BEEN THROUGH TOGETHER?
OH, ALEX...
CRAFT KITCHEN & TAPHOUSE
WE JUST MET! BESIDES...
IT'LL GIVE YOU SOMETHING TO LOOK FORWARD TO NEXT TIME WE MEET.
I GUESS IT WILL.
THE END

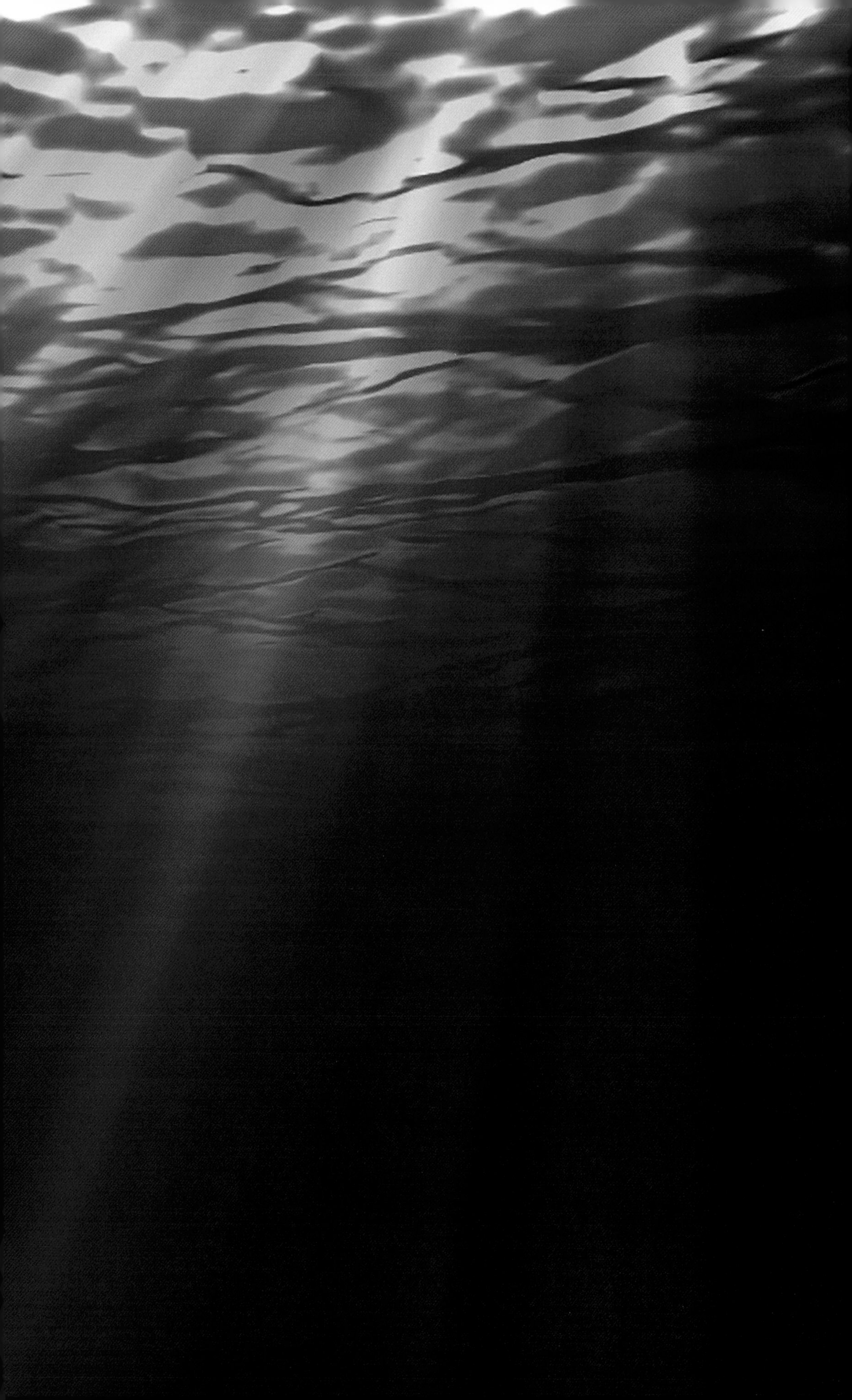

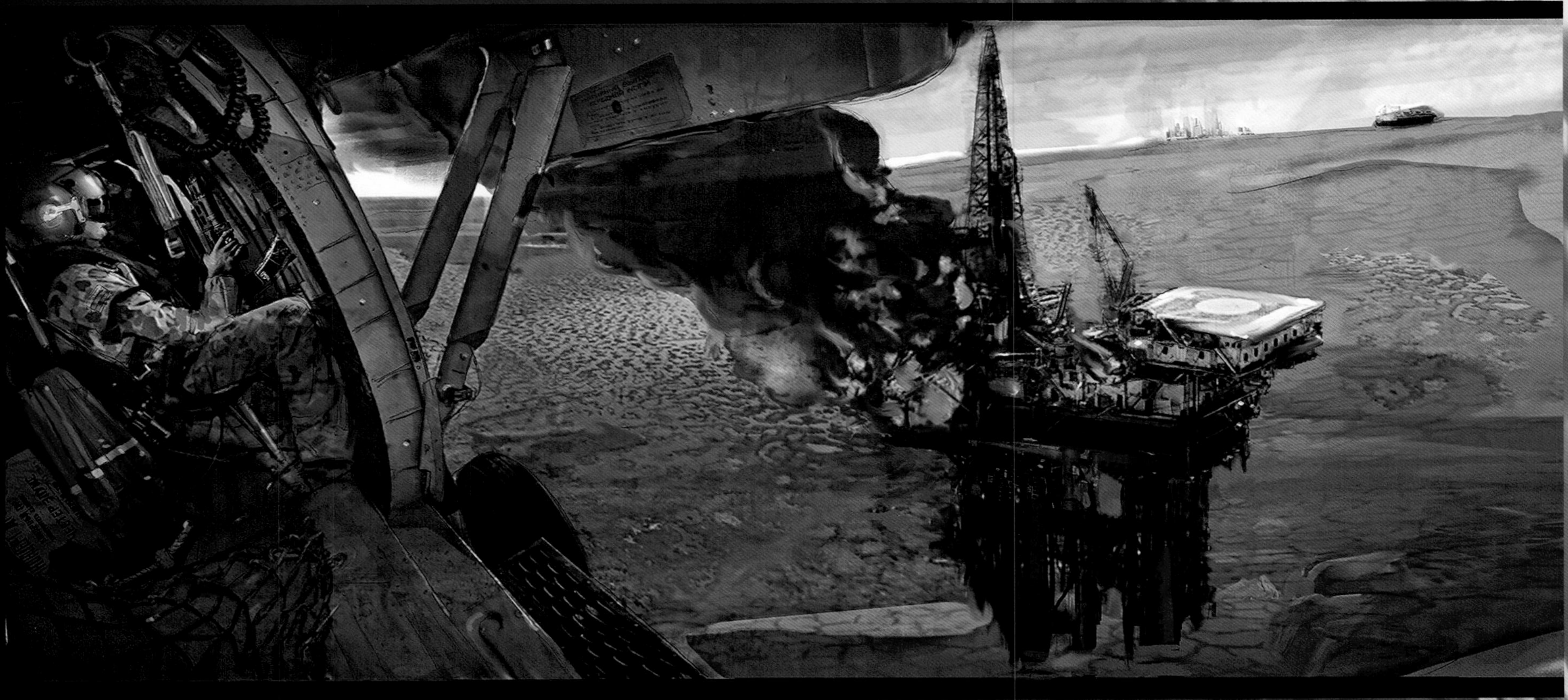

Pre-Production Art by Paul Allen Ballard

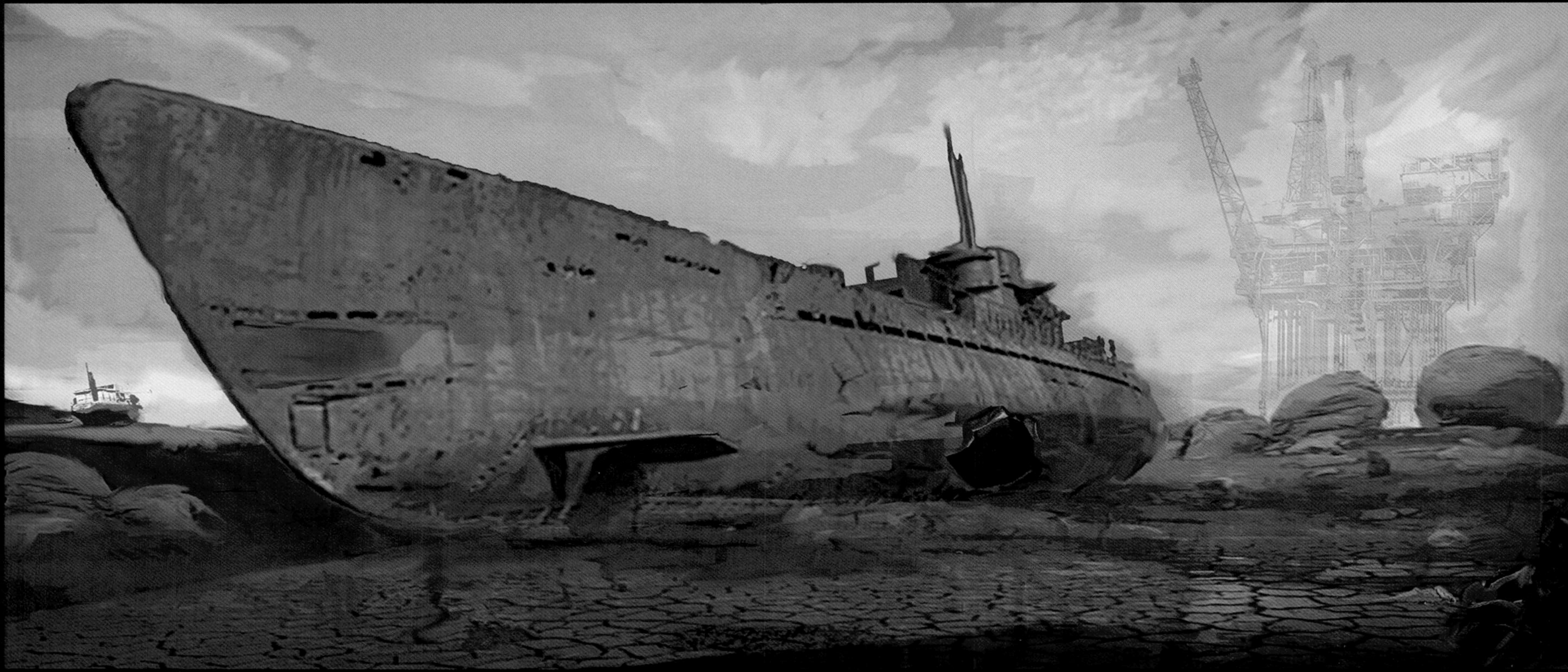

Pre-Production Art by Paul Allen Ballard

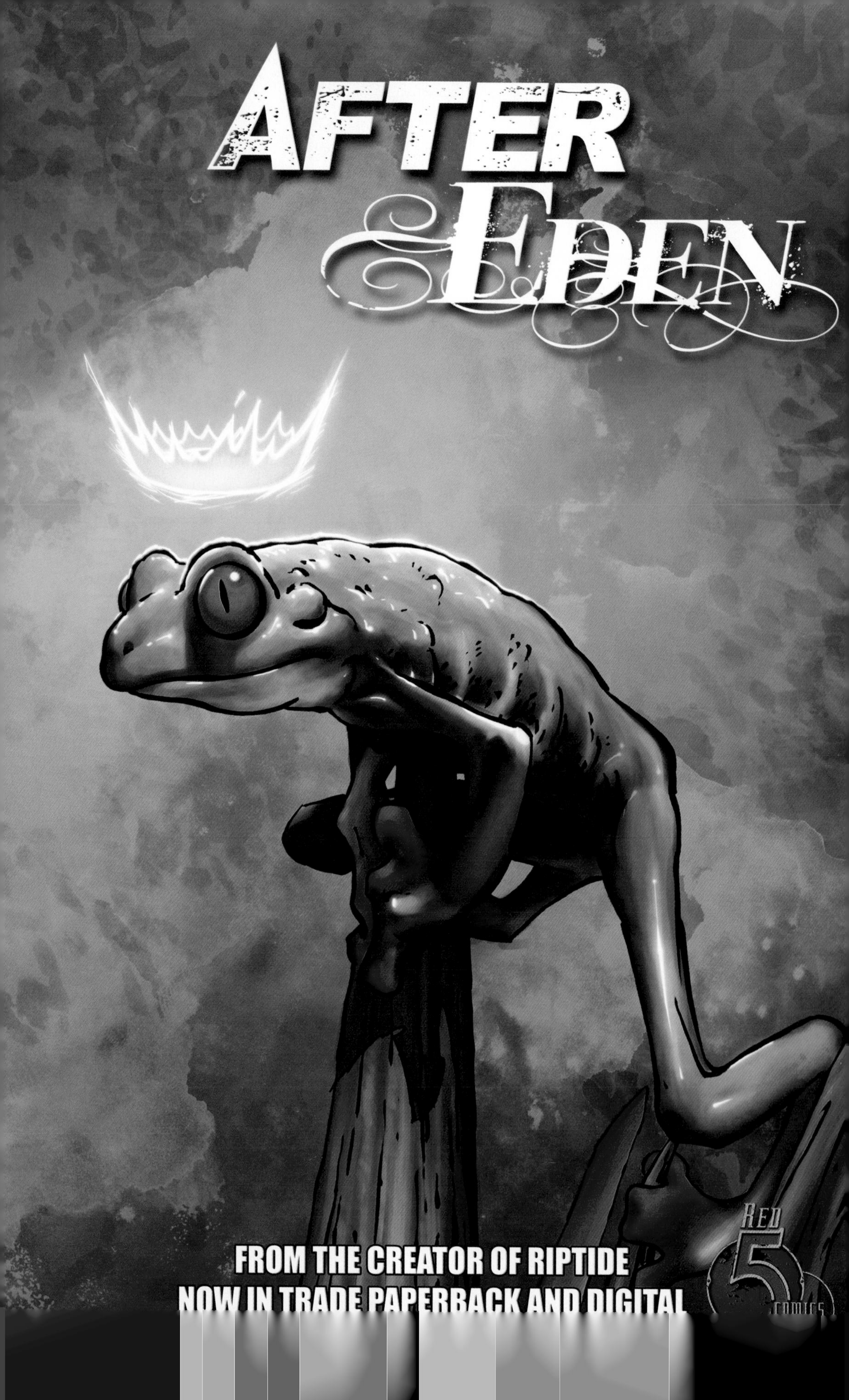
AFTER EDEN
FROM THE CREATOR OF RIPTIDE
NOW IN TRADE PAPERBACK AND DIGITAL
RED 5 COMICS

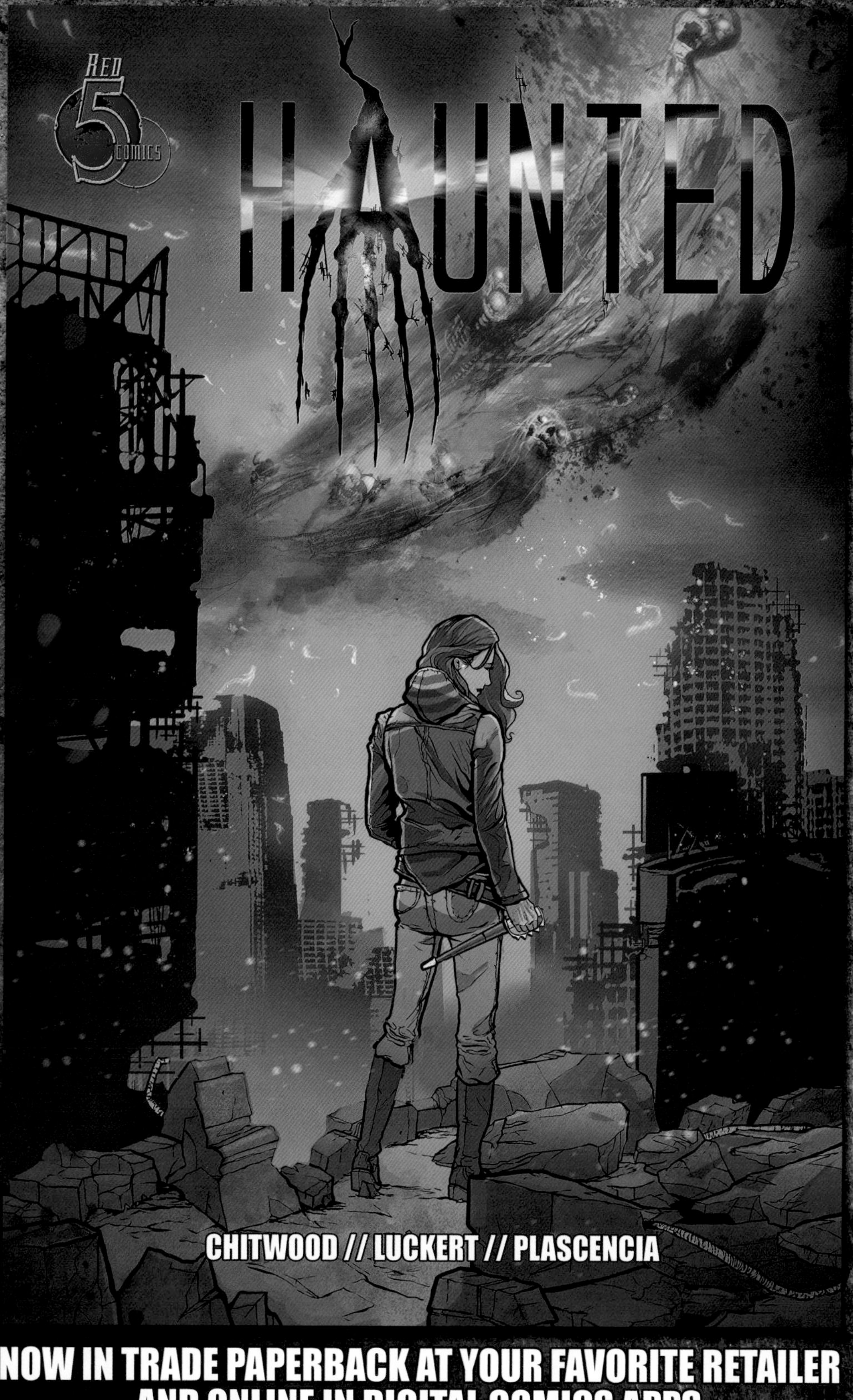
RED 5 COMICS
HAUNTED
CHITWOOD // LUCKERT // PLASCENCIA

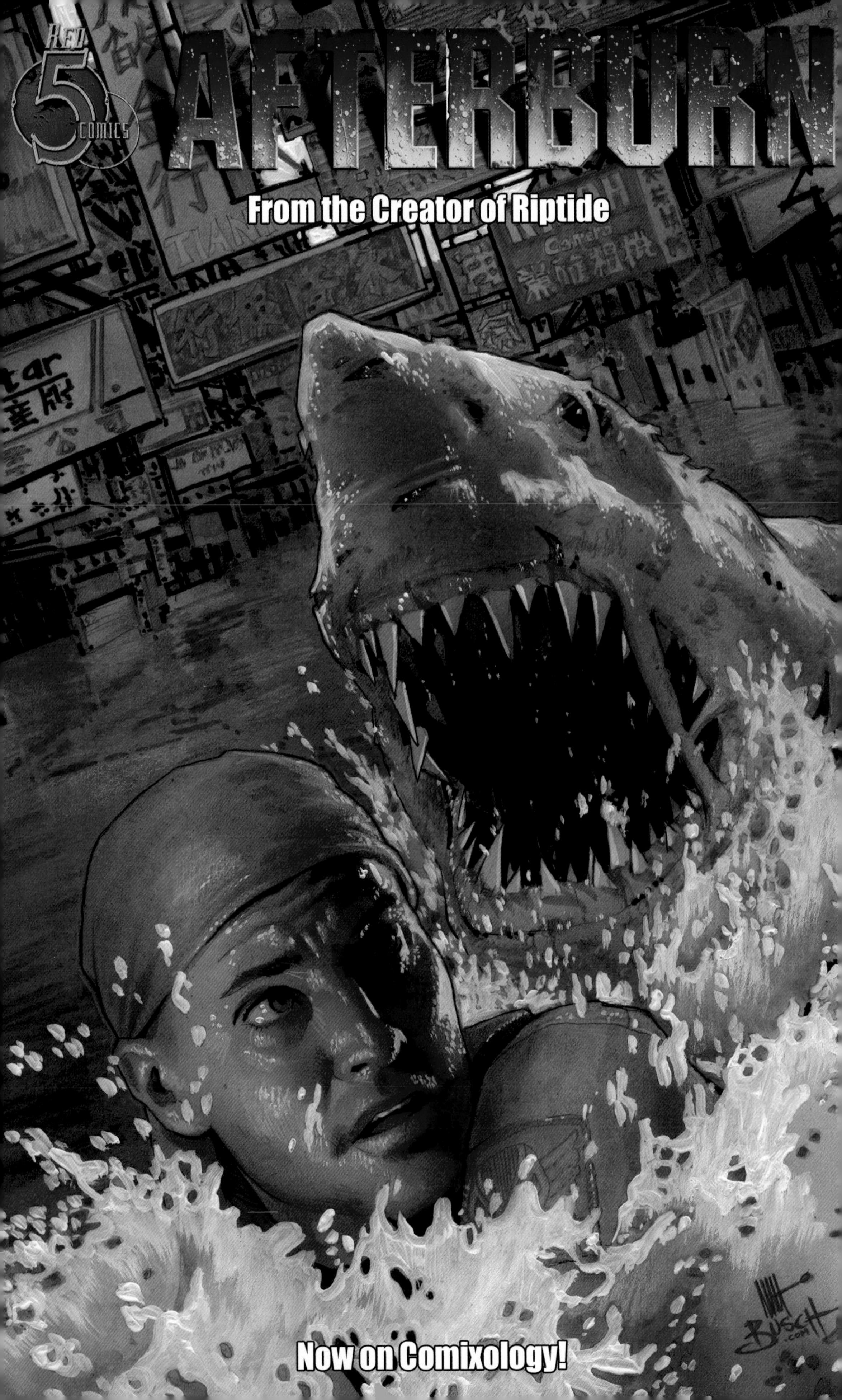

Red 5 Comics
AFTERBURN
From the Creator of Riptide
Now on Comixology!